Clean,
Sweet
Wind

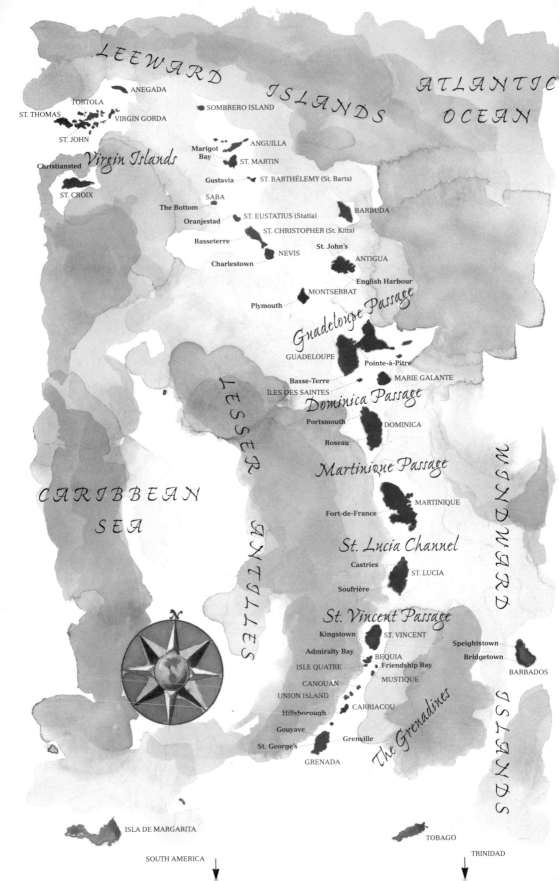

Clean, Sweet Wind

Sailing with the
Last Boatmakers
of the Caribbean

Douglas C. Pyle

International Marine • Camden, Maine

New York • San Francisco • Washington, D.C. • Auckland • Bogotá
Caracas • Lisbon • London • Madrid • Mexico City • Milan • Montreal
New Delhi • San Juan • Singapore • Sydney • Tokyo • Toronto

International Marine/
Ragged Mountain Press

A Division of The **McGraw·Hill** Companies

10 9 8 7 6 5 4 3 2 1

Library of Congress Cataloging-in-Publication Data
Pyle, Douglas, C.
    Clean, sweet wind: sailing with the last boatmakers of the Caribbean/by
Douglas C. Pyle.
      p. cm.
    Includes bibliographical references and index.
    ISBN 0-07-052679-6 (alk. paper)
    1. Sailing ships—West Indies. 2. Navigation—West Indies. 3. Sailboats—
West Indies. I. Title.
VM321.P94 1998
623.8'22'09729—DC21   97-49256
                                                                               CIP

Questions regarding the ordering of this book should be addressed to:
    The McGraw-Hill Companies
    Customer Service Department
    P.O. Box 547, Blacklick, OH 43004
    Retail customers: 1-800-262-4729
    Bookstores: 1-800-233-4726
    Visit us on the World Wide Web at www.books.mcgraw-hill.com

This book is printed on acid-free paper.

Printed by Quebecor Printing Company, Fairfield, PA
Design and Page Layout by Faith Hague
Map on page ii by Shane Reiswig
Photographs and drawings by the author
Project management by Janet Robbins
Production assistance by Deborah Krampf and Shannon Thomas
Edited by Jonathan Eaton and Kathryn Mallien

Dedication

To the people of the West Indies,
with love and admiration
for their kindness and courage,
their wisdom and skill,
this book is respectfully dedicated.

Acknowledgments

First of all, I must thank Michael Doran, who, with a persistence that defies expectation, refused to let this work lie quiet in its grave; and his wife, Pat, whose experienced eye diagnosed the work's fatal malady, furnishing the key to its resurrection. My debt to Professor Edwin Doran is now in its second generation.

My thanks are likewise due to Jon Eaton and Kate Mallien, the editors who have coaxed the work into its present form, and to my wife and constant friend, Nancy. Without her willingness to act for me amid the daily demands of a cattleman's life, the efforts of all these others would probably have come to naught.

Introduction

Quiet magic wraps the harbor in dawn twilight as the small West Indian town of Kingstown, St. Vincent, slumbers away the last cool hour of night. Another tropical day of heat and bustle awaits the sun, which will soon climb from behind the island's high volcanic cliffs.

A triangle of weathered canvas glides into the angle between sea horizon and a headland's dark green mass. First the headsail and then the gaff mainsail of a wooden sloop ease into view, moved by a breeze too faint to ripple the glassy sea. In a moment the wedge of faded canvas hesitates, then slowly shrinks into a single vertical slash. The work-scarred sloop is swinging her bows up into the faint land breeze. I hear the slap of idle canvas, and the squeal of wooden sheaves drifts across the water.

As the sails fill and take shape on the new course, I set my coffee on the deck. The steersman stands motionless at the tiller, more observer than captain, while the vessel glides across the outer harbor. At his nod, the foresail is let go and comes rattling down the forestay. A figure moves methodically forward, bunching the sail and stowing it along the rail. In the same unhurried manner the gaff is lowered and the mainsail secured. Momentum carries the cargo-laden vessel the remaining distance to the concrete quay. Lines are heaved, and the *Delight B* snugs into her berth.

The sequence was so timeless and hypnotic that I might have thought I dreamed it were it not for the reassuring warmth of the coffee. Yet it was real in 1970. Anachronistic as they seemed, wooden vessels were then still part of daily life in Caribbean ports from Puerto Rico to Trinidad, enabling West Indians to catch fish, move cargo, and transport passengers. On palm-shaded beaches in certain island communities, caulking mallets still sounded their hollow, ringing notes as vessels took shape from piles of hand-hewn timbers.

Today the old sailboats and their makers are almost gone, replaced by outboard rigs and motorsailers. Vanishing with them are the traditions and skills of wooden boatbuilding. But odd vestiges of the life of sail live on. Baltic traders now at work in island shipping occasionally can be seen with auxiliary stay sails rigged to their derricks, and the knowledge of making and sailing wooden boats and vessels is retained in a few places and honored in wooden sailboat races.

Accident put me in the position to write the story of the boatbuilders and boatbuilding in the island chain of the West Indies. After finishing my Master's degree and teaching for a year at a college, I took my savings and went to England to buy a sailboat. I sailed *Eider*, a lovely 1939 Robart Clark sloop, back across the Atlantic, fetching up in the Virgin Islands in 1968. Short of cash and liking the place, I took a job teaching in St. Croix that kept me happily occupied until 1970.

I intended to end my tropical sojourn that year at summer's end, after which I would return to the United States and begin graduate studies. But curiosity and a strong admiration for local wooden boats and their makers held me. At first I thought vaguely of doing some enjoyable summer sailing while I collected notes for a graduate school paper or thesis. I soon found that

The port of Kingstown,
St. Vincent. March 1974.

I had badly miscalculated the scope of what I wanted to do and, in fact, found the project itself growing and changing as I pursued it. The project acquired a life of its own, broadening and deepening until it had gone well beyond the original time allotted. Five years elapsed before my inquiry finally ran its course, leaving me with a mass of notes, data sheets, and photographs.

I had discovered the historical traces and current examples of no fewer than twenty-eight types of sailing craft between the Virgin Islands and Trinidad. In addition, I had collected observations, impressions, and opinions, all of which were intertwined with my understanding of the maritime history I had uncovered. And I had doubled and redoubled my scope of friendships with the wonderful people among whom I had wandered so freely and so long.

In 1975 I returned to the United States and began trying to put everything together. It was then that the shimmering, mosaic quality of island life got the better of me. Despite repeated and determined efforts, I never was able to get the scientific data into outline form. The exuberant rhythm of West Indian life mocked my initially stolid attempt to achieve the detached, objective tone of good technical writing.

When I found myself unable to separate the vessels from their builders, the people from their traditions and culture, and my observations from the enjoyment of observing, I realized that writing down the information still embedded within the experience of gathering it was my only hope to finish the exercise. When I finished, to my delight I discovered that not only had I accomplished the original scholarly goal, I also had both a story of how learning actually occurs and an organized picture of the islands and islanders in that time pocket of observation. It is my hope that in setting down this description of the watercraft, the builders, and their life as I saw it in its unique island setting, I succeed in conveying the uncommon pleasure of their acquaintance.

Lighting the Flame

~ ~ ~

R eady?" Bill called as he slipped the tiller into the rudder head. He was sitting at the captain's station in the sternsheets. "Let's go on the next good puff."

We were getting ready for a Sunday sail on the waters around St. Croix, southernmost of the U.S. Virgin Islands. A breeze riffled the bright blue surface of Christiansted Harbor. Picking my way gingerly over the pile of large cobbles that made up our ballast, I slid past the spindly mast toward Bill and handed the mooring line around one of the frayed rope shrouds. The strain on my arm increased as the foresail filled.

"Okay, let go."

I drew in the mooring line and Bill released his grip on the quay. With me handling the foresail's running rigging and Bill adjusting that of the mainsail, the sails filled and the little sloop began to gather way.

It was my first sail in *Flame* and only the second for my friend Bill Sparks. He had bought her and sailed back from the island of Tortola in the British Virgin Islands the week before, a distance of some forty miles.

"The old man who built *Flame* showed me how to sail her," Bill had assured me earlier as we stepped the mast through a hole in the thwart, then swigged tight the forestay to which the foresail was sewn. I looked around skeptically at the gray, patched canvas, the furry ropes, and the whittled pegs for cleating them home.

"Pretty rough," I said.

"Yeah, but the old man said she was the fastest of the Tortola sloops," Bill laughed.

"For whatever that's worth," I nearly said—and was soon glad I hadn't.

The smooth waters of the harbor gave me an opportunity to look for a comfortable spot on the ballast stones while we learned the drill for tacking: sail full for a moment to build up speed, put the helm down, haul the mainsail in tight until the jib backed and pushed the bow around, then quickly pull loose the jib sheet and relead it through a thimble on the opposite side. All this had to be done quickly, while sprawled on the stones out of harm's way when the mainsail swung over to be adjusted on the new course.

"The old man told me to sail her on the leech," Bill said. At this reference I eyed the outer edge of *Flame*'s mainsail, where the wind was blowing across the only truly shipshape airfoil. The rest of the sail was backwinded over half its surface in cheerful defiance of all conventional sailing theory.

Soon we were through the reef and out of the harbor, bang in the middle of the Sunday yacht traffic making the five-mile beat out to the beaches of Buck Island. Sail to the right of us, sail to the left, sail all around us. My first reaction was defiant embarrassment, something like what one might feel if bursting out of the starting gate at the Kentucky Derby astride a sway-backed plow mule. I kept my head down and tried to pretend I was busy bailing or trimming ballast—until slowly it dawned on me that there was nothing to be embarrassed about. We weren't able to sail as close to the wind as some of the better-tuned yachts, but we were footing better and clawing up to windward as fast as anyone out that day. Humble *Flame,* her pine planks fastened to hand-hewn frames with rusting nails, frayed lines running through thimbles and rope-stropped blocks, and baggy sails of weathered canvas, was sailing as well as yachts of fiberglass, Dacron, and stainless steel built solely for speed.

The return trip late that afternoon was less of a surprise but no less a thrill. With her big, billowy mainsail eased way out to starboard and the jib "goosed" to the opposite side, on the downwind course we cleanly outran all contenders. In the exhilaration and amazement of that afternoon was born my conviction that the sailing craft of the islanders represented one of their most notable achievements.

In 1959, when Fidel Castro's regime came to power in Cuba, its failed relations with the United States quickly resulted in displacement of the Cuban tourist business elsewhere around the Caribbean. At first it seemed to the struggling island communities that tourism offered an ideal solution to the economic stagnation that had plagued the West Indies since the decline of sugar prosperity in the nineteenth century. But in practice tourism frequently disrupted the fragile economic relationships of small and unsophisticated communities, offering in exchange chiefly jobs for waiters, chambermaids, and taxicab drivers. The attractive and lucrative positions were usually filled by outsiders with specialized skills.

During the time I lived and worked in St. Croix, I came to feel that the capacities of the West Indians were being undervalued by the tourist industry and, in consequence, by themselves—an even more serious matter in the long run. Perhaps it was for this reason that my afternoon sail in *Flame* stirred me so. In her ropey, make-do way she was pure West Indian, yet at first I had rated her below her worth because of how she looked. To find her sailing ability the equal of any high-tech design made me aware of how misinterpreted and patronized the West Indians were.

Several weeks after meeting *Flame* I had a week's vacation during which a fortuitous combination of circumstances put me on the path to learning something about the island boatbuilders. I had planned to spend my vacation cruising in *Eider*. My intended destination was the British Virgin Islands, *Flame's* birthplace, usually an easy day's sail to the north. In this case the breeze that wafted me out of Christiansted Harbor weakened all morning and died completely by noon. After waiting patiently for an hour or so, drenched in perspiration, I concluded that we were in for an "Irish hurricane" (the expression on St. Croix for flat calm). I roused myself from languid musings induced by the gently heaving sea and got the engine going, deciding in the process that if I had to motor I might as well head in an unaccustomed direction.

The failure of the prevailing easterly trade winds, which I had relied on to carry me to Tortola, presented a rare opportunity to steam due east to Anguilla, a destination normally dead to windward from St. Croix. The name had long nibbled at the back of my mind. The big two-masted schooners that called from time to time in the U.S. Virgin Islands hailed from Anguilla, and I had heard people in Christiansted say that schooners formerly had been built there. The chance was too good to miss: I dropped the jib, sheeted the mainsail flat, and began to motor.

The calm continued all afternoon, until at sunset a light breeze lifted out of the northwest, just enough to flap the mainsail and wake me when *Eider* got off course. Later in the night the weather closed in and a gentle drizzle started, obscuring the beacon on nearby St. Martin that I was counting on for my bearings. I was feeling a bit uneasy when at daybreak the drizzle thinned enough for me to see the distinctive, high volcanic cone of Saba far off to the southeast. I took a bearing, guessed at the distance, found an approximate position, and adjusted my course with what I hoped was the right bearing. Shortly thereafter I saw first the mountain of St. Martin and then the lower bulge of my target. As the overcast cleared, the trade winds resumed and I was able to finish my trip with a spanking sail along the leeward coast of Anguilla.

My chart showed no off-lying hazards except in the vicinity of Dog Island, so I had ample opportunity for sightseeing, if only there had been some scenery. In those days, tourism on Anguilla amounted to a grand total of three guest houses, not like the white towers one sees today. All I could make out was low, dry scrubland with little sign of human occupation. The shoreline was formed of rocky headlands separated by shallow bays rimmed with gleaming white sand. Road Harbor, when I found it, was just another of these bays, only a little wider and deeper.

As I eased the sheets and stood into the bay, it seemed as if I had slipped backward in time. A dozen or so sloops and schooners swung at anchor; about the same number of brightly painted cinderblock houses were set among the palms edging the white beach. After letting go the anchor, I stood looking about me, trying to understand the powerful sensation of well-being I was feeling, for there was in fact very little to see or hear—no powerlines, no automobiles, no hotels, no billboards. In the stillness of that tropic noon, I heard only the slap of halyards and the anonymous creaking of working vessels as they rested from their labors. There was nothing present that would have positively identified the century as the twentieth rather than the nineteenth.

Shaking off the hypnotic effect, I launched my dinghy and rowed ashore. In the tiny, yellow-plastered police outpost, I tendered my passport to a tall young man in tropical shorts and military blouse. As I was cleared, looking out upon the bay I made casual small talk about schooners and their builders, and my interest in West Indian sailing lore.

"Schooners, is it?" the young man said. "Did you see that one just along there?" He pointed at the shore of Road Bay and its lonesome jetty. "And then you have Forest Bay. An even bigger one there. I can drive you over tomorrow if you'd like to see it. Eight o'clock suit you?"

I accepted the offer gratefully, then set off hiking along the shoreline, ducking under palm trunks that leaned over the steep beach until I reached an open area where seagrape branches arched onto the wave-smoothed sand. Just behind the crest of the beach stood the gaunt carcass of a schooner, hauled out and repairs evidently being undertaken by a small gang of carpenters. I walked over to look at it.

My intention had been to watch quietly from the sidelines, but at my approach the workmen all laid down their tools and waited expectantly. Under the circumstances it would have been downright unfriendly to remain silent, so I pitched right in: What were they doing? How were they going about it? Without any formal declaration of intention, or organized preparation, I found myself conducting an interview.

MacDuff Richardson spoke for the group: It was he who was in charge of stretching (lengthening) the present vessel. It was he who was also responsible for construction of the new vessel over at Forest Bay. Above all, it was he who had been off the island and worked overseas. Everyone took an extemporaneous break during this interchange, some men hunkering down and others flopping on the sand in the shade of the palms or the hull.

After answering my questions for a while with patient good humor, Mac asked me one of his own. He vehemently stabbed his forefinger at me.

"What do you think of the Man in the Moon?" he demanded.

I blinked. "Well . . . I don't really know," I replied, nonplussed, not knowing whether to run or stand my ground.

"That right. That right!" Richardson exclaimed. "That what I think, too." He eagerly seized me by the hand and shot a triumphant glance toward his smirking crew. "There never was a man on the moon and there never will be. It against God. The Bible say . . ."

The exact passage of scripture passed a substantial distance over my head as I groped wildly for understanding. It slowly dawned on me that we were talking about the NASA lunar landings, the first of which had occurred the summer before, in 1969. Mac's crew, I now noticed, were openly grinning as they watched the sport. Apparently Mac battened on to all newcomers. Later, when I had time to reflect on it, I realized that Mac's version of space travel—fooling all the people all of the time—would have been an even greater technological achievement than what actually was the truth.

In addition to sharing his views on space travel, Mac told me about working in a shipyard in St. Thomas, about building a schooner in Tortola, about how the dimensions and proportions of a vessel are determined. My first interview was going surprisingly well. Mac could not be at the other construction site tomorrow, but he welcomed me to talk to anyone there.

The next morning at Forest Bay (not a tree in sight) I found the second vessel under construction, as well as two boats intended for lobstering. Here, too, the carpenters were easy to approach and eager to share their knowledge.

In island terminology, *boats* are those watercraft that can be pulled ashore when not in use; *vessels* are watercraft too large for that. Vessels are further divided into *sloops*, which have one mast and generally are under fifty feet in length, and *schooners*, which generally have two masts and are over fifty feet.

One of the first things I learned from the island shipwrights was how they set up the hull. Their design work was done full-scale in the process of building, not from drawn plans. After the keel was laid, the builder attached the angled stempost and the sternpost. In many cases, particularly with large sailing craft, a "navel piece" was butted on top of the sternpost so that part of the hull could be built back above where the rudder would eventually be fitted. Next, he set up his "modeling" frames: bow frames at the forward end of the keel, main frames at the one-third mark on the keel, and the main transom

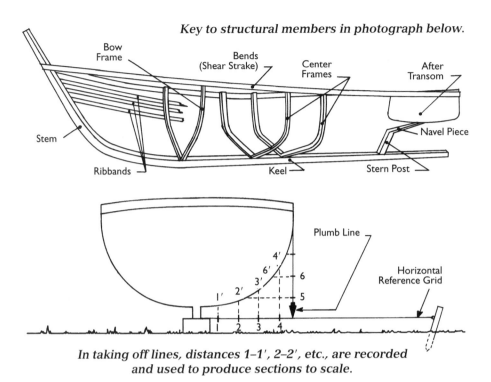

Key to structural members in photograph below.

Bow Frame

Bends (Shear Strake)

Center Frames

After Transom

Stem

Navel Piece

Ribbands

Keel

Stern Post

Plumb Line

Horizontal Reference Grid

4'

6'

3'

2'

1'

6

5

1 2 3 4

In taking off lines, distances 1–1', 2–2', etc., are recorded and used to produce sections to scale.

Small vessel being "set up" at Charlestown, Nevis. April 1974.

frames at the top of the sternpost. Thin strips of wood called "ribbands" were bent around these modeling frames and nailed bow and stern. The remaining frames were then fitted into this basketwork shape, the fairing being done with hatchets, axes, or adzes by sighting along the ribbands for bulges and hollows. Designs were modified according to whim, instinct, or experience of the builder by slightly changing the shapes or locations of the modeling frames.

At the end of my visit to this parched but friendly island, I found I had collected several pages of notes and taken a roll of film showing the vessels and their makers. I had also learned from helpful residents about several other centers of boatbuilding around the islands. To supplement my interest in West Indian watercraft, I had verified that there was concrete information in the form of a fleet of trading vessels and active boatbuilders.

By accident I had stumbled onto enough material to begin a study. My head was filled with ideas about how I could go about it as I ran back down to St. Croix.

TWO

Passage to Grenada

The Anguillans had told me that while their island was the important center of wooden ship building in the northern Lesser Antilles, there was an equal or greater center down in the Grenadines. That was new territory for me; a reconnoitering trip in search of the southern builders was the obvious next step if I wanted to learn about maritime matters in the West Indies.

A sailboat bound for Grenada from St. Croix has two choices: Beat ninety miles upwind to Anguilla or St. Martin, then follow the arc of the Lesser Antilles southward to Grenada; or sail a close reach directly there, much the shorter trip. This latter seemed the best idea, but one slight difficulty appeared as I studied my charts. The direct course from St. Croix to Grenada passes very close to Aves Island, an isolated patch of shoals and coral reef capped by a bit of sandbar, lying one hundred miles due southwest of Guadeloupe. This was precisely the sort of hazard one did not want to pass when sailing single-handed back in the days before satellite navigation.

The safest plan, I decided, was to *try* to land on the tiny island, thereby rendering it impossible to find. The morning after leaving St. Croix I took a sun altitude and got a good line of position. Shortly before noon I got a second line and the intercept showed Aves Island five miles dead ahead. A few minutes later a ring of breakers was visible with a sandy islet inside. So much for irony as a navigational principle.

With the sun high it was fairly simple to enter the small lee behind the curved rim of sand, no more than a few dozen yards from end to end. The holding was good, in clean coral sand. But as soon as the mainsail was down *Eider* began to roll from gunwale to gunwale in the swells that bent around both ends of the island and reentered the lee in a dizzying criss-cross. Launching the dinghy was clearly impractical, but swimming ashore seemed feasible.

Going in with mask, fins, and a spear gun made me feel a little less exposed but couldn't entirely ward off the loneliness of the spot. In the shallows rested a dozen sea turtles waiting for the full moon and spring tide to aid them in coming ashore and laying eggs. I left the water and stood dripping on the steep beach, sending clouds of mewing sea birds screaming and swirling up into the air. There was no plant life on the islet except patches of the low-growing succulent called ice plant. A short distance along the beach I saw a piece of galvanized pipe sticking out of the sand with a tattered Venezuelan flag fluttering at its top. At its base a plaque stated that the Radio Club of Venezuela had visited the place two years before.

Abruptly I was swept by a sense of futility and desolation that left me acutely uncomfortable. After a scant half hour, my plans for a Robinson Crusoe picnic seemed pointless. I gladly swam back to *Eider* and got under way on the course to Grenada.

Landfall after a four-day passage is always welcome, but my first view of the port of St. George's from seaward was so picturesque that it is still indelibly fixed in my mind. The sun, already dropping behind me into the western sea, had highlighted the neat brick facades and red-tiled roofs of the little town, transforming the whole scene into the stage set for some impossibly romantic light opera. Behind a steep headland capped by a fort lay the inner harbor—the same brick facades but here all the activities and noise of a busy sailing port.

A few days after getting *Eider* snugged into the yacht anchorage I began to realize that my plan to complete my study of boatbuilding culture by

Port of St. Georges, Grenada. June 1970.

summer's end was unrealistic. There was, first of all, the period of relaxation justified by an offshore passage: mornings of shopping and reprovisioning, long lunches at the Nutmeg Cafe looking out over the harbor, afternoons of siesta and inspired idleness, evenings of rum punch and conversation with new acquaintances, followed by nights of blissful sleep cradled under the tropic stars by the gently rocking yacht.

Then followed a period of chores and undertakings: a line to splice, a seizing to redo, a touch of paint or varnish. Then a round of bigger jobs: rebuilding the dinghy, which was proving too small; replacing a bearing in the gear box; and of course, the continuing obligations of coffee aboard in the cool of early morning, visiting with the yacht community, and inquiries now and then about boatbuilding.

It was late July by the time I set out to stalk my elusive quarry aboard that monument to free enterprise, the Grenada bus system. Unhampered by any consideration other than getting there firstest with the mostest, the buses are individually owned and locally built. Straight-backed wooden benches are set as close together as possible on the back of a flatbed truck, then roofed over from side to side. As a final expression of concern for the comfort of the passenger, canvas curtains can be rolled down in case of a change in the weather. Bright paint and an affectionate name are all that are needed to complete the turnout.

Passengers mount a two-step ladder at the rear and shuffle forward to wedge into any empty space. A friend of the driver rides at the back to collect fares, shout directions, and act as a living guard chain when the bus fills to overflowing. Scheduling and routing are equally straightforward: The bus runs from the home village of the driver to the market square in St. George's and returns, stopping anywhere, anytime, as passengers require. Buses run as often as they get a load and leave when they are filled. As a consequence, the market square is a seething, milling maelstrom of people, parcels, and machinery, all surrounded by the roar of unmuffled exhausts echoing off the brick facades surrounding the square.

Into this bedlam I wandered, looking for a bus to Grenville, the island's second-largest town, on the eastern shore. From St. George's on the southwest coast, it is reached either by sea or over the rugged mountain soaring eight hundred feet above the surrounding waters. Traveling by road offered a look at the interior of the island and was a happy alternative to sailing around and anchoring in a roadstead, not a harbor.

Seeing neither posted destinations nor any other suggestion of a system, I timidly asked a man with a chicken under each arm how I could get to Grenville.

"Grenville?" he screamed. "Is Grenville you want?" I nodded. "See over there? Is that one going." He gestured frantically with his head toward a confused tangle of buses and people.

"No, man, no!" a new voice chimed in from the left. "Over here, over here!"

"Try me, man, try me!" came from still another direction.

The best strategy seemed to be to find a bus that was nearly full and scramble aboard. I jumped into the nearest candidate, handing the assistant my fare. Soon thereafter we got under way, exhaust roaring, driver honking and shouting for room. Virtually by lung power alone we propelled ourselves through the jam of the market, lurching and jerking up the steep streets and finally out into the countryside.

The two-lane road crossing the backbone of the island to Grenville is in constant use by taxis, trucks, and rival buses; by school children in uniforms, field workers with their machetes tucked under the left arm, and women carrying improbable loads balanced on their heads; by dogs, donkeys, and an assortment of domestic fowl. The rules of the road for motorists are simple in the extreme: Blare the horn at intersections and blind spots—in other words, almost constantly—and forge ahead while traffic scatters out of the way. Unless, of course, the oncoming vehicle is bigger and more determined, in which case it is your turn to screech aside.

Our driver, a paragon of dexterity and singlemindedness, went unchallenged until he swung out to pass a poky taxi on a winding upgrade, a technique that had doubtless served him faithfully many times before. This time, however, a heavily loaded truck on its way down the mountain hove into view just as he started the maneuver, and it was at last his turn for the shoulder. But there wasn't much of a shoulder on that seventy-degree mountainside, and we teetered to a halt with the left rear wheels hanging out over the void, barely supported by a tangle of dense tropical undergrowth. As soon as possible I leaped out, hastened by visions of the bus tumbling end over end down the mountainside in a cloud of splinters and tossed riders. Standing on good old terra firma, feeling more than thankful, my eye for the first time lit on the name our intrepid driver had chosen for his vehicle: *Why Worry?*

When another bus happened along I did not linger, as many did, to wrangle with the driver for a refund. I chalked it up to experience and proceeded onward to Grenville.

Once there it was an easy matter to get directions to a stretch of beach north of town where a large schooner was being set up. The keel, stem, and sternpost were in position, and the modeling frames had been fastened in place. Two men were shaping additional frames with adzes. They worked carefully on the outer face of each frame where the planks would be attached, but for the three other surfaces they merely knocked off the high spots from the sides and the inner face and called the job done. The frames, once shaped, were erected in pairs connected by a long batten and leveled by sighting across the batten to the sea horizon, thereby taking advantage of the world's largest spirit level.

A third man, with tape and chalk, moved between the vessel and a pile of crooked timbers lying nearby, laying out and marking work for the other men. I asked him if there were enough timbers in the pile to finish the framing.

"Oh no," he answered, laughing. "If all be brought at once, then is too discouraging." He explained that when this lot of timbers was exhausted, the crew would spend a week in the foothills, finding and cutting more crooks. This gave them a break in the work routine and provided an opportunity to look for specific shapes as they were needed.

When I asked how the proportions of the vessel were determined on Grenada, the builder outlined essentially the same system I had found in Anguilla and would find everywhere in the islands: With keel, stem, and sternpost in position, center frames are shaped so the center section has a beam equal to one-fourth the intended length and a depth in the hold equal to one-half the beam.

Although the method and proportions were substantially the same in all the islands I would visit, the shaping and positioning of the modeling frames varied from island to island and builder to builder. In fact, most builders were rather secretive about their molds, considering them the critical ingredient that made for greatest speed—the thing on which their reputations were built.

I asked the builder where he learned to set up vessels. He replied that his name was Steill and that he had grown up in Harvey's Vale, Carriacou, as if that were answer enough. Later I found it was.

Since my visit to Anguilla I had decided that, while photographs were a start in recording the characteristics of West Indian vessels, lines drawings would be more precise—if I could get them. But at best builders only carved half-frame models of their boats before setting them up. No one had ever heard of "lines drawings." If I wanted them, I was going to have to take them off the boats myself.

To illustrate a vessel's three-dimensional shape on paper, naval architects employ the same methods surveyors use to depict topographical elevations. A profile, or sheer plan, shows the buttock lines, or the curve or flatness of the sides. The half-breadth plan shows the vessel as if it were turned on its side and half buried, illustrating waterlines at different stations rising from the keel. Last, entry through the water is indicated through a body plan, whose lines show front and rear images, placed side by side.

In the field, one can take lines using surveyor's tools where they are available, or measuring tape, spirit level, and plumb bob where they are not. The eager boat-measurer lays out a reference grid beneath a chocked-up hull and jots down all data in a neat and orderly manner while maintaining unruffled calm in the face of blowing sand, biting insects, flapping paper, and curious children. After all is measured, the boat-measurer retires to the confines of his yacht, shoves aside the accumulated clutter of life under sail, balances his drawing board on his knees while bracing against the roll, pitch, surge, wind gusts, or whatever else might be the peculiar joy of the night's anchorage, and—still with unruffled calm—turns his data into clear, clean lines drawings. Nothing to it.

Steill's vessel was not far enough along to be measured accurately; not all the frames were in place. However, he told me of another vessel, not visible from the road, being built at Soubise, south of Grenville, by a man he had taught. I was to ask the bus driver to let me off on the low-lying stretch of coast just before the road cut inland and began to climb. I was to ask for the house of George Justlyn.

When I arrived, Justlyn was not at home, but his wife consented to let me take the lines off the medium-sized schooner lying planked and decked among the palms behind their house. This occupied me fully for two hours. The lines I later sketched out show a hull with a strongly marked "sheer" (the fore and aft curve of the deck). There was a good deal of overhang in the stern and a long, curved stem. The waterlines and buttock lines both appeared to have good waterflow characteristics.

I never had the chance to verify this in action. Four years later, when a further concatenation of circumstances brought me back to Grenada, the schooner at Soubise was still unlaunched, unrigged, and unnamed. The owners in Trinidad had stopped sending money and Justlyn had stopped working.

It is possible to imagine the sail plan, since I later took photographs of similar vessels built in Grenada and Carriacou. There is a strong generic resemblance between the vessels of these two islands, as well there might be. My conversations in Grenada turned up the interesting tidbit of information that Steill and Justlyn were typical of most Grenada builders in having their roots in Carriacou. In most cases, relocation came about when a Carriacou builder came to Grenada to build a vessel near the abundant timber resources, and stayed. Thus it happens that the wooden trading vessels of Grenada were merely built there, whereas in tradition and design they were specifically of the Carriacou model.

Before I left Grenada, however, I did discover two types of small boats that were unique to that island. North of St. George's, in the lee of Mt. St.

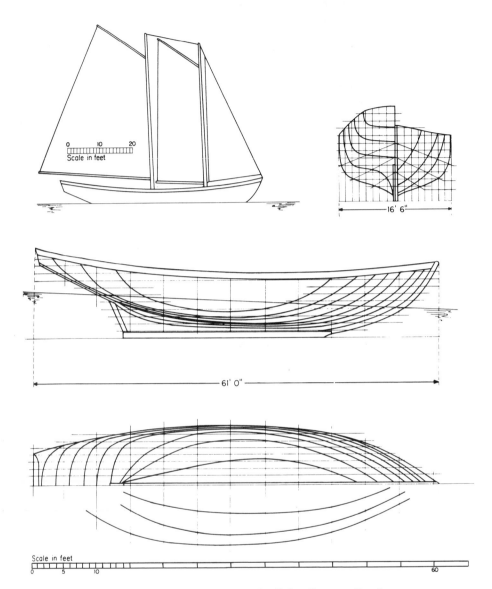

Lines of unnamed schooner built by George Justlyn,
taken at Soubise. Taken off June 1970.

Catherine, lies the village of Gouyave, even today a straggle of houses and shops between the coast road and the black sand beach. Like most of the coastal towns, Gouyave depends for at least part of its livelihood on fishing, which at the time of my inquiries was done on this stretch of coast in a curious sailing canoe. Today sail has been supplanted by outboard motors, and the canoes are largely abandoned.

The canoes were made from a small hollowed log with three raised planks added to form the sides. These "strakes" were fastened directly to the log,

Sailing canoes at Gouyave, Grenada. March 1974.

with widely spaced frames fitted after the strakes were in place. The lines show very clearly that no effort was made to give the hull any shape other than that assumed by a hollowed log wedged slightly open at midsection. They were propelled by sailing and rowing simultaneously, a practical mix in the flat water and fluky breezes that prevail in the lee of all high islands such as Grenada.

The canoes were versatile, however, capable also of operating in the open sea. I watched a contingent of eight of these craft when they turned up for a 1970 regatta in Carriacou, twenty-five miles to the northeast. They were easy to follow in the races because all had dark blue denim sails. Not, you understand, that denim makes very good sailcloth; it probably accounted, at least in part, for the canoes' notable lack of success against the small double-enders that had come down for the first time from Bequia, to the north. Denim was simply the cheapest cloth at the dry goods shop in Gouyave.

It was well that I saw them when I did. Two years later the Gouyave canoes stopped coming to the regatta, discouraged, I imagine, by their poor showing. In 1975 I returned to Grenada to take lines off one of these canoes and could find only a handful still in use. Their places on the beach had been taken by roughly built imitations of the Bequia double-enders, a vivid example of cultural diffusion.

*Construction detail of sailing canoe, Gouyave, Grenada.
March 1974.*

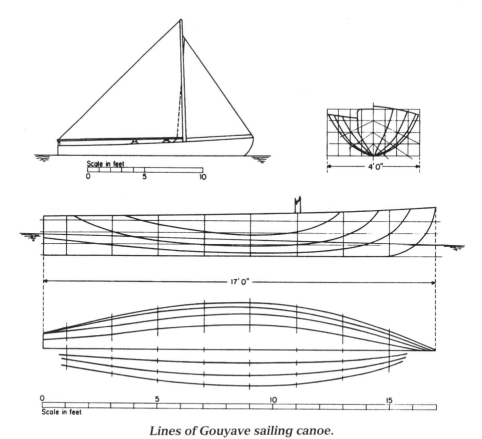

*Lines of Gouyave sailing canoe.
Taken off March 1974.*

Elsewhere on Grenada, fishing was being carried on in double-ended motor launches as cheap fuel propelled the decline of working sail. These were so characteristically Grenadian, and symbolic of what was happening all over the Caribbean, that I took some time to examine them and talk with their builders.

At first glance, the launches appeared to be a sailing craft converted to power by replacing the sails with the typical single-cylinder Stuart-Turner engine. But this turned out not to be the case. The rather sophisticated teardrop shape was the work of an English fisheries officer stationed some years before in Grenville. No one could remember his name. Had the man been a notable drunkard or womanizer his name would be a household word in Grenada; alas, merely creating something with which to land fish economically doomed the creator to anonymity.

Except for the launches there was surprisingly little boatbuilding under way in Grenada, despite abundant resources and a need for waterborne com-

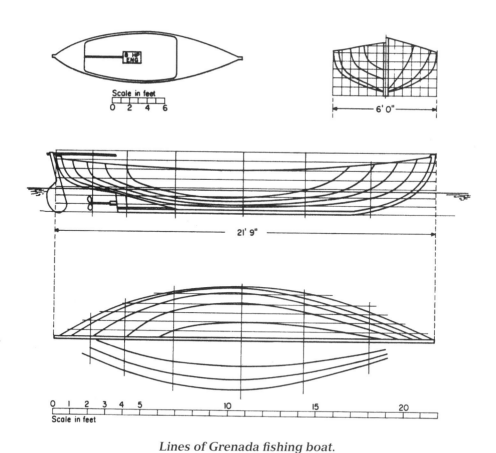

Lines of Grenada fishing boat.
Taken off March 1974.

merce. As I spoke with the carpenters I learned that even in the past activity had been sporadic and mostly done by men from Carriacou. Moreover, nearly all the trading vessels I saw coming and going in the busy port of St. George's were not owned or crewed by Grenadians. They were based in Carriacou. Grenada, for all its resources, seemed to stand in maritime affairs very much in the shadow of its sparsely inhabited, small, dry neighbor.

This apparent anomaly was to be found again and again during the course of my travels, so persistently that it gradually became a paradigm. "Is boatbuilding you want, is Carriacou you going," Grenadians said repeatedly. The notion of maritime specialization in particular islands was ground for thought and an eventual visit there.

One of the encounters I had in the exuberant midst of the produce market in Grenville underlined how the individualization of duties is one of the cornerstones of our world.

One morning I found myself in the market. Fascinated by the abundance of exotic fruits and vegetables, I asked a vendor about the little heaps of round, golden fruits she displayed.

"Them's govers, sor," she explained.

After a moment's reflection I decided that "govers" might be guavas, until then known to me only by name.

"What do you do with govers?" I asked.

"You makes gover jam, gover jelly, and gover cheese," she replied cheerfully.

Jams and jellies seemed pretty obvious, but the notion of cheese made from fruit was intriguing.

I ventured a second question. "How do you make gover cheese?"

The lady smiled indulgently. "Well, sor, you does buy some of my govers and you takes them to your cook and you says, 'Cook, make me some gover cheese.'"

Bearing this in mind, I concluded my first visit to Grenada and set off to see what was going on in Carriacou.

THREE

Carriacou You Going

~ ~ ~

I t's a stiff sail against wind and current to Carriacou from Grenada, but well worth the effort, especially if you arrive for Bank Holiday, the first weekend in August, when the island comes alive for the annual Carriacou Regatta. Sloops and schooners from up and down the Grenadines gather in the roadstead; canoes and fishing boats line the beach. The main street of Hillsborough, seat of the race, swirls with people stirred into a West Indian jump-up of bright colors, plentiful refreshments, and the inevitable beats of calypso and Jamaican reggae. All is in honor of the workboats, large and small, that gather every year to race during the Bank Holiday.

Boatbuilding in Carriacou is a tradition whose origins are steeped in legend. But it owes its contemporary existence in part to J. Linton Rigg, an American yachtsman who settled in Carriacou after cruising the islands in 1960 and writing a book about it called *The Alluring Antilles.* Rigg founded the regatta and initiated the revival of wooden boatbuilding in Carriacou and the Grenadines.

Large sloops class, Carriacou Regatta. August 1972.

The Mermaid Tavern, across from the police station on Hillsborough's only paved street, forms the landward cornerstone of Rigg's island holdings. The jangling cacophony of the street in front was tempered by the gentle breaking of waves at the back door, blending, in the low hum of the overhead fans, into a tranquilizing harmony of the tropics. In the jalousied dimness of the bar, regulars mingled with passing yachtsmen. Presiding over this setting, with his red neckerchief and Panama hat, his fund of stories punctuated by "don't ye know," Rigg epitomized the white man in the tropics. And nodding gently at anchor on the windward side of the island lay *Mermaid of Carriacou,* the other half of Rigg's domain, and the sloop to beat on race day.

Naturally I found my way to the Mermaid Tavern soon after anchoring and clearing customs. I learned from Rigg that boatbuilding had all but stopped on Carriacou when he arrived. He set out to arrest this decline, not from antiquarian sentiment but out of concern for the economic well-being of the island and its people. Being small and dry, Carriacou offered little opportunity for local enterprise. At any given moment, a substantial proportion of the island's young men and women were working abroad. Their remittances to relatives and deposits in island banks played an important role in keeping the economy afloat, as in other islands where tourism was virtually nonexistent. Typical local enterprise consisted of opening a small shop for the convenience of the neighbors, but this did nothing but circulate money brought in from elsewhere. Building a vessel, on the other hand, takes local skills and some local materials, transforming them into a capital asset that can then generate new money by freighting between islands in good times and by going fishing in others.

For the first part of his revival, Rigg financed a forty-four–foot sloop named *Mermaid of Carriacou,* built by Zepharin MacLaren in the little Carriacouan village of Windward. Rigg bought materials and had a suit of sails cut by Ratsey and Lapthorn, while MacLaren earned half equity by doing the construction. With *Mermaid* at his disposal, Rigg organized and sponsored a regatta for workboats in six classes: large-decked sloops, small-decked sloops, three categories of open boats, and canoes. In each class, the competitors raced without handicaps or formal rules, with points awarded for the first four places in each of three races. The vessel with the highest total for the series was to be awarded a purse of $500 Eastern Caribbean, and smaller prizes would be given through fourth place.

Rigg assumed that the sporting inclination in humans may well be stronger than the desire for economic independence or even the instinct for survival. Racing for substantial cash prizes certainly produced greater stimulation of boatbuilding activity than any amount of urging or explanation of

Mermaid of Carriacou *running the line at the start,*
Carriacou Regatta. August 1974.

economic benefits. Once built, Rigg reasoned, the vessels would surely find
useful employment no matter how frivolous the original purpose of building
had been.

Over the years *Mermaid* proved unbeatable, giving rise to a certain
amount of grumbling about Rigg's and MacLaren's "yacht" with her stainless
steel rigging and Dacron sails, but challenges continued to be made. Many
builders eventually adopted the amenities of stainless steel and Dacron, not
such a bad influence in the long run. During the four years that I followed the
regatta, six large sloops were built and made their debut racing against
Mermaid.

The results were all Rigg could have hoped for. At the time of his death in
1976, a new fleet of sailing vessels had been built on Carriacou and a new
generation of builders had acquired the skills of setting up and building sea-
worthy sailing craft. One such accomplishment would be a worthy memorial
for anyone; Rigg, in fact, had two to his credit. The Out Island Regatta in the
Bahamas is also his creation, established during his earlier years there, with
similar intent and effect.

Mermaid's racing record made me especially eager to have her lines. It
turned out the Mermaid Tavern had a scale model that both Rigg and Mac-
Laren certified as accurate. Finally I was able to take off a set of lines as it

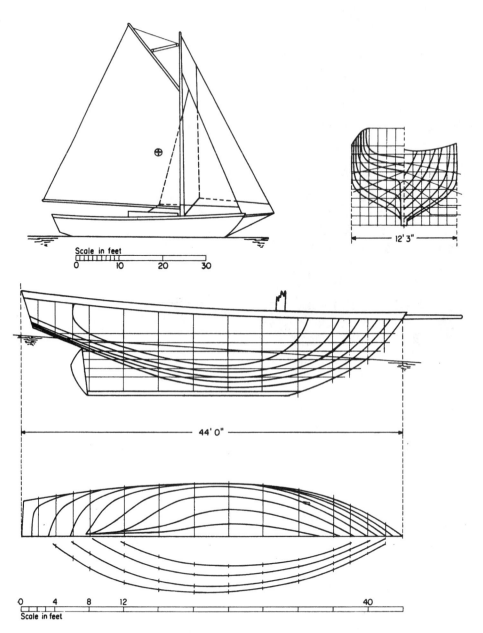

Lines of **Mermaid of Carriacou, *built in 1964 by Zepharin MacLaren at Windward, Carriacou. Taken off August 1974.***

should be done: seated at a table on the terrace of a tavern, shaded by gently swishing palms, cooled by the balmiest of breezes, and watched over by an attentive barman.

The resulting lines show a straight-sided vessel with sharp floors, extreme deadrise, a high V-shape, and a graceful entry. The long, straight run starts at the midsection and is carried onto the wide counter without any cramping of the buttock lines. Under sail *Mermaid* showed little inclination to heel over, mainly because her length-to-beam ratio made her wider than most island sloops. As MacLaren told me, "If a vessel build long and narrow, is sailing more on the side. You must give she sufficient beam to sail more up on the keel—so you could walk upon the deck." He made this pronouncement as he counted his share of the previous day's first prize. Few who have seen *Mermaid* race would dispute his judgment.

Mermaid was too large and too busy to sail in circles for me while I collected performance data. However, I was able to hitch a ride as she sailed back to Windward, her home port, after the races. Sure enough, whether on the wind or off, her performance was comparable to that of a fast, modern cruising yacht, a remarkable achievement for a working vessel built by eye to traditional lines.

In competitions, *Mermaid* did not always lead on the downwind leg, but once around the mark she invariably showed her stuff, outpointing and outfooting all challengers by substantial margins. Her big advantage lay in her deep draft and marked deadrise, which gave very good lateral resistance for tacking into the wind, while her beaminess enabled her to stand up to her lofty rig. And, inevitably, her well-cut Dacron sails were superior to the hand-sewn canvas sails used by her challengers.

Once the merits of polyester sail cloth became apparent to other captains, some set out to neutralize *Mermaid*'s edge. In 1974, during a period of lawlessness in Grenada occasioned by the petition for independence, a nighttime raid was made on the yacht anchorage at St. George's. A considerable quantity of boat gear went missing, including a number of sails. Several months later, some of these sails reappeared magically at the Regatta on a competitor, reincarnated in a novel configuration of tints and easily spotted shapes. It gives me great satisfaction to report that crime doesn't pay, at least in this case, since the challenger with the stolen Dacron was still handily beaten by *Mermaid*.

The little community where *Mermaid* was built lies near the end of a road that winds out of Hillsborough, rises to cross the backbone of the island, and then descends again to the shore before turning north to end on a rocky headland facing Union Island. Two small islands, Petit St. Vincent and Petit Martinique, lie to the east, adding to the haven in the coral reef that forms the shallow but well-protected harbor where the vessels of Windward swing at anchor.

I made my way on foot down the road to Windward to verify that a vessel was being built there. Small houses with unglazed windows and wooden shutters fronted the road, their back doors opening onto the sandy shore. There, half hidden by the curving palm trunks, I found a large hull, planked and decked. It was waiting, bows toward the sea, for the day when it would be launched.

I found the owner, Hobin Roberts, a smiling, soft-spoken man. Could I take off the lines of his craft? "No objection," he said. "Is no objection." Little work was going on because everything was essentially completed. Roberts and his assistant carpenters watched curiously as I measured the new vessel.

The resulting lines provide a good example of the larger class of Carriacou-

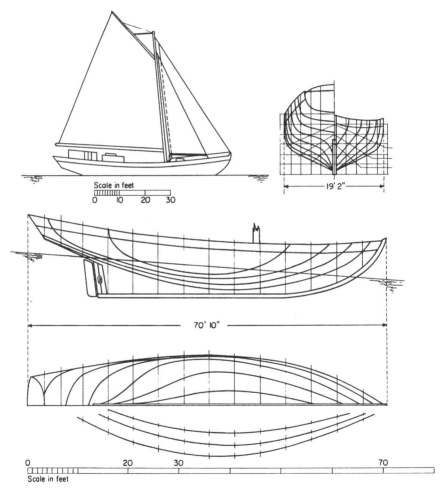

Lines of sloop **Yankee Girl R**, *built in 1970 by Gordon Patrice at Windward, Carriacou. Taken off August 1970.*

Sloop **Yankee Girl R** *anchored at Hillsborough, Carriacou. August 1974.*

built vessels. Their defining hallmarks had always been, I learned, a stem curved and strongly raked, a long overhanging stern, strong drag to the keel, moderately sharp floors, and, like *Mermaid,* straight sides with no tumble-home (that is, no inward curve of the sides below their maximum beam). In times gone by, a vessel of *Yankee Girl R*'s size, more than seventy feet in length, would without doubt have had the two masts of a traditional schooner rig. But with the increasing availability and reliability of marine diesel engines and low fuel costs, the move toward power was well under way. Vessels such as this one were beginning to be designed as motorsailers, foresail and jib retained to lend stability and a reduction in fuel costs, not to mention a safeguard should the engine ever fail.

I was to find that all decked vessels built in the Lesser Antilles had overhanging sterns with the exception of those built in Antigua and the British Virgin Islands. But in Carriacou this overhang was proportionately longer than elsewhere.

On most islands, in setting up a vessel the frames of the main transom were butted into the top of the sternpost. To create the overhang, or "after transom," a thick navel piece was attached to the top of the sternpost, extending back several feet. Once provided with several frames, planked, and caulked, the weight of the overhang was supported by only the side planking with some help from the decking. As vessels aged and the hull worked through many seas, the planking loosened and warped, and "de starn droop."

This was not the case for vessels built in Carriacou and Grenada. Builders here, recognizing the need for reinforcement of the after transom lest it "droop," used heavy supports called "ledges" fastened to the frames of the overhang. These extended forward and were attached to the sides of the sternpost and two or three frames forward. In this way, the stern was strongly cantilevered with the sternpost serving as a fulcrum. It is revealing that a structurally sound method of supporting the overhang of the after transom should exist in Carriacou and not, for example, in Bequia, only thirty-five miles away.

When I showed Roberts the completed lines for his motorsailer, he was politely interested and seemed flattered that I would take the time to carry out such a task. Clearly, though, he did not see the point in what I was doing. Why write down information on boatbuilding that was common knowledge? Nevertheless, he was very cordial and invited me to come to his vessel's up-coming launching.

I was delighted to accept his offer since I had already heard something of the folkways associated with such an important event in the islands. According-ing to a Grenadian who had been there, the most recent big vessel to be launched in these parts was built at L'Esterre, a community on the leeward side of Carriacou. The launching began tamely enough, with a priest chris-tening the *A.L. Sea Author M.* in the accepted manner. This individual then discreetly remembered a pressing engagement elsewhere on the island and departed, upon which the shaman, still a personage of some importance in Carriacou, took over for the remaining observances. First, a cock was killed and its blood sprinkled on the deck amidships so there would always be plenty to eat on board. Next, a ewe lamb was stuck and bled at the stempost so the vessel would be docile and go where she was pointed. Finally, a bull calf was sacrificed on the ground near the sternpost to give the vessel drive. The entire sequence was so bloody, and undertaken with such gusto, that sev-eral of the white spectators decamped forthwith. Despite the elaborate prepa-rations, the launching went awry and the heavy hull was stuck for four days in the shallows before it could be floated on a spring tide.

These lurid details were very much in my mind as the date of Roberts's launching approached. Launchings are generally held on Sunday so as to draw a larger crowd. On the day before, I arrived to find Roberts smoking a pipe and working quietly around the vessel, driving tight the water pins in the joint between stem and keel and touching up the paintwork. A ladder stood against the side of the vessel, so I asked if I might look around. At the forward end of the deckhouse, on the main hatch cover, a small checked cloth was spread and a simple meal set out: a plate with several fried cakes, a bottle of Scotch whisky and a glass, a folded napkin, and a small vase of plastic flowers. When I asked Roberts about the food, he shyly explained. "Oh, is an old belief hereabout. Some people does think that jumbies come in the night to take food and you must not disappoint them."

Further whetting my appetite for folklore, a young black bull was tethered to the smooth gray trunk of a palm tree near the stern of the vessel. Additional questions seemed inappropriate; I simply made it a point to be ashore as early as possible the next morning. I was not quite early enough, for when I got there the little bull was nowhere to be seen. Roberts was, though, and held in his arms a fine rooster with a glossy tail of green and black plumes. I watched as he deftly wrung its neck, then spoke to it in a low and encouraging voice during its death dance. When the legs stopped moving, he picked up the body and slung blood along the keel. No one else was there to see this, and I remained at a respectful distance. Roberts's demeanor was that of a person who observes the proprieties, as if he were not himself superstitious but had no intention of offending public sensibilities in these matters.

A short distance along the beach in a well-shaded spot, Roberts's wife and her helpers were setting up tables, tending fires, and stirring the deep iron pots that are the common cookware of the islands. A big feast was in the offing, partly because a launching is a festive occasion but also because an offering of food and drink is a sure way to draw a crowd. And a crowd is essential at a West Indian launching. Human muscle, known in those parts as "Norwegian steam," is the cheapest and most portable source of power.

Bottles of Scotch and "jack iron," a formidable local white lightning, were set out on the refreshment table as people began to collect around midmorning. Wood smoke and the aroma of curry mingled with the scent of oakum and pitch. At the far side of the table, a sheet of plywood was set up facing out over the crowd toward the new vessel. Openings, both round and rectangular, had been cut in the plywood, giving it the appearance of an enormous primitive face. Ever alert to the ritual aspects of the occasion, I took the opportunity to ask Roberts what it was.

"Oh," he informed me, "a fella over by Bogley have a very good hi-fi he does bring to all fete and thing. It having a very good bass. You wait and hear."

So much for folklore.

Shortly after eleven o'clock, when Mass was over, the village priest arrived with a flock of his parishioners. Most headed straight for the refreshments, particularly the alcoholic section. Shortly the Bogley hi-fi began demonstrating its very good bass, which signaled a move over to the waiting vessel. The priest and his acolytes carefully climbed the ladder onto it, followed by the vessel's godparents, a little boy and a little girl, shy and awkward in stiffly starched Sunday clothes. The rite of baptism was read on the foredeck and the name of the vessel revealed by unfurling a red banner on which were the white letters spelling out "Yankee Girl R." A murmur of speculation and appreciation ran through the crowd because the name had been known only to the owner until this moment.

When the priest and his party had backed carefully down the ladder, the little godmother in her bright yellow dress skipped happily around to the stern of the vessel. She handed her purse to Roberts and stepped back while he tied it to the sternpost, then again stepped forward and stuffed a folded banknote into the shiny plastic bag. This was a signal for others to come shuffling forward with goodwill offerings of their own.

While these formalities were taking place, a small group of men quietly made final adjustments to the launching gear with the slightly aggrieved air of ants in the vicinity of grasshoppers. They fastened a two-inch diameter hemp cable to the sternpost, led it forward to the bows, and then used a lacing of lighter line to position it along the sides of the vessel. At the bows, this heavy strop was made up to the near end of a six-part launching tackle (pronounced "tay-kel") whose far end lay on a little raft in the bay, held in its turn by a heavy kedge anchor.

Yankee Girl R had been shored up by braces placed along the sides as the vessel was built. The first step in launching had to be the removal of the braces along one side so the hull could be laid over onto the waiting rollers that would be the eventual means of moving the heavy hull across the beach to the water's edge. In the islands, this first step was known as "cutting down," because the shores were literally chopped away at the base, all being shortened slowly and simultaneously until the hull came to rest gently on the rollers.

Obviously this was to be a very delicate operation. If the cutting down was not carefully coordinated, too much weight would be thrown onto too few shores; and once breaking began, it would accelerate and bring *Yankee Girl R* smashing down onto the turn of the bilge—not a strong point, since the frames were overlapped there. To perform this delicate operation, I imagined a team of the oldest and most trusted men of the community swinging their razor-sharp machetes in stately unison, perhaps to the measured rhythm of some old chantey.

It turned out that there was no chantey and no unison. In their stead was boundless enthusiasm, in direct proportion to the number of pulls taken at the jack iron jug. Also, there was an apparent belief that speed was of the essence. Some chopped high, some chopped low, and all chopped rapidly. The mass of observers cheered, and I held my breath, fearing the worst. Fortunately the sharpened ends of the shores sank into the soft sand, which moderated and integrated individual effort. In a surprisingly short time the vessel was lying on the rollers, her weight divided between the keel and a strip of planks nailed along the turn of the bilge to protect the new paint job.

After the cutting down, there was a brief intermission while another round of refreshment was prescribed. Then eager hands were laid onto the tackle, and sheaves began to squeal in the heavy wooden blocks. A current of excitement ran through the onlookers as the heavy rope rose dripping out of the water and began shuddering under the load. But the fifty-ton hull didn't budge, and the eager haulers stumbled to a halt. Another excited rush was made, and again the rope stretched its limit before recoiling and pulling the crowd with it.

After several of these fruitless efforts, an ancient woman, wizened and brown as mahogany, her braids done up in the bandanna of a field worker, dipped into her past and began to chant.

"Long TIME on the labor GANG; YO, heave HO. Had a good TIME on the labor GANG; YO, heave HO!"

Up and down the line, older people began to take up the heavy beat of the chant. Slowly, the confused and ineffectual heaving of the crowd subsided as the rhythm became established and made itself felt. Now the stretch was pulled out with slow steps taken in time to the plodding beat. Now when the strain came on the heavy hull there was no recoil, and *Yankee Girl R* began to move.

Once started, she moved readily enough. There was an outcry as she crossed the flat foreshore and approached the last gentle slope down to the water's edge. Then, without warning, an old man at the stern wrapped the end of his check line around a palm trunk and held hard. There was a groan, then angry shouts and taunts from all the haulers as the life went out of the rope and the vessel stopped. The old man paid no heed, quietly directing his helpers to bring four rollers already left astern down to the water's edge ready to receive the weight of the bows when the water was reached. It was failure to do this that had caused the *A.L. Sea Author M.* to stick in the shallows for four days, six years back.

Rollers set in place, it was time to start again. The vessel advanced easily this time. The heaving became a walk and then a run across the beach. People stumbled backward, laughing and falling as the rope went slack and the burden began to move under its own weight. With a rush and a cheer from the crowd, *Yankee Girl R* slid into the water and floated free of the rollers. A swarm of boys swam out, clambering aboard and wrestling in an island version of king-on-the-mountain. Ashore, the festivities, congratula-

The Yankee Girl R *afloat for the first time.*
Windward, Carriacou. October 1970.

tions, and glow of accomplishment continued until the soft hour of island twilight settled on the jubilant Carriacouans.

Rigging and fitting out of *Yankee Girl R* took another year because Roberts worked carefully and to a high standard. The following summer he sailed her down to St. George's and installed the engine. Another year went by before I ran into him one morning in St. George's and asked how he was doing with the vessel. He smiled his cautious smile and replied that he was just on his way to close a deal with a young American who wanted to buy *Yankee Girl R* so he could haul fruit from the Dominican Republic to the Virgin Islands. Roberts volunteered that he had been offered $70,000 Eastern Caribbean (about $200,000 U.S. today) and was well pleased. I heard some while afterward that the deal fell through when the American was unable to raise the money, but it did give me some idea of the value an owner placed on such a vessel.

The last time I saw *Yankee Girl R,* Roberts was freighting biscuits and soap powder from Trinidad to St. Lucia under contract with Lever Brothers of Trinidad. The contract was especially favorable since the cargo was light and easy on the vessel and the trips were scheduled, thus avoiding both agent's commissions and long waits in the sweltering inner harbor at Port-of-Spain. Most vessels commonly spent two or three weeks there locating a cargo, finding space at the dock, and loading—just to make a single two-day trip with no assurances of cargo for the return.

With the launching of *Yankee Girl,* my principal aims in Carriacou were accomplished. It was time to move on to Bequia, the next island along the chain that had a widespread reputation for boatbuilding.

FOUR

Bequia Sweet

~ ~ ~

The trade winds dropped to nothing as the sultry afternoon wore on. A dark cloud appeared to windward and came drifting slowly down as *Eider* approached the two rocky cays that lie just off the south-western tip of Bequia. The squall hit just as I brought the cays abeam, and for a few moments I was fully occupied hauling in the mainsheet and getting my bow as close to the wind as possible. When I looked up to get my bearings, a small, blue open boat had cut through a narrow pass between the two cays and taken up a windward course just ahead of me. I could make out two sailors aboard, one handling steering and trim of the sails, the other standing on the windward gunwale and hiking out while holding on to the weather stay.

The wind was strong, but in the lee of the island there was only a small chop—ideal conditions for a brisk sail and an upbeat finish to what had been a dull day. The prospect of a brush with another boat added the frosting, and I leaned eagerly into the tiller.

When I did not gain an inch in the course of ten minutes, I concluded that *Eider* was carrying too much sail, heeling out of her best waterlines and generating too much water turbulence. Ordinarily I would not have taken the trouble to shorten sail so close to port, with no danger to the yacht or her gear, but it vexed me not to go powering past that bobbing, impudent little boat. I hastened forward and rolled down the mainsail until the helm was balanced again.

"*Now* we'll see what new sails and a longer waterline can do," I thought. I settled again at the tiller. But the little blue boat continued to dance provocatively ahead, the helmsman flinging water over his shoulder with a bailing gourd. His companion, on the windward gunwale, appeared to leap with joy in the gusts.

I bore down grimly, concentrating all my attention on overtaking the upstart. No luck. Although *Eider* was the larger boat, on this course she could not catch her opponent.

At last I sensed a slight weakening, a sag to leeward not fully recovered by the captain of the blue boat. "Well," I thought, "if I can't outfoot him, surely I can outpoint him." In theory, a taller rig and better cut sails always count when you steer as small as the design will take. If I could beat the blue boat to windward, I could win the race without being faster.

Soon the angle of *Eider's* course was indeed closer into the wind than that of the blue boat. We were standing well over it. Then, suddenly, the helmsman eased sheets and bore away two points. It took a couple of seconds for me to register that the little boat was not bound for Port Elizabeth at the head of the bay as I was. He was off across the channel to St. Vincent, nine miles of open water with a strong tide running against the winds of the squall.

The blue boat leaped ahead, seemingly from wavetop to wavetop, then into a wave with a burst of spray. Any chagrin I may have felt was swept away in admiration of the performance of the little craft. Clearly, a closer look at these unique double-enders was going to repay the trip to Bequia, even if nothing else was going on.

Riding the wave of my enthusiasm, I set out the next day to do some boat measuring. As it was Sunday, a good selection of fishing boats were pulled ashore at Friendship Bay.

There was one that was especially well maintained that also had an un-usual flared bow. Choosing *Country Girl* to measure turned out to be a partic-ularly happy inspiration; I later discovered she had won the medium-sized open boat class for the last three years at the Carriacou Regatta. As a result, a new generation of double-enders had been built with her characteristics.

The hull lines of *Country Girl* held the answer to the mystery of her speed: extremely fine entry through the water, sharp floors in the midsection to re-duce lost ground clawing to windward, and a fine run aft at the double-ended stern for minimum turbulence and drag. As a matter of fact, the lines are so fine that one might wonder if the drawing is an exaggeration. It isn't. A glance at Ian Child's photograph of *Leopard* under full sail, a boat built to the same lines as *Country Girl,* dispels all doubts.

Two other features of these craft, the daggerboard and the spritsail rig, deserve comment since they are characteristic of the double-enders of Be-quia, or "two-bow boats," as they are called. The retractable daggerboard is a big factor in the weatherly ability of these boats, important since the better fishing grounds lie to windward of Bequia. The spritsail rig, in its turn, is a handy means of increasing the height of the sail profile without using a taller, more expensive mast or a heavy gaff.

Just as I finished measuring *Country Girl,* a pedestrian halted his erratic progress along the beach, stared for a moment, then wobbled over.

Bequia fishing boat **Leopard** *at the Whitsun Regatta,*
Admiralty Bay, Bequia. (Photo by Ian Child.)

"You must pay to take the model," he announced in a no-nonsense tone.

I paused, taking him in, and played a hunch. "Are you the owner, then?" I asked.

My visitor drew himself up importantly. "I is know him. You pay me and I giving to him." Bloodshot eyes measured me from the seamed black face.

I stalled a little longer by explaining what I was doing and why I wanted the lines. It seemed best to lay it on pretty thick, and the light of inspiration went on as I recounted the preceding day's impromptu race as the reason for my admiration.

"Oh, is you in the little yacht, then?" interrupted my new acquaintance. It had been he at the helm of the little blue boat bound for St. Vincent in the squall. Waving aside my continuing apologies, he proceeded with great gusto to tell me of his trip.

"After the fish done sell, we having a good time. Having a Good Time with the boys. Having a Good Time with the girls. Having a general, all around Good Time."

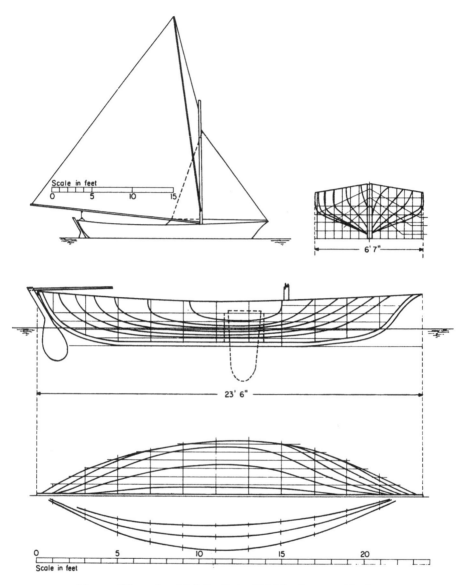

6' 7"

23' 6"

Lines of Country Girl, *built in 1963 by Lennox Taylor.*
Taken off October 1970.

And still having one, by the look of it.

Later, after spending more time in Bequia, I learned what my beach-side informant was enthusiastically describing was, in fact, the downhill portion of a typical day for Bequia fishermen. They leave the beach at 4:00 A.M. for the nine-mile beat out to the fishing grounds northeast of Mustique, trolling on the way out and hand-lining on the grounds themselves. If the catch is good, they set sail shortly after noon for St. Vincent, a distance of about fifteen miles.

After the fish are sold, they sail home, again about fifteen miles. In round numbers, this makes a daily outing of some forty miles, all of it in an open boat, and most of it in the open sea.

At a later stage in my understanding of these matters, I decided that it would be good to have some hard data on performance. *Country Girl* having been sold by then to someone in St. Vincent, I arranged a sailing trial on *Big Stuff,* one of the boats built to *Country Girl*'s design and that year's winner at Carriacou. *Big Stuff* would point as close as forty-five degrees apparent, making up to 5.4 knots, astonishing for a twenty-three–foot boat. With the wind on the beam, she attained speeds up to 6.5 knots, and downwind she made as much as 4.8 knots. These are numbers any boatyard with modern facilities might envy.

In Bequia there are several classes of open boats, all of which are double-ended, spritsail-rigged, and equipped with some form of daggerboard. The parent type undoubtedly is the New England whaleboat, to which it bears a close resemblance. This agrees with local lore concerning the origin of the boat. "In Bequia, it having aplenty whalerman," anyone will tell you. In fact, whaling remains such a focal point of Bequia's island life that it merits a chapter of its own, as will be seen.

The lines of *Dart,* one of the two actual whaleboats still in service when I was last in Bequia, are very similar to those of the Nantucket and New Bedford whaleboats, though perhaps just a little higher at the turn of the bilge. Also, the after sections are fuller than the forward sections, showing a greater asymmetry in this respect than the lines of the whale boat I eventually used for comparison. This difference may well be the result of late and individual innovation. Athneal Olliverre, the builder of *Dart* and head harpooner, told me that he had made *Dart* fuller aft so that she would not "squat" when being towed by a harpooned whale.

Along the south shore of Bequia, I found several fishing boats so similar to the whaling boats that I did not make a separate set of lines. These boats set sail with a large seine entirely filling the midships and patrol back and forth across the Grenadines Bank until they locate a school of the small, pelagic carangids locally known as "robins." The seine is paid out as the boat circles until the school is penned. Then the fish are dipped up in hand nets from the edges of the pen. Sometimes, by careful management, a single school can be worked by several boats for two or three days. During this time the boats shuttle to markets in Bequia or St. Vincent as quickly as they are filled, which is why fast sailing is a particularly important characteristic of this type.

In recent years, as small outboard motors have become available in the islands, many of the Bequia two-bow boats have begun to sport a 7.5 horse-

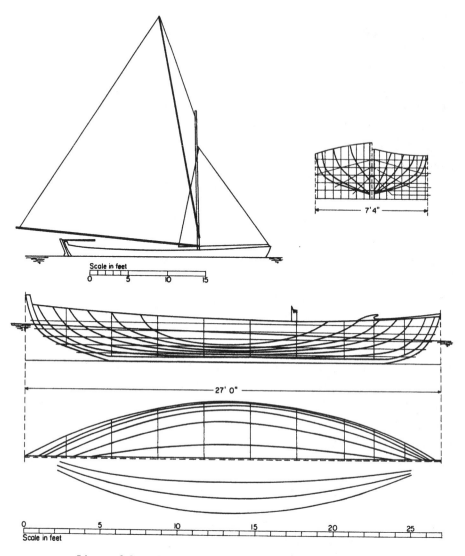

Lines of the whaleboat Dart, *built in 1955 by Athneal Olliverre. Taken off August 1973.*

power motor on an offset bracket fastened to the port side in the stern. When the outboard is in use, the rudder is unshipped; when sailing, the outboard is cocked up and securely lashed.

Port Elizabeth, at the head of Admiralty Bay, was still an active schooner port in the 1970s, although by then there were no longer any active builders. When I asked the "old heads" who gathered to decide these matters in the shade of a large almond tree, they were all in agreement: *Friendship Rose,*

Schooner **Friendship Rose** *beating up Admiralty Bay*
on a failing breeze. March 1971.

launched in 1969, was the last of the Bequia schooners. Smaller sailing vessels, the sloops, continued to be built, but in declining numbers. While smaller boats continued to be a live industry both here and elsewhere in the islands, only occasionally were vessels for cargo transport being built in the traditional fashion.

In the course of my research under the almond tree, repeated mention was made of a famous vessel builder and captain known as Reg Mitchell. Lost at sea during World War II, he has taken on the dimensions of legend with the passing decades. While his surname is a common one in certain islands of the Lesser Antilles such as Bequia, the man himself assuredly was out of the ordinary. He was seven feet tall. He was the only known West Indian to master celestial navigation. And he went missing under circumstances absolutely guaranteed to endow a considerable body of folklore.

Further information, first-hand and factual, was readily available in an early visit to Bequia, just down the beach at the Frangipani Hotel. It was owned by the Hon. J.F. Mitchell, son of Reg and elected representative in St. Vincent for the Grenadines constituency. "Son" Mitchell talked interestingly and well about his father and his father's last vessel, *Gloria Colita,* reputedly the largest schooner ever built in the Lesser Antilles.

Builder's half model of the schooner Gloria Colita,
owned by the Hon. J.F. Mitchell.

Son Mitchell produced a snapshot of the 1939 launching of *Gloria Colita.* Noticing my obvious interest, he asked if I would like to see a model of the schooner. To my delight and wonder, he brought it out—not a painted toy to be admired politely and put aside, but the actual builder's half-model from which the vessel was framed. I was therefore able to take lines directly from the instrument carved and used by Reg Mitchell himself.

The lines of the model might have been taken by unpinning the lifts and measuring them as was originally done—the ends of the pencil marks were still visible at each station. However, I hesitated to take such liberty with an object of obvious sentimental value. Instead I devised another method. The model was fifty-five inches long, which made it convenient to designate stations at five-inch intervals. At each station, I pressed a short length of copper wire against the model and then traced the curve onto graph paper, thus creating the body plan of the hull, from which I could develop buttocks and waterlines.

Gloria Colita is interesting not only for her size (165 feet overall; 178 tons) but for her sharp bottom, extreme deadrise, and three-masted rig. Sharp floors and marked deadrise are generally recognized as important characteristics of a fast-sailing hull. There is also the fact that the V-bottom formed by sharply rising floors would have much greater longitudinal strength, an important consideration in such a long vessel.

My luck continued and I was able to make a sail plan from the recorded length of the vessel and a photo Son Mitchell had among his memorabilia.

Even allowing for the inflationary tendencies of folklore, the builder of *Gloria Colita* must have been a man of unusual abilities. Himself the son of a schooner builder, Mitchell owned two schooners before building *Gloria Colita.* His first was *Water Pearl* (ninety-four feet long; sixty-eight tons), built in partnership with his father and launched in 1932. Two years later the schooner failed to come about when tacking near Bequia Head and was blown ashore and lost. Next came *Juliana,* a schooner built up in the Bahama Islands in a Nassau boatyard, about which nothing is known except that she

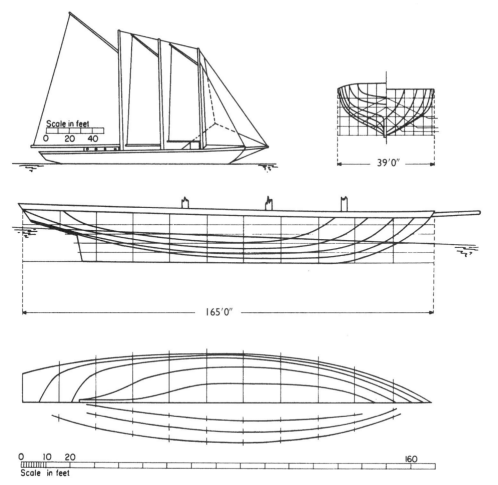

Lines of the tern schooner Gloria Colita, *built in 1939 by Reginald Mitchell,*
Admiralty Bay, Bequia. Taken off March 1974.

was larger than *Water Pearl*. With her, Mitchell freighted between British
Guyana and Cuba and on one occasion set out for New York but was turned
back by heavy weather off Cape Hatteras.

Reg Mitchell's widow, still living in St. Lucia, told me these and many
other details of trips she made sailing and trading with her husband. She told
of loading rice in British Guyana for Cuba, loading sugar in Cuba for Mobile,
Alabama, and returning to Cuba with lumber. She had particularly pleasant
memories of Batista's Cuba—everything was very cheap and customs officers
brought fruit and flowers to the schooner as she lay at dock. Mrs. Mitchell recalled holding the deck watch when Reg made his sights at noon and four
o'clock, thus confirming one of the legends about him without my asking. She
spoke fondly of the luxurious master's accommodations aboard *Gloria Colita*,

less fondly about her responsibility for cleaning out the crew's quarters when the vessel returned to Bequia for a refit.

On his last voyage, Mitchell again loaded rice in British Guyana for Havana, and then in Havana loaded sugar for Venezuela. But before leaving, he discharged his Bequia crew without explanation and sent them home. He shipped a Spanish-speaking crew and returned to Mobile, where he loaded lumber and cleared for Havana. No overdue report was ever made. *Gloria Colita* was simply found abandoned and awash in the Gulf Stream by a United States Coast Guard patrol plane. The schooner was towed to Mobile and sold. The mystery of what happened to Mitchell and his crew was never solved.

Although much was of interest to me in Bequia on my first visit in 1971, there appeared to be no further building of larger vessels. It saddened me that in an island where seafaring was so much a part of an independent and enviable life such a thing could have happened. But everywhere I inquired, the answer was the same: "No more vessel is building in these times." So I set a Monday in November for my departure, and on the preceding Saturday afternoon I took my last stroll around an island that I had come to admire.

I climbed the steep, winding road that leads from the harbor to the top of a ridge, then drops down again to Friendship Bay and communities along its south side. At the top of the ridge, for no particular reason, I left the paved road and took an unpaved fork that dropped down to the Bay at a new point. I came to a stop at the beach and stared. Across the water on a low bank above a small pebble beach stood the gaunt carcass of a small vessel in frames! Everyone had been so definite about no further shipbuilding that at first I doubted my eyes. But the long rays of the afternoon sun highlighted the far shore quite clearly. There was no chance I was mistaken.

I walked along the water's edge. Presently the sand narrowed until I was forced to scramble up a steep bank and make my way along a footpath through the dry, thorny scrub. When the path emerged from the bush, I found myself looking across a cultivated hillside at a small wooden house painted light blue. An old white woman sat at the front window, her arms folded on the sill and her chin resting on her arms. As I approached, a small girl spotted me, scampered up the steps, and disappeared into the house. The woman sat up and looked in my direction.

"How do, sor," she called.

Inside, the urgent voice of the little girl was saying, "Mama, mama. White man coming."

A slender, brown-skinned woman came to the half-door, wiping her hands on her apron. She repeated the old woman's greeting. When I asked who was building the vessel I had seen, she answered obliquely. "Yes, sor. Is he down by the bayside now."

She stood quietly with the little girl clinging to her skirts as I made my way past the house, over a low stone wall, and down another footpath to the bay. There I found a man sitting on his heels among shavings and wood chips, staring up at the frames of the vessel. He was wearing faded shorts, a short-sleeved white shirt, and a billed cap.

I greeted him and asked if he was building the vessel.

"Yes, sor," he replied. "The keel laid in August month."

"You're moving along very well, then."

"Well, is very hard these days, you know," the man said quietly. "Materials is very dear and no one want to work at all."

The remarks were pessimistic, and yet I sensed determination. He was lean, of medium build and deeply tanned, with a reserved and diffident manner. As he turned to speak to me, I noticed that his left hand was gone at the wrist, and that he had a long scar on his left thigh.

The builder's name was Haakon Mitchell. He rented from the government the thirteen acres that formed Point Hilary. The products of his grazing sheep had provided his principal source of income since losing the hand in a fishing accident. In addition he owned two adjacent acres upon which his house stood, where he planted his ground provisions and reared his family of seven.

As we talked, he dropped the "sor" and began to speak with greater animation. Although he had never been to the Carriacou Regatta, he knew of *Mermaid* and was planning to challenge her. He told of trips he had made in his father's schooner as a boy, of the Nova Scotia–built schooners he had once seen in Barbados. He told about the stockpile of suitably curved timbers under his house that he had been gathering for six years and that he and two teenage boys hoped to turn into a vessel.

We talked until the sun was behind the island and it was time for me to start back to the harbor. Our conversation had produced much useful information about methods and possible design influences. Moreover, I felt a strong empathy for the man's aspirations. He was building more than a vessel: Haakon Mitchell was trying to provide growing room for his family, which otherwise had two acres of rocky hillside as the limits of their world.

A delay of a day or two to take off the lines of Mitchell's craft would not have mattered, but nothing like it could be done before the hull was planked. That was still a long time off.

I wished Haakon Mitchell well and walked back to the anchorage through the night. Two days later I went ahead with my departure as planned.

FIVE

Anguilla Once Again

As I made my way north from Bequia, island-hopping and looking for signs of sloop and schooner construction, it began to seem as if my project was in the home stretch. The end of the island chain of the Lesser Antilles was already in sight, and with practice I was getting much better at taking off lines.

Anguilla, as I knew from my earlier visit, was still an active boatbuilding center and had long been known for its fleet of schooners. These two facts, however encouraging for a boat measurer, constituted a somewhat startling defiance of certain realities. Anguilla, being low and flat, does not force the moisture-laden trade winds to rise and cool; consequently it receives little rainfall. What's more, the scant rain hardly slows down as it either soaks into the loose, limestone rubble or instantly evaporates. As a result, there are no timber resources *at all* on the island, and I wonder whether there ever were.

Another problem is apparent from the configuration of Anguilla's coastline. There are many shallow bays, but not a single well-protected harbor. The upshot of these two troubling factors was that Anguilla had a boatbuilding industry without timber and a schooner fleet that was annually in jeopardy during the hurricane months of August and September. And these were not the only surprises, as I soon discovered.

One sun-baked afternoon, while walking the dusty road near Sandy Ground, one of the few settlements, I pondered the marvel of a desolate and unproductive landscape dotted, in defiance of economic expectation, with houses. Not just any houses, mind you: solid houses built of cement blocks, brightly painted, and each showing, by many small signs, the pride of ownership. The Reverend Carty stopped to offer me a lift and explained the phenomenon as he drove.

"Anguilla is a remittance society. The money here comes from islanders working overseas. Husbands, sons, boyfriends—they work somewhere and send back what they can so that a house is ready when they return. Why, did you know that there are more Anguillans in Perth Amboy than in Anguilla?"

I had not known, but could see the point. There was very little to do in Anguilla. In the past, a long-staple variety of cotton was grown here, and seed from Anguilla was in demand as far away as Louisiana. But synthetic fibers put an end to all that.

There has long been a small salt works operating at Sandy Ground. For this, at least, the climate of Anguilla is ideally suited. The large, shallow lagoon lying behind the beach is flooded with sea water in late December at the beginning of the dry season (that is, when it is even drier than usual). By March, sufficient water has evaporated so that large crystals of nearly pure sodium chloride begin to form and settle to the bottom. Then the harvest begins. Workers pushing small, flat boats wade the lagoon, scooping up the wet crystals, which are dumped on the beach to dry. Gradually a gleaming white mountain grows as salt piles up, after which it is ground and bagged. Much of this salt is sold in Trinidad and used in the oil fields.

Apart from salt and, lately, a burgeoning tourist industry on the north coast, Anguilla produces little except Anguillans. For those with the requisite skills, boatbuilding is an alternative to leaving the island. In boatbuilding, materials acquired elsewhere are brought to the island, to be assembled there into an asset that can return to the outside to earn.

I found that boatbuilding Anguilla style was carried out in an informal manner ideally suited to the rhythm of island life. It would all begin when someone with money engaged someone like MacDuff Richardson or Egbert Conner, in the 1970s the senior maritime craftsmen of the island. Whichever man was available put together a team of carpenters and arranged to use a section of beach. The keel was brought from Guyana by schooner, the framing timbers cut on nearby St. Martin or St. Eustatius. The materials were dumped on the beach, and work continued as long as money and materials lasted. When either ran short, the carpenters returned to fishing and subsistence agriculture until work on the vessel resumed. No rent was paid for the building site, there were no formal contracts with delivery dates or penalty clauses, no minimum wages, no taxes, no bookkeeping chores. In short, there was very little overhead and no reason to make haste, which only got folks vexed and created additional delays.

This was definitely the method followed in the construction of the first vessels I measured in Anguilla (the largest I saw being built anywhere in the islands). *New London,* set up by MacDuff Richardson, had been three years under construction when I measured her and was not launched until two years later. At the time I took off the lines, Egbert Connor had taken over as master carpenter and was working with two helpers and a caulker.

The large size of *New London* made her something of a chore to measure,

Schooner New London *under construction at Forest Bay, Anguilla. March 1970.*

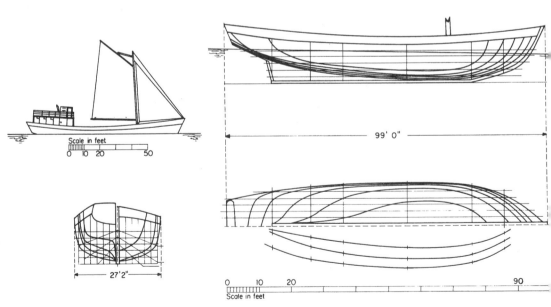

Scale in feet
0 10 20   50

99' 0"

27' 2"

0   10   20   90
Scale in feet

Lines of the New London, *built in 1972 by MacDuff Richardson and Egbert Connor at Forest Bay, Anguilla. Taken off January 1971.*

Mack Conner (right), owner of the Lady Mack (background), at Blowing Point, Anguilla. January 1971.

but on the other hand the flat floors and full bow sections made it easy to draw and fair the lines. The result is a very full-carrying hull that was later said to carry up to 140 tons of cargo for her owner, Albert Lake. Although decidedly unglamorous in other respects, it is interesting to note that the run of *New London* is smooth and well-formed. The broad, flat transom would immediately mark her as Anguilla-built in any port in the Lesser Antilles.

In her rig *New London* went one step beyond *Yankee Girl* in yielding to the attractions of diesel power. *Yankee Girl,* though rigged with only a single mast, was proportioned for a full sailing rig; *New London* was rigged as a schooner without a mainmast. There was a logic to this, since *New London* was built to trade primarily between Anguilla and Puerto Rico with stops in

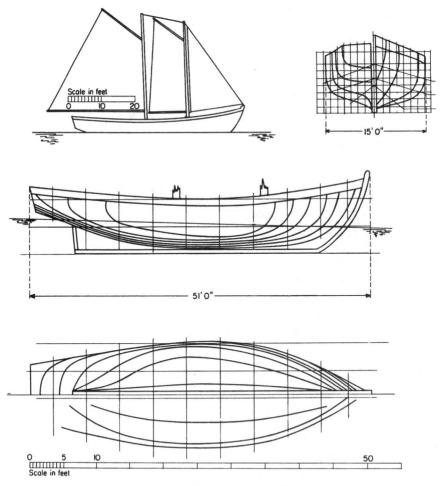

Lines of schooner Lady Mack, *built in 1966 by Mack Connor at Blowing Point, Anguilla. Taken off January 1971.*

the Virgin Islands. On this route the wind is either dead ahead or dead astern, and the schooner rig is not best suited to either point of sailing.

At Blowing Point, a reef harbor near the southwest tip of Anguilla, *Lady Mack* had been hauled ashore for repairs, giving me an unusual opportunity to take the lines off an older-style vessel. Although *Lady Mack* was built in 1966 and fitted with an engine at launching, she had the unmodified lines of a traditional all-sail schooner. The marked sheer of the deck provided generous freeboard despite relatively little drag to the keel. The stem, less raking and curved than in *New London,* gave *Lady Mack* the correspondingly finer entry that might be expected of an all-sail vessel. The floors of the midsection were a compromise between the flat floors of a full-carrying hull and the sharp floors of a fast sailor.

Lady Mack was the third schooner built, owned, and captained by Mack Connor. His earlier vessels were lost in hurricanes, underscoring the hazards of not having an Anguillan hurricane hole. In setting up his vessels, I learned that Connor used the common four-to-one length-to-beam ration with an additional variation all his own.

Speaking of his first schooner, *Baby Mack,* which had a long, overhanging stern, Connor said, "When she load heavy, the stern steer the boat." After a couple of near disasters when the vessel was hard to bring about, Connor concluded, "If is a longer vessel you want, then put a longer keel." And in fact, *Lady Mack* was noticeably short ended. For a length overall of fifty-one feet and a beam of fifteen feet, she was some nine feet shorter than the traditional four-to-one ratio would dictate.

Fishing and fishing boats are an integral part of the subsistence livelihood still found among over one-fourth of the people of the islands, including Anguilla. In addition to everyday practical employment, these boats are spruced up and raced on New Year's Day, Whitsun, the August Bank Holiday, and on Bastille Day in the French part of nearby St. Martin.

Egbert Connor's boat, *Bluebird,* was an obvious choice to measure since I now knew the owner. The upright stem and straight bow frames produce so fine an entry that the waterlines forward appear to be hollow, though they are not. Sharp floors and a very high "tuck" result in a smooth run and a very easy bottom. Much time and thought have been given to modifying these boats for racing, with the result that they have acquired some impractical traits. The sharp bottom makes them a little unsteady, and the deep draft makes them difficult to haul ashore. In compensation, they are graceful and fast, though I am not sure how fast since I never had the opportunity to get sailing data.

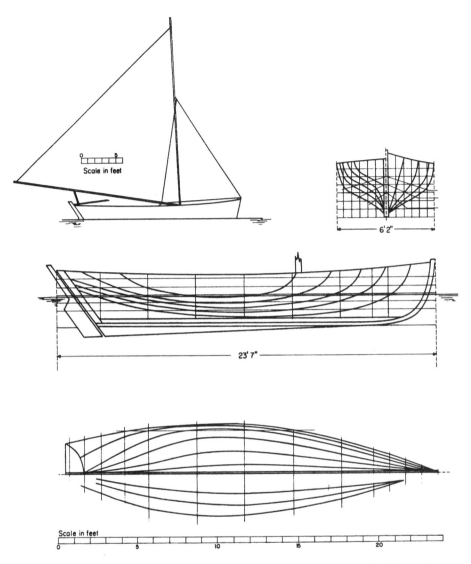

Lines of Bluebird, *built in 1960 by Egbert Connor at Sandy Ground, Anguilla. Taken off January 1971.*

On my second trip to Anguilla I stayed longer, became better acquainted with the people, and as a result got the chance to sail aboard old *Warspite*. In addition to her monthly trips carrying salt to Trinidad, *Warspite* had the contract to carry supplies and relief crews twice a month to the lighthouse on Sombrero Island, forty miles northwest of Anguilla. Emile Gumbs, owner of *Warspite,* suggested I go along to get the feel of a schooner at sea.

Departure time was 4:00 A.M., but I was awake by 2:30, too excited to stay in my bunk any longer. The moon was down, and *Eider* rocked gently in the soft, inky darkness. After a time, sounds began to reach me from the shore—the murmur of voices, the hollow grating of a boat dragged across the beach, the thud and splash of oars being shipped. I hailed the rowers softly, was picked up, and went aboard *Warspite* with the crew. Several of them began to clear off gear while a couple took the dinghy back to the beach for passengers and supplies.

Four men moved to the foredeck in the darkness and set about shackling the two-part jib halyard to the heavy anchor chain. Three men tailed onto the halyard and began to take out slack. At the right moment, the fourth man cast off the chain from where it had been secured to the samson post. Then all four began to heave, transmitting the rhythm of the work with body and breath until all had settled smoothly into the load. At each heave the rattling chain rose dripping from the water, sinking again as the men shifted their holds on the halyard.

When the jib halyard was "two-blocked," with the tackle hauled as far as it could go, a man stopped the chain at the hawse pipe and the jib halyard was let run. Down came the chain along the deck. The floor block was unshackled and taken forward to the hawse pipe so the sequence could be repeated. In this unhurried manner, it took a little over a half hour to bring *Warspite* short on her anchor, ready to get under way.

Once the lighthouse crew and supplies were aboard, the dinghy was quickly lifted on deck using the throat and peak halyards of the foremast. Then the vast mainsail was raised, using its two halyards. I noticed that as each job was finished the crew moved without instruction to the next. Soon the big mainsail was peaked up and flopping idly in the faint morning breeze, a pre-dawn harbinger of the trade winds. The engine roared into life, coughed, and settled into a low grumble. There were calls from the wheelhouse to the crew, and I detected motion forward. We powered over the anchor, breaking it out. Two men brought up the rusty monster and catted it. Another group hoisted the jib and the staysail. The wind was pulling the vessel back and turning her; the sails bellied out, inch-thick sheets squealing through the blocks. With the engine steadying her, *Warspite* filled away and began her journey to Sombrero Island.

Once clear of the bay, *Warspite* took the freshening breeze on her starboard quarter and quickened to her sails. The helmsman leaned forward, peering into the dark as he piloted the schooner past the shoal patches that lie to the south and west of Dog Island. After half an hour he relaxed visibly and lit a dim light inside the cabin, slid aside a small wooden panel, and exposed the compass mounted on the cabin trunk. He glanced up and nodded me to a seat beside him on the wheel box. I slid into place as he rose, and I realized he wanted me to steer. I gingerly grasped the iron spokes of the wheel while the helmsman stepped back to the big cleat where the mainsheet was secured.

"Shake her, boy," he called. "Shake her."

The command came as a complete surprise to me, but the expression was so apt that it took only a second to grasp what was wanted. I spun the wheel and luffed while he overhauled the mainsheet.

"Again," he urged, then stood for the space of a few seconds looking at the mainsail, stretched in a taut curve upward to the gaff. Apparently satisfied, he made up the sheet on the heavy cleat and returned to the wheel box. I started to yield my place but he motioned me to stay.

We were going at a good clip, and the schooner held her course with little help from me. As the overtaking waves rose under the starboard quarter and gurgled forward along the keel, *Warspite* first lifted, then surged diagonally across the face of the wave to settle softly into the trough as the next wave gathered. Out away from the island, where the trade wind was well established, I waited expectantly for the engine to be shut off, now that its work was done. I wanted my night passage on a windjammer pure and undefiled by the whine of a General Motors diesel.

The engine droned on, however, oblivious to the delicacy of my sentiments. As it became clear that it would be with us for the duration, I gave the matter a little further thought. However romantic it might be for me, this was not, for the captain and crew, a nostalgic journey to recapture sensations of the great age of sail. For them it was simply another day's work and not an especially easy one at that. An engine makes passages quicker, easier, and safer; for these benefits, a little unromantic noise and stink are not too high a price to pay. Besides, the worst thing in the world for a marine engine is to be used briefly and then shut down to sit in the salt-saturated damp of the bilge until needed again.

So we continued, the whine of the engine punctuated by the squeal of a gaff as it swayed with the lift and roll of the swells that sweep through the Anegada Passage into the Caribbean Sea. The sun rose behind us, slowly warming into activity the passengers and crew, drawing them out of the corners where they had been sheltering from the night's chill. Soon the cook, muttering and grumbling to himself, began to serve tin cups of hot, sweet tea along with a thick slice of bread and a cold piece of fried barracuda.

Two hours after we set sail, the loom of Sombrero Light became visible. By nine o'clock we were lying-to in the lee of the island, a high-sided disk of pitted limestone punched up from the ocean floor to stand as a sentinel in the middle of the Anegada Passage. There was, in the lee, a three-fathom bottom

Sunrise aboard the Warspite *en route to*
Sombrero Island. January 1971.

over a rocky shelf, but holding was poor and the chance of fouling too great to anchor. In consequence, *Warspite* lay-to with the mainsail sheeted close and the helm lashed hard over.

The dinghy was gotten over the side, and the first load of passengers started ashore as the schooner slowly side-slipped downwind. When the boat was ready to return for another load, the mate put the engine in gear and edged closer to the cliffs. All of the crew not otherwise occupied got fishing lines over the side and were soon hauling in snapper and grouper in profusion.

I went ashore in the second boatload to see what there was to see: the concrete tower that housed the light, concrete living quarters for the crew, and the twisted and rusting girders of the former light tower, destroyed when waves swept the island during the hurricane of 1950. The base of the old tower was located at least fifty feet above the surface of the sea, and the disintegrating girders had been made of structural grade steel. The storm that destroyed the station must have been fearsome indeed.

The relieved crew was aboard by noon, and the dinghy was again stowed on deck. The return trip was sailed on a close reach, bringing us to Anguilla at 4:00 P.M., forty miles in four hours exactly, an average of ten knots. Later I asked *Warspite*'s captain, Arthur Connor, about some of the schooner's passage times. He replied eagerly, with obvious pride in *Warspite*'s reputation:

Anguilla to Sombrero, 40 miles in three and a half hours; eleven and a half knots, light.

Anguilla to Guadeloupe, 195 miles in twenty-six hours; seven and a half knots, loaded.

Anguilla to San Juan, 170 miles downwind in twenty-two hours. Past seven and a half knots, light.

And then he told again, in loving detail, the story of *Warspite*'s most famous passage, when he was no more than a boy. In the 1920s, workers went from Anguilla to the Dominican Republic every year to work in the sugar cane harvest. On these trips, *Warspite* carried as many as three hundred cane cutters. She and the other schooners making the trip had to clear from St. Martin, since British regulations did not allow such overloading.

On the return trip in 1929, *Warspite, Eagle, Betsy, Ismay, Gladys,* and *Industry* cleared together from La Romana in the Dominican Republic. The rest of the schooners began the long beat home in the usual way, tacking off and on under the southern coasts of the Dominican Republic and Puerto Rico, hoping for relief from headwinds and currents by hugging the shore. *Warspite* took a chance and held on the port tack, taking a long board to the south until even the heights of Puerto Rico were lost to view. Two days out, the trades backed well into the north. *Warspite* got home in three and a half days, still on the port tack, hardly having to be trimmed throughout.

The straight-line distance for this passage is 360 miles, but a vessel going to windward sails roughly twice that. In addition, I figured 84 miles of leeway due to the opposing current. This brought an average speed for the passage of 9.8 knots—on the wind and without an engine! Using 11.5 knots, Captain Connor's reported best speed unladen to Sombrero, and this remarkable 9.8 knots figure, I calculated speed/length ratios of 1.44 and 1.22, respectively. In *The Search for Speed Under Sail,* Howard Chapelle, who devoted much of his life to these matters, remarks: "Long and intensive observation shows that the highest service speed usually recorded in a seagoing sailing vessel of good design, with an efficient rig, is in the neighborhood of a speed/length ratio of 1.25–1.35."

From the foregoing, it is clear that *Warspite* has been a remarkably fast sailor by international standards as well as in local Anguillan legend. She was built in 1918 by J.T. Hughes to the design of her original owner, A.R. Carty. Materials were so scarce (then as now) that timbers were used from an abandoned sloop, *Gazelle.* Originally, *Warspite* was 62 feet long, 18.3 feet in beam, 7.6 feet in the hold, and 37 registered tons. Later, in 1928, she was "stretched." She was cut in two, a 14-foot piece was scarfed into her keel, frames were added, and the vessel rebuilt to new dimensions of 76 feet in length, 20 feet on the beam, 9.6 feet in the hold, and 72 registered tons.

The details of *Warspite*'s colorful career seem worth recording, not only because they form an important part of the folklore of Anguilla, but also for the clues given about her long and profitable life. In this I was fortunate, because Emile Gumbs, *Warspite*'s owner and master, was a nephew of the original owner and exceptionally well informed about his venerable schooner.

Gumbs laughingly said that the schooner had been repaired and rebuilt so extensively over the years that she contained none of her original wood. She sank twice at moorings and once was abandoned at sea. Always she returned to service, largely from the persistence and ingenuity of Gumbs.

In 1954, on a return trip from Trinidad, the schooner was sailing to leeward of the Grenadines when water was found in the hold. Pumping did not reduce the level and the crew put the boat over the side. Captain Carty refused to leave the vessel and shamed the crew into returning aboard. Between them, they managed to get *Warspite* into Admiralty Bay and beached her. After making temporary repairs, Carty then took *Warspite* to Bequia and stayed for several months, supervising the replacement of the vessel's keel— while careened!

On another occasion, Gumbs himself was captaining *Warspite* on a return trip from Trinidad with a load of cement. They passed the heavily trafficked northern mouth of the Gulf of Paria at sunset and Gumbs took the wheel through the night. Toward dawn, he raised the light at Point Salines, Grenada, and called the mate to relieve him so that he could get some sleep. In mid-morning he awakened with a captain's sixth sense that something was wrong. Hurrying on deck, he found that the schooner had fallen into the morning calm that prevails behind Grenada and was aground on the coral patch lying off Long Point. The sea was flat and the day fair, so the mate was admiring the green splendors of Grenada's heights and waiting for the minute Caribbean tide to float the vessel off.

Without hesitation, Gumbs roused the crew, got the hatch cover off, and began to throw sacks of cement into the sea until the schooner had been lightened enough to kedge off the coral. He judged it the height of folly to sit idly while the vessel was in danger, however remote the danger might seem.

Such a response is unusual in the islands, where sailing conditions are so nearly ideal that it is easy to become careless. Few captains have formal training, navigational aids are scarce and unreliable outside yachting circles, but above all it is simply hard to believe that danger can exist in such a warm and wonderful world. In this case, however, there is a strong surge that occasionally sets onto the leeward coast of Grenada out of a clear blue sky and sends breakers smoking across the shoal where the schooner stranded that day.

Gumbs's response, to my mind, represents the very highest calibre of seamanship. Many people are capable of prudence when facing a clear and present danger, but it is much rarer to find someone able to anticipate hazards while the sea is calm, and who, moreover, does not hesitate to take measures that may appear unnecessary, even faint-hearted and foolish. In the long run such prudence pays off, as I believe the age of *Warspite* admirably demonstrates.

There were many excellent reasons for taking off the lines of *Warspite*, but

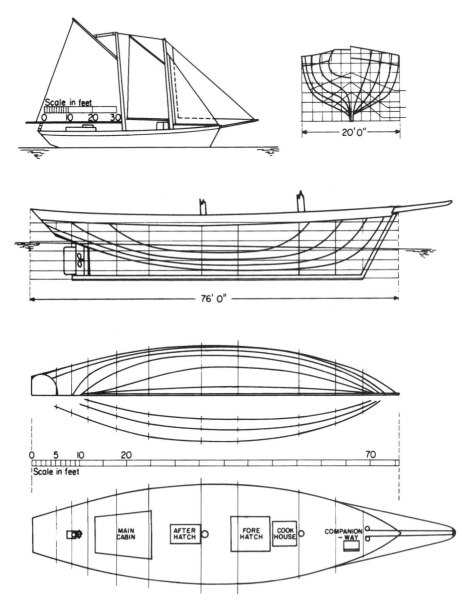

Lines of schooner **Warspite***, built in 1918 by J.T. Hughes at Sandy Ground, Anguilla. Taken off May 1975.*

it meant catching her when she went up on the marine railway in St. Lucia, which I never managed to do. On my final trip to Anguilla, it occurred to me, *in extremis,* that the job might somehow be done with the vessel in the water. The method I adopted was simple enough in conception: I marked stations on the rail where convenient, measured the beam at each station, and hung over the side a string, weighted and knotted at one-foot intervals. With diving mask, snorkel, and a waterproof carpenter's rule, I dived into the water to measure the horizontal distance from the knots on the string to the hull, calling out the measurements to a helper on deck. It was all pretty straightforward except for the communications link. For each measurement—and there were a lot of them at each station and ten stations in all—I had to surface, remove the snorkel from my mouth, spit out my ration of sea water, and call out the numbers loud enough for them to be heard over the slap and creak of the schooner.

The method, however cumbersome, did work, and I got my measurements. But by the time the job was done, I was so cold, hoarse, and waterlogged that I had stopped regretting that the method had not occurred to me earlier.

The lines of *Warspite* are an excellent example of the principal characteristics of a fast-sailing hull: sharp floors in the midsection, with a high, easy turn of the bilge; a fine entrance, with slight hollow in the lower waterlines; and a long, easy run begun well forward and carried smoothly past the stern post and onto the transom. The rigging plan is much shorter than the original. The masts have twice been cut down, first when an engine was fitted, later when a larger engine was installed. Once, during World War II when materials were particularly scarce, the mainmast broke and the mainsail was set on the foremast for a time. With that ersatz sloop rig, Gumbs told me with a chuckle, she sailed even faster than before.

At the time I made my measurements, the foremast was out and Gumbs was considering rigging her again with topmasts. He had an eye on the day charter business in nearby, tourist-booming St. Martin. I hope he did so, for it would be a grand thing to see once again a schooner with top hamper standing into Road Bay.

In a conversation with Arthur Conner, *Warspite*'s captain, the following interesting fact came to light.

"In Anguilla, we does sail on the shares. Can't get people to sail on the month, only on shares. Been so since ancient time. If the owner is buy a car, we is buy a chair."

He was referring to the fact that in Anguilla, alone among the islands I visited, trading vessels operate on a traditional share plan similar to that used by fishermen the world over. From the gross earnings of the vessel, running expenses (food, fuel, harbor dues, commissions, etc.) are deducted. Of net earnings, the owner takes one-third and the crew share equally in the remaining two-thirds. Then the captain is paid an additional half-share from the owner's portion.

Arthur Connor, captain of the Warspite, *at Road Harbor, Anguilla. May 1975.*

The advantage to the owner is obvious. When the vessel is not earning, there are no labor costs. The advantage to the crew is less obvious, and intriguing. It would appear that it suits the crew to work intermittently and to know that they have an assured share of a profitable venture. I was surprised to learn that all members of the crew share equally, from captain to cabin boy, but Connor was very definite on that point. It was another of those discoveries that, taken altogether, constitute the unique character of Anguilla.

The skills and traditions of boatbuilding were already well established in Anguilla when official records began in the 1840s—this in spite of the island's complete lack of timber resources. Of the island's four anchorages, three are reef struck and difficult of access. The fourth is shallow and subject to rollers from the north in winter months. None provides a secure, all-weather moorage.

By contrast, the nearby islands of St. Martin, St. Barthelemy, and St. Eustatius have better resources, be they timber or harbors or both, and appear to have similar ethnic and cultural backgrounds. Yet these islands have seen only sporadic maritime activity, whereas Anguilla has had a well-founded and continuous industry since early times.

My best explanation for this enigma is that the difference is to be found in the Anguillans themselves. Though they come in all shades from black to white, they seem to have the cohesion and shared attitudes that may be an outgrowth of their common poverty. In conventional terms, Anguilla is poor and unproductive; since it has no history of successful plantation activity, this must always have been the case. It is my observation, however, that to be barren and unproductive in the Caribbean is frequently a blessing in disguise. There is little to attract the exploiters who come in the first wave, and therefore little to do for the reformers who come when times change. This is certainly the case in Anguilla, where the people have been left almost entirely alone to make their own way in a harsh environment, developing in the process a sense of purpose and independence that is their heritage and principal natural resource.

Make Thee an Ark

T he big tamarind tree cast a welcome shadow in the glare of a sharp afternoon sun, strong even in January, and I was glad to stop. The road that winds upward from the harbor of Friendship Bay was steep, and the view of Bequia and the surrounding seascape from the crest spectacular as ever. Back to the right I could see the hotel for off-the-beaten-track tourists; on the other side of the bay was the little village of La Pompe, quiet and serene.

I rested and drank in the always-new panorama of sea and islands while my eagerness struggled with a nagging uncertainty. While still in Anguilla, it had seemed a fine and workable plan to return to Bequia and help with the building of the little sloop I had seen on the shore at Friendship Bay. This plan, already stirring the first time I talked with Haakon Mitchell, had teased at the back of my mind for three months now. Now, with new arrangements and a more flexible schedule, I was back for as long as it took.

I felt a bit sheepish, however. How much help could I really be? I had some tool-handling ability, but certainly not the skills of a ship's carpenter. How would the solitary builder on Point Hilary regard my offer of help? I felt entirely incapable of walking up and announcing the simple truth: that I was deeply moved by the dreams and plans of a poor and simple man to provide for his family and himself by building a vessel; that I wanted to watch and learn from him. Such an announcement, no matter how sincere, would surely convince Haakon Mitchell that I was eccentric if not actually dangerous. I felt more ill at ease with each passing moment.

From the branches above my head a white-eyed grackle called "bek-wee, bek-wee, tsweet, tsweet." The grackles in Bequia really say this and say it clearly. Elsewhere, even in St. Vincent only nine miles away, other members of this species sing a different tune. Having stated his opinion, the glossy black bird edged a little closer, rolled his pearly eye at me, then retreated to a higher branch. Taking this as a good omen, I allowed eagerness to prevail over uncertainty and resumed my trek, downhill now, on the narrow road leading to the bay.

When I reached the little blue house, the old lady was seated at the same window in the same attitude as three months before. Haakon Mitchell was sitting on a plank nailed between the two palm trees that grew in front of his house. Both of them gave me a greeting that was warm and natural, as to a returning friend. My uncertainty vanished. These were unaffected people, glad to welcome a face that a single visit had made familiar. I asked how they were and how the vessel was progressing. No other explanation of my presence was necessary.

Down by the bayside, the vessel now stood with all frames in place and secured by the "bends," as the sheer planks were called. The builder and I squatted on the wood chips in the shade and talked. We talked of high prices and the difficulties of getting materials. We talked of what it cost to build a vessel and what one might earn with one. We talked of *Mermaid* and what it would take to beat her. In fact, we talked ourselves onto familiar ground and then onto personal ground.

Mitchell's vessel in frames at Friendship Bay, Bequia. January 1971.

Mitchell explained what had gone into the vessel thus far. He had begun to put aside money and materials half a decade earlier, soon after he returned from the hospital, knowing that his days as a fisherman were over once he lost the hand. Under the little house began to grow an assortment of bits and pieces that might someday be woven into the fabric of a vessel—pieces of timber with a useful curve, lengths of rope, odd blocks, pieces of iron rod . . . An odd collection, it seemed to me, until I more fully recognized the difficulties of supply in the islands. All manufactured goods are imported and may well be scarce even on the larger islands. Items as common as nails are sometimes unavailable for extended periods. It is a good rule, I learned, never to pass up anything that might eventually be useful.

When everything seemed right, Mitchell sent to Guyana for the keel, relying for transport on the good offices of his half-brother, mate on the schooner *Lady Angela*. Once arrived, the keel was laid on a low bank above the pebble beach below the Mitchells' house. The sternpost was mortised into the keel eighteen inches ahead of the butt and raked to a degree that "seemed right." Next the stem, a single curved timber, was butted onto the forward end of the keel, with a small shoulder left on the upper surface of the stem to support it where it joined the keel. Both stem and sternpost were held temporarily in place through a mare's nest of posts and props until framing and primary planking could be completed.

The next step was to set up two pairs of frames at the midpoint of the keel and another pair of bow frames at the forward end of the keel. Then the main transom frames were butted onto the sides of the sternpost at the top of the tuck, or deadrise, the area from the keel up to the point where the run passes the sternpost and opens out onto the transom. The height of the tuck is a major factor in providing lateral resistance, hence the windward sailing ability, of a hull in this tradition. It also contributes materially to the difficulties of planking up later, due to the complex geometry.

The shapes of the bow, center, and transom frames, called the "modeling frames," were made prior to erection using molds nailed up from rough lumber. Like other builders, Mitchell was secretive at first about his molds and did not show them to me until much later, after we became good friends.

With the key elements defining shape in place, the long strips of wood called "ribbands" were nailed to the stem and bent around the modeling frames to form a shell into which the intermediate frames would be fitted one by one. This was a slow process. First, scraps of sawn lumber were nailed together and cut to approximately the shape required. Then this shape was scribed onto a naturally curved timber and rough-faired with saw, ax, and adz. Final fitting required several rounds of lifting the timber into place, sighting and marking high spots, and returning the timber to the ground for more shaping. When the frame fitted into the ribbands without producing any unfairness, the lower end was spiked to the keel and the upper end braced across to the top of its opposite counterpart frame. Shores to secure the frames were placed as needed.

All the structural timbers of a West Indian vessel, except the keel, are shaped by hand from West Indian white cedar (*Tabebuia heterophylla*). This wood is so important in the islands that it deserves additional comments, the first being that it is not really a cedar at all. In fact, it is a deciduous tree with glossy, dark green leaves and pale purple, trumpet-shaped flowers. Except for the flowers, it might better have been called "West Indian oak," since like oak the wood is light in color, tough, rot-resistant, and it holds fastenings extremely well.

In habitats with abundant rainfall, this species forms a tall, straight tree. On arid, salt-sprayed windward coasts the tree grows tougher and denser, forming the curved and twisted shapes that are ideally suited to boatbuilding. Mitchell, like many other builders, preferred to cut his timbers during the waning of the moon, a time when, it is believed, the sap is out of the wood, allowing better curing and greater resistance to wood decay. When possible, the timbers were worked while still green and relatively easy to shape.

One afternoon I walked around from where I had *Eider* moored to see if anything new had taken place with the vessel. Mitchell's wife, Winnie, came out as I approached the house.

"No one down by the bayside, sir," she said. "Gone to Ravine to cut a timber."

She indicated a direction up and over the ridge that lay behind the little house. After a steep climb and a scrambling descent, I came to a tiny bay where a dry watercourse entered the sea. I followed the sound of an ax, climbing the steep-sided gut until I found Mitchell and his second-oldest boy, Earlin, felling a white cedar. When trimmed out it made an eight-foot log, about as much as two men could carry. Until this writing, it never came to me to wonder how Mitchell had intended to move this log prior to my arrival. It was too heavy for a man and a twelve-year-old, and my visits at that early stage were too irregular to be counted upon.

In any case, Mitchell gladly accepted my offer of help and we set out along the rocky trail that angled upward to the ridge. I took off my cap to make a cushion where the log rested on my shoulder. It took all my strength and balance to follow the barefoot, bare-legged man ahead. He walked with his knees bent, in an easy, gliding gait that I later imitated, walking barefooted on stony ground. We had traversed about half the hill and my teeth were clenched with the effort when Mitchell grunted and signaled a halt.

"I didn't think I could keep up," I gasped after we dropped the log.

"I was testing you, Douggie," Mitchell laughed. "Ravine plenty steep, man."

It was the first time he had addressed me by name and he used a diminutive form of it into the bargain. I felt a genuine measure of acceptance. By the time we reached the top of the ridge and stood looking down into Friendship Bay, however, I was past caring about acceptance or anything other than my trembling, aching legs.

We rested for a long, leg-gladdening time, looking out over the Grenadines. With the air of a bright child making a recitation, Earlin called out the names of the islands: to windward, Baliceau, Battowia, and Mustique; near at hand below us, Semple Cay, Petit Nevis, and "Oily Cot" (Isle du Quatre); farther away, Canouan, Mayero, and the Tobago Cays; and finally, because it was a clear day, Union and Palm Islands.

Haakon stood silently until the recital was finished and then asked me, "You ain think that beautiful, Douggie?"

I murmured my agreement but was thinking more about the heavy log and the distance yet to haul it. Fortunately Earlin had another plan. He uncoiled a length of rope from his waist and made a timber hitch around the small end of the log. The three of us began to drag the log, which was much easier than carrying even on the level at the top of the ridge. Soon we were moving at a trot and then a wild run, whooping and dodging as the log bounced behind us.

Once down at the bayside, work started immediately to turn the log into a four-inch-by-four-inch "scarlin" (carling), a fore-and-aft connection between two deck beams to frame a hatch or some other opening in the deck. While I was still wondering how the job was to be done, Earlin grabbed a straight-handled hatchet and set about it. He stood atop the log and worked within inches of his bare toes, chopping first a series of cuts at forty-five degrees to the axis, then making a quick swipe to shear away the chips and leave a surprisingly smooth surface. The hatchet was sharpened at frequent intervals on an oil stone, and one face of the log was quickly flattened as I watched in fascinated horror.

When this was finished, we laid the log on a pair of saw horses and Haakon scribed a straight line on the flattened surface. Orbin, the older of the two Mitchell boys, had come in from fishing and now began to help with the sawing. He stood facing the work, the saw held in both hands with blade down and the teeth away from him. Keeping his legs straight, he sawed using the strength of both arms while the other boy steadied the log. The saw was sharp and cut evenly; nevertheless it was tiring work, and we had all taken a turn before the long rip was completed. The two remaining faces of the timber were then quickly dressed with the hatchet, leaving me puzzled why we had bothered with the laborious sawing. Mitchell explained that a hatch coaming was to be fitted against the sawn face, which had to be absolutely straight so that a tight seam could be fitted. Taking more care with the other faces was unnecessary, and in fact really was a waste of energy.

We spent the entire afternoon on that single timber. I looked up at the skeleton of the little sloop in despair. What sort of foolishness had I let myself in for? How many more timbers were needed? With only a hatchet and a hand saw to cut them? Mitchell, on the other hand, seemed well pleased with the afternoon's work and thanked me politely for my assistance.

Later, when the tools were put away in the tiny shed by the sloop, he asked, "You wouldn't care to take tea with us, Douggie?"

I was gratified by the invitation and followed him up to the little house. We sat on the bench between the two palm trees while the boys flopped on the steps of the house, displacing a flock of smaller children who studied us silently.

"Winnie-O," Haakon called toward the house. "You ain have some tea for us?"

An answer that I didn't catch came from the kitchen, and Earlin ran inside, returning quickly with a tray that he held out to me. It held a large enamelware cup of hot milk and coffee, a thick slice of buttered, homemade bread, and a cold piece of fried fish. Haakon Mitchell soon had the same repast in hand. We talked idly as we ate, watching the wave patterns refracting over the surface of the water while the sun sank below the ridge across the bay.

Thus began my labors in the building of *Skywave* and a friendship with the Mitchell family that continues to the present.

When I first visited the Mitchells, I simply watched the work, taking an occasional photograph and asking questions. Soon I was being asked to pass a tool or go for a nail, then to do this or that simple task, until, in the tradition of Tom Sawyer's fence, I was working full days and taking all my meals with the family. At no point did I ever state my purpose, and by like token, I was never asked just what I was doing there. Slowly I came to realize that it never really occurs to a Bequian to wonder why a stranger is in Bequia. The people know that their island is the only place in the world truly worth living in, and they charitably assume that the rest of the world has the good sense to share that opinion.

It had taken Haakon Mitchell five months to lay the keel, place the stem and sternpost, and set up the frames. During the next month, as I insinuated myself into the project, the "beaming off" of deck beams was accomplished. By the third month I was working full time and fitting "knees" to brace the deck beams against the bends. The knees, short natural crooks approximating a right angle, were dressed on the ground and then held in place while a saw was used to make a final smooth fit. Two $\frac{5}{8}$-inch holes were drilled through each arm of the crook into the adjacent timber and an iron pin dipped in pitch driven into each. The pins were cut as needed from a length of common construction reinforcement bar and, when in place, were peened over a washer to tighten the joint. The assembly was called a "bolt"—not a threaded bolt, mind you, for that is an expensive item in the islands. Threaded bolts generally were used only when a joint had to be closed over a greater distance, such as when the keelson timber was drawn down to the keel, locking the butts of the frames in place.

The workday began a little before eight in the morning, when one of the younger children rowed across the bay to fetch an experienced carpenter from La Pompe who had begun to work on the vessel during the beaming off. The early hours of morning were best and the pace of work was brisk. At eleven o'clock Winnie sent down one of the younger children with "breakfast," the main meal of the day, which we ate in the shade of the vessel. Afterward we lay talking or dozing until work was resumed. The afternoons were hot as the sun beat against the hillside behind us, and the hours sometimes dragged until tools were put away at four o'clock and the carpenter was rowed back across the bay for tea.

After the knees were all fitted, we began to set in the scarlins for the hatches, cabin, cockpit, companionway forward, and "lazareet" (lazarette) in the stern. With the scarlins in place, half-beams could be fitted to complete the deck layout. The frames were cut off even with the bends, and finally the top timbers were shaped and slipped into place between the beam shelf and the bends to form a framework for bulwarks and the top rail.

The hired carpenter, named Napoleon Olliverre, III, and called Uncle Nappy, was a relation of Haakon's but was nonetheless earning the going rate for a carpenter. He was also a great raconteur (a talent common to Bequians), and willingly set himself the task of initiating me into the joys of life in Bequia and the mysteries of boat carpentry. He was particularly proud of his ship-lap joint, which he insisted should be used on all scarlins and coamings because it gave a caulking seam on both faces of the joint. "Ship-lap and double-lock," he would intone with satisfaction each time he completed a joint and drove it tight.

One afternoon after work, Uncle Nappy invited me home with him for

Uncle Nappy and the ship lap joint. February 1971.

evening tea. There he introduced me to his wife and showed me a painting of the schooner *Emeralda,* fifty-one tons, which he built in 1940 and which he and his brothers owned. In his lifetime he had set up and built eleven vessels including Haakon's and had given assistance on many others.

Another month and the hatch coamings and cabin trunk were completed, the mast partners and samson post were in place, and the top timbers were fitted. Down below, the outer sternpost was in place and the rudder case had been hollowed out and fastened to it.

The outer sternpost is a recent West Indian innovation for dealing with the problem of where to fit a propeller when an auxiliary engine is installed in a sailing hull. In yacht construction the propeller is generally fitted into an aperture in the rudder, which means reducing both steering leverage and strength. For modern yachts, strength reduction at least is overcome by laminating the rudder or by using a welded rudder stock, but neither of these options is open to island builders.

They choose, instead, to erect a second sternpost a short distance behind the first and also butted into the keel. The outer sternpost then carries the rudder case and rudder, while the inner sternpost is drilled for the stern tube and propeller shaft. The method is structurally sound but has the disadvantage of producing considerable frictional drag as water swirls in the large aperture and around the unfaired edges of the after sternpost.

During this period of work, Mitchell became increasingly worried about securing the milled boards necessary for planking the hull and deck. His intention was to use silver balli (*Cordia alliorda*) from Guyana, but there were interminable delays in shipping his order. And there was no way to expedite matters other than by sending queries via *Lady Angela* when she sailed twice monthly to Guyana. While we waited for the planking, we worked at small jobs that, while necessary, didn't give the satisfaction of visible change.

One day we cut a rabbet in the after face of the rudder case and set in the navel piece, a thick plank that fastens to the lower side of the transom frames. Working in the Bequia tradition, Haakon was prepared to leave it at that, although as I pointed out earlier, this approach provides weak structural support for the overhanging transom stern. I mentioned to Haakon the ledges I had seen used for this purpose in Carriacou.

"Oh," he said, "that why I see plenty Bequia vessel with the stern droop but I never see Carriacou vessel droop yet. Must be why."

Once the navel piece was in place, we added the pointer, a straight, raking timber mounted atop the navel piece and running up toward the extension of the top rail. Next in place were the horn timbers, small, inverted frames running from the tip of the pointer down to deck level, which form the characteristic oval shape of the transom.

The next morning, Uncle Nappy called me to come down to see the proper method of rabbeting the keel. He began by shaping a small piece of plank to use as a guide. The piece was beveled one eighth of an inch out of square, then held against the keel from time to time as the rabbet was chiseled out. Uncle Nappy explained that this was done so that the lowest plank next to the keel, the "garboard streak" (strake), would lock into the bevel chiseled into the keel, providing a joint into which caulking cotton could be driven without forcing the garboard away from the keel, a common cause of leaking in vessels whose builders did not take the time to do the job right.

During the months that I had thus far worked with them, the Mitchell clan had come to regard me as more good natured than genuinely helpful. I was unable to take the hatchet and produce a surface as smooth as if it had been

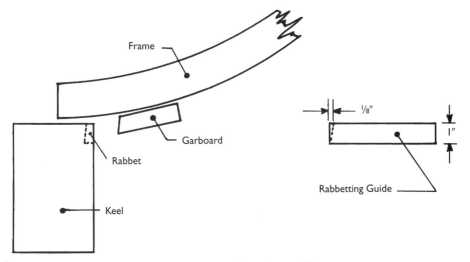

Detail of the rabbetting guide
used by Uncle Nappy.

planed; I couldn't tell from the placid surface of the bay when sprat were running; and I sheeted the boom too close when sailing to windward.

But one day as we were having our breakfast, conversation came around, as it frequently did, to the difficulties of getting supplies. This time the focus of concern was a seven horsepower outboard motor of the Mitchells' that had been out of service for several months because of a broken shift lever. Obtaining a new shift lever had proved impossible. I asked to see the motor and was surprised to find that the lever in question was in an accessible place and not very complicated. I went aboard *Eider* for some tools—a hacksaw, a tap and die set, a piece of bronze flat bar, an electric drill, and a portable power generator.

Back on the beach, at first I had only the younger Mitchell children as spectators, but by the time the simple task was finished the gallery was full. When I turned off the generator, Charles, the spellbound youngest boy, was muttering, "Douggie is a magic man."

"Man, you got tools you ain touch yet!" Earlin chimed in.

The Mitchells, although highly skilled and inventive in working wood, were deeply in awe of all things mechanical, and their estimate of my worth soared. Never have I achieved so much effect with so little effort. I became the person to consult on a host of subjects, from broken tools and toys to the authenticity of the twice-weekly westerns projected against a patch of whitewashed wall in Port Elizabeth. It was a solid boost for my ego, but far more importantly, it later provided me with the opportunity to make something more than a token contribution in the building of Haakon Mitchell's sloop.

By this time Easter was at hand, and work stopped. Uncle Nappy had a visit from his son living in Canada; the rest of us took a holiday.

Earlier, Orbin had mentioned that on Easter Monday the La Pompe National Bar usually organized a boat race. When asked if he planned to enter, Orbin replied that he didn't have the entry fee. I took my cue and volunteered to put up the backing in exchange for the right to crew in *Cedar Blossom,* a two-bow boat built by Haakon before his accident and used now by Orbin for fishing and lobster diving.

And so it happened that on race day I found myself standing waist deep in the sea, holding the bow of *Cedar Blossom* into the waves that were breaking onto Friendship Beach. Bo-So, the other crewman, was holding the stern, and Orbin was standing with the other skippers in a clump on the beach. We were among a dozen or so boats all standing at the ready with mainsails up and flapping in the breeze.

Suddenly a shout went up, and Orbin and the other skippers came sprinting toward us. Orbin tumbled into the boat, Bo-So and I gave a shove, and we were off.

"Buss out the jib!" Orbin shouted, and he began to haul in the mainsheet.

Bo-So yanked hard on the jib sheet, pulling the jib from its loose knot around the forestay. The sails billowed out and we quickly filled away. But somehow Bill Bynoe was a little quicker and already had a small lead as we stood out past the shoals off Point Hilary and began to beat up toward Hope Rock. Orbin perched on the gunwale with the tiller in one hand and the mainsheet in the other, springing up in every little puff, then hauling off, occasionally pumping the tiller back and forth in sheer impatience. Bo-So held the jib sheet wrapped around his hand and sawed in and out, hauling in on the rise of each wave, easing out in the trough. Lacking other instructions, I crouched on the ballast stones and tried to stay out of the way.

As we sailed, Bo-So kept up a constant barrage of advice, instructions, and encouragement:

"Hold she! Hold she hard!"

"No, no! Let she shoot out!"

"Study, study!"

"Go back, man, go back! Got to go back! He cutting we!"

Sailing with a Bequia crew could be a shock to any graduate of the William Bligh Academy of Maritime Procedures. The tradition of an unimpeachable, unapproachable skipper, grim-eyed and aloof on the quarter deck, making his inscrutable decisions unchallenged, has simply not taken root in Bequia. According to the Bequia Code of Unparliamentary Procedure, advice and criticism may be freely and constantly offered by all ranks from highest to lowest, regardless of the circumstances or the skipper. In all matters pertaining to the sea, Bequians are astonishingly and—once you get used to it—refreshingly democratic.

However, despite this free flow of information, we failed to gain on Bynoe and were a couple of lengths behind as we stood over Hope Rock and eased sheets to shoot through the narrow, surging channel between the rock and Bequia.

Once out of these tight quarters, Bo-So snatched up the bamboo pole we had stumbled over each time the ballast stones were shifted. He used it to goose the jib, holding it out taut on the side opposite that of the fully extended mainsail to help us with the downwind leg. As we ran back past Point Hilary, Haakon trotted along the shore, urging us to shift the ballast aft and "get she shooting." But in spite of all our heroic efforts we gained nothing on Bynoe on the long run down to the West Cays and nothing on the beat back to Friendship Bay. We brought second by the same margin that we had held throughout the race.

A half hour later Orbin and I were back on the beach below the Mitchell house. After the boat was hauled and washed out, we went up for breakfast with the family. The meal was accompanied by lively discussion of racing technique and tactics, as might be expected in the afterglow of a close race.

I assumed that the festivities were over until Haakon Mitchell stood up late in the afternoon and spoke. "Well, Douggie, let we go. It be time for spree." And to my surprise, in a short time I found myself around at the La Pompe National Bar, where a feast was set for contestants, friends, and relations—with, in short, all the males in the community. To eat, there was rice-with-peas-between, stew chicken, corn meal mush (called "coucou" by white Bequians and "fungee" by black Bequians), West Indian potatoes, and a salad of onions and Irish potatoes. To drink, there was "strong rum" (140 proof), Scotch whiskey, and Heineken beer. It began to seem as if my entry fee had been bread cast upon the waters. The crowd was warm, noisy, and friendly; everyone urged me to partake of the bounty and make myself at home.

From a table near the open window a voice hailed me by name. A large man with a natural air of authority motioned me over and poured me a drink from his bottle. No introductions were necessary: Athneal Olliverre was already known to me by reputation and, apparently, I to him. Olliverre and his brothers owned the whale fishery that operated from Petit Nevis, and he was the head (and for that matter, only) harpooner.

His manner was quiet and unassuming, and yet I felt somehow as if I were in the presence of an elemental force of nature. He seemed to know without asking that I would want to know about whaling, and so, without preamble, he launched into a description of that art as practiced in Bequia. After a while he beckoned me to follow and led me along the road to his home where he showed me the tools and trophies of his trade. As an aid to understanding the intricacies of his art, he was steadily pouring shots of rum, which we washed down with everything from beer to banana soda pop. When rum and conversation had imparted as much learning as Olliverre deemed essential, he suggested that if I really wanted to know something about whaling, then awhaling I must go.

Meanwhile, back at the bar the spree was in full swing, though the initial offering of liquor was exhausted. I bought my own bottle of rum and set out to repay obligations. Eventually I found myself seated on a wooden bench looking out over a yard in which the small fry of the community were gathered to gawk at the sight of their elders at play. My neighbor was assuring me that everyone was glad to make welcome "the fella what giving Haakie a help" when we were interrupted by angry voices.

A bench was overturned with a sudden crash as bottle and glasses went flying. Bill Bynoe jumped to his feet and began to announce in a high sing-song voice what he was going to do to his adversary when he laid hands on him—which was hypothetical for the moment, since both men were being restrained by their friends. However, disagreements quickly arose among the friends and subgroups began to surge and shove. As the altercation showed signs of becoming general, I eyed the open window, gauging the distance to the ground.

"No, no," my neighbor laughed. "Is not for you, man. Is only for show. They ain doing *you* nothing."

Cyril, a half-witted castaway adopted by Bynoe, saved everyone's face by pushing his way through the crowd to seize Bynoe around the waist and wail piteously. Gradually the commotion subsided, then was abruptly forgotten when, on the stroke of nine o'clock, the women who had been gathering outside resolutely invaded the premises and grabbed partners. It was time for the dance that was to complete the evening.

When it was time to go, I said goodnight to Haakon and prepared to walk back to Admiralty Bay where *Eider* was anchored.

"Douggie, you ain want Earlin to walk with you?" Haakon asked.

I gestured toward the crowd and repeated what my neighbor had said earlier. A little unsteadily I said, "They ain doing *me* nothing."

"No, no," he said anxiously. "Is dark moon tonight. You don't frighten of jumbies?"

I assured him that I would be fine, and I made my way back aboard without mishap. I was asleep within minutes.

Launching *Skywave*

L ate the following morning I rowed ashore for the usual walk over to Point Hilary. I was surprised to find Haakon and Earlin Mitchell on the beach waiting for me. They had walked to town to buy several lengths of purpleheart (*Peltogyne pubescens*). Haakon preferred to avoid retailers and retail prices, but his lumber had still not come from Guyana and he wanted to keep the job moving. Could I help haul the lumber for him? Of course. We put the long planks on the deck of *Eider* and sailed around to Friendship Bay, now my usual anchorage in Bequia.

That afternoon we began to put down the covering boards (the outermost planks of the deck, which cover the upper ends of the frames), a tedious job requiring very few materials. Uncle Nappy was taking time off to plant his "provisions" (Bequian for garden) so Herbie Olliverre, another carpenter from La Pompe, was standing in for him.

With the covering boards in place, the top timbers could be "bolted" to the frames below, and the top rail could be mortised onto the tops of the top timbers. While Earlin and I worked at that, the others toiled below, fitting the keelson onto the top of the keel and drawing it down with "screw bolts" to lock the butts of the frames securely to the keel. Next, the bilge stringers were fastened along the insides of the frames halfway between the keelson and the beam shelf. With the addition of these members, the frames were rigidly locked in place and needed only the planking to attain the vessel's full strength.

One day, after we had eaten breakfast and were resting in the shade, the younger children of the family came down for a swim in the bay. Charles, the youngest boy, brought with him a little sailboat, which he tried out in the sea. When I asked to look at it and expressed my admiration, the two other boys ran back to the house for their models.

Usually made from wood of the gum tree (*Bursera simaruba*), these were called gumboats. They were shaped with a pocket knife and smoothed with a piece of rough stone. The ballast keels were made of lead, melted over a charcoal fire and poured into a beach sand mold. Much care and skill had gone

The Mitchell children with their gumboats. From left to right: Roderick, Charles, Alvie (rear), Dorathie, and Osrick. May 1971.

into the shaping and decorating of these models, and all the boys had produced by hand and eye very sophisticated designs. It seemed to be part of the process by which they began to acquire adult boat carpentry skills.

In fact, the oldest of the three model builders had already begun to hang around the Mitchell vessel after school, happy to run errands, fetch tools, and perform some of the simpler jobs. The older boys, both of whom had gotten their school-leaving certificates at fourteen, were rapidly acquiring skills and were able workmen by the time the vessel was completed. The evolution from model builder to boat carpenter occurred so smoothly and naturally that no one seemed to realize that it was education and should therefore be distasteful. And at every stage, the children had the satisfaction of knowing they were making a real contribution to the welfare of the family.

About now, Haakon decided to brace the stern with the "ledges" I had mentioned seeing in Carriacou. Two cedar timbers were fastened inside the frames of the counter stern and extended forward past the two sternposts onto the frames of the tuck. When pinned from side to side through the two sternposts, the full weight of the stern was cantilevered onto the sternposts and keel, making a very strong assemblage. If this new method catches on in Bequia, then I myself will have become an agent of cultural diffusion.

By late spring, everything had been done in readiness for decking and planking, and still the materials had not come from Guyana. Mitchell asked if I would take Earlin down to Grenada to buy Douglas fir for making spars, none being available in St. Vincent. He was still planning to race against *Mermaid* in August and wanted to put some part of the project forward. On the trip down, Earlin and I kept company as far as the Tobago Cays with Orbin and Bo-So, who were going to camp there and dive for lobsters for a month or so.

In St. George's, Grenada, it didn't take long to discover that there was no Douglas fir of the length required. Everywhere we asked, the response was substantially the same.

"No, we have nothing of the kind. No one builds schooners anymore. No reason to stock the spars or gear."

As long as we were in Grenada, it seemed like a good idea to sail around and check on the progress of the two schooners near Grenville. And as Earlin and I walked through Grenville I noticed several long straight logs lying in the street near the concrete jetty. I asked whose they were and was directed to a shop owned by Hyacinth MacLaren, a Carriacou man and former schooner owner. The logs had been cut up in the government experimental forest at Grand Etaing and were destined to become the spars of *Yankee Girl R.*

The logs were Maho pine (*Thespesia populnea*), a flowering tree called pine only because of its rapid, straight growth and its medium-light–colored wood. I had seen the quality of work that went into *Yankee Girl R* and figured that any spars good enough for Roberts were good enough for us. MacLaren warned us that, although the cost was reasonable, the trees were bought "where is, as is."

The following morning I stuffed some gear into a sail bag, and Earlin and I set forth in a bus. The road wound upward past small, unpainted wooden houses propped against the slope of the land, each surrounded by its aureole of red-brown earth, kept bare and smooth by the feet of dogs, chickens, and children. At the outer edge of this inhabited circle grew the trees of life: breadfruit, banana, mango, avocado, nutmeg, cocoa. Beyond them lay the tangled growth of tropical rainforest.

As we climbed, it grew steadily cooler until we entered the zone where the sun was obscured and the atmosphere became clouds and swirling mist. At the top, past all houses and other signs of human habitation, the bus pulled over and the driver informed us that this was what we had asked for—Grand Etaing, the lake lying in the crater of the volcano that had formed the island.

There was no one to give us further instructions, but after turning around a few times we struck a dirt track that went neither up nor down, and we followed it through a plantation of bananas to a clearing that held a small wooden hut and an open-sided shed. Under the shed, a barefoot worker in faded trousers rolled to the knee turned the handle of a heavy grindstone while a comrade sharpened a cutlass.

We asked for the person in charge, and when he arrived we explained what we wanted: a mast, a boom, and a gaff. There followed a period of reflection during which the foreman sucked his teeth and looked us over. Finally he announced that the aforesaid timber came to a price so reasonable that it seemed indiscreet to inquire into either his pricing policy or the true destination of our money. After we paid, he indicated with a sweep of his arm the area in which we were free to make our selection.

We followed the road in the direction indicated and entered a stand of Maho pine, growing in a network of ridges and ravines where the only level ground was occupied by the road itself. The boom and gaff were not difficult to locate. Many suitable trees were near the road. We quickly felled and limbed our selections with an ax borrowed from the foresters.

The mast was another story.

A tree able to yield a spar thirty-six feet long and eight inches on the butt was about the upper limit in this stand of timber, and we looked long and hard to find one. The only candidate we could locate happened to be on the other side of one of the steep-sided ravines. Felling and limbing were no problem, nor was the first leg of the trip to the bottom of the ravine. From there we had only some three hundred feet to reach the roadway. The only difficulty was that it was up a slope that would have been too steep to stand on without trees and undergrowth for a handhold.

Being not completely green as to the way things get done in the islands, I reached into the sail bag and pulled out *Eider*'s mainsheet and two double blocks. I confidently rigged a four-part tackle, one end hitched to the butt of the log, the other fastened to a tree partway up the slope. We were pulling downhill, and on the first heave we straightened the log and got it started across the ravine. As we refastened our tackle to a tree higher up the slope, I felt very pleased with myself and was glad that a small crowd of foresters had gathered to watch our efforts. Again we heaved, and the log advanced until it spanned the ravine. But its butt was jammed firmly into the soft earth. It was no longer a matter of skidding the blamed thing; we were now pulling against the full weight, and the harder we heaved, the more the butt dug into the side of the hill.

At this point the fundamental flaw in my plan became apparent. In a sort of hysterical reflex for tackling the hard part of a job first, I had hitched to the butt of the log. Now that it was well and truly jammed, it was obvious that if the log had been pulled from the smaller end, it would have been much easier to lift and unjam.

The foresters, whom I had been so eager to impress, at this point rallied around, courteously withholding comment on my methodology. Even with their help, it was still very near a draw match. We cut saplings to use as levers, shifted the tackle to a new direction, and gradually wriggled the butt sideways. Gaining an inch or two with each heave, we finally worked the butt to one side and pulled it far enough up the slope that the log began to skid again. Even so, the slope was greater than forty-five degrees and progress was heavy going.

It was past noon before we rested with the three logs lying by the roadside. Earlin and I had had nothing to eat since early morning and had brought nothing, another bit of bad planning. The foresters, in the camaraderie of common hardship, shared with us their midday meal: an appetizer of bananas, a main course of bananas washed down with cold water, followed by a dessert of bananas. I relished every mouthful.

Even with the logs lying beside the road, we were not, as the saying goes, out of the woods. It was still a long way down a winding mountain road to Grenville, and the only link was a trucker with the easily remembered name of Ivy Forrester. He lived in the last village passed before entering the cloud forest. An hour's walk, discussion of terms, and payment for rented labor and vehicle secured for us the aid and ability of this professional, who assured us on the way back up the mountain that unwieldy loads were all in a day's work.

We slung a block from the crotch of a convenient tree and lifted the butt of the biggest log while our friends, the foresters, provided the "Norwegian steam" to lift the smaller end directly onto the bed of the truck. After that, the boom and gaff were child's play. The mast and the boom both dangled off the bed in the rear and extended beyond the cab on the off side. It looked wildly precarious to me, but the driver was blithely confident. Earlin and I used the full forty yards of the mainsheet to truss the load before crawling into the cab from the driver's side and bracing ourselves for the descent.

On every hairpin curve I held my breath and gave it all the body English at my command, dreading the thought of reloading without our gang of well-wishers. My gritted teeth, combined with the luck or skill of the driver, saw us through, and with the last of the daylight we dropped our putative spars on the waterfront, an easy roll to the water's edge. The first stage of the journey was over, and in my relief and fatigue I had not yet begun to worry how my poor *Eider*, at thirty-nine feet long, was going to bear such a burden.

My reeling mind was just coming to grips with the prospect of *towing* the blessed things forty miles hard on the wind when Earlin piped up.

"Look, Douggie. *Lady Angela* done tie up over there. Uncle Davis going tow she to Bequia land."

He ran off to make the arrangements while I sank down upon one of our logs, my knees weak with relief.

Shortly after the spars made their way to the construction site below Haakon's house, he finally located some silver balli—in Bequia, of all places. Another Bequian had bought a stock of 1,300 board feet for a project that had not materialized. The quantity was sufficient to plank the hull, and the prospect put new life into everyone. For too long the work had gone slowly with little to point to at the end of the day, or even the week. Now, for a pleasant change, the work went rapidly and the entire hull was planked in sixteen days. No small part of this speed was owing to my generator and electric drill, which proved to be my most important contribution to the building of the vessel.

The planking began at the bends and proceeded downward to the turn of the bilge, before starting again at the garboards and coming upward. This is certainly not the strongest method of planking, since it leaves several short planks to be fitted in the critical zone between wind and weather. However, it is economical of time and materials, since most of the "spiling" (tapering and shaping) is left to be done on those few planks.

It was apparent to me even as a novice that planking consists of more than simply nailing planks of uniform width over the frames. Planks must be wider in the middle and taper toward the ends since the hull itself does this. Furthermore, the edges of each plank must pretty closely match those of its neighbors, so that caulking joints of uniform width will be formed. And a final constraint is imposed by the fact that a plank will bend across its thickness but not across its width. Any matching with the edge of another plank must be done by cutting, not by springing. Most of this was obvious. What surprised me was that a shaped plank may taper, then widen before tapering again. The method for laying out this nonuniform curve, essential to the good fit of a plank, "spoils" the plank, hence the term "spiling." It was the most technical aspect of boat carpentry I observed in the islands.

The plank next to the keel, the garboard, must be an especially good board: wide, straight grained, and knot free. With the unshaped garboard plank lying handily nearby on saw horses, Haakon located a straight batten long enough to scribe a reference line the length of the plank. A cross mark was struck at the midpoint of this line and a corresponding mark made on the center frame of the hull. Then, with a carpenter's rule, Haakon measured the distance forward to the centerline of the next frame and had one of the boys

*Haakon Mitchell with the recently planked sloop at
Friendship Bay, Bequia. July 1971.*

lay off this distance along the reference line on the plank and make a cross
mark. This was continued both forward and aft until all the frames were represented by cross marks on the plank.

At this point, an important matter of judgment came up and was dealt
with in the usual manner—free-flowing advice, contradiction, and comment.
What was under discussion was the nailing of the batten to the frames. It had
to be positioned so that its lower edge would correspond to the reference line
on the plank. When the decision was made, the batten was bent across the
frames from stem to sternpost and nailed lightly, particular care being taken
not to "spring" the batten—that is, bend it from side to side.

Mitchell went to the tool shed and returned with an ancient pair of dividers, iron ones with a brass pivot and brass points. With these he began the
"pricking"—gauging the interval between the lower edge of the batten and
the rabbet in the keel—and then transferring this to the plank at the cross

mark corresponding to the frame gauged. When he finished, there was a line of little holes, pricked by the divider points, which defined an edge for the garboard. The batten was removed from the frames and bent around the prick marks, so that a smooth curve was formed for the lower edge of the garboard. This line was cut with a hand saw and then beveled with a plane so it would "hook" into the keel rabbet Uncle Nappy had so carefully chiseled weeks before.

When the plank was ready to fit, Mitchell solemnly returned the dividers to their place in the shed. The forward end of the plank was set into place on the stem rabbet and securely fastened with cleats laid over the end of the plank and nailed into frame and keel on both sides. Using clamps hooked inside the frames, we gradually brought the plank down onto the frames so holes could be drilled and nails driven through and clenched tight. If the plank was too tight against the keel, Mitchell had the boys slack off the clamp so he could "take a rub" with the plane. If, on the other hand, the joint seemed too open, a cleat was nailed to the frame at the upper edge of the plank, and a thin wedge driven between the cleat and the plank to close the seam.

As successive planks were added, the lower edge of each was spiled to fit against the upper edge of the preceding plank. Both edges of all planks were beveled so that they would later form a good caulking seam: one wider on the outside than on the inside, so a cotton wick could be driven into the seam and tightened without coming through on the inside.

With the completion of the hull planking, Haakon's spirits improved substantially. The odds, initially against him, now were tipped decidedly in his favor, and the chances for a successful outcome had become rather good. As a further contribution to the lifting of spirits, the long-awaited purpleheart lumber arrived from Guyana and the deck was laid without further delay.

When the planking was finished, I made a set of lines measurements. The lines were fair and harmonious, and I began to share the general feeling that the vessel would be a fast sailor. Aside from the obvious difference made in the stern when we strengthened the counter support, the body plan of Haakon's vessel showed a strong resemblance to the whaleboats and other two-bow boats of Bequia in the moderately flat floors and very slight drag to the keel. Both traits reflect the fact that the two-bow boats rely on a centerboard for their lateral resistance, rather than their tuck. From the lines alone, it was clear that all of Haakon's previous experience had been in building small, two-bow boats.

However, the inward turn of the frames and hull shape a short distance above the waterline, clearly apparent in the topsides, was a very unusual feature, one that I saw on no other West Indian vessel. This intrigued me, and I tried, without making any leading remarks, to learn where Haakon had gotten the idea.

"Is 'tumblehome' they call it," he informed me. "When I just a boy, I did sail to Barbados in my father schooner, and I see plenty Nova Scotiamen. They all having tumblehome, and they plenty fast."

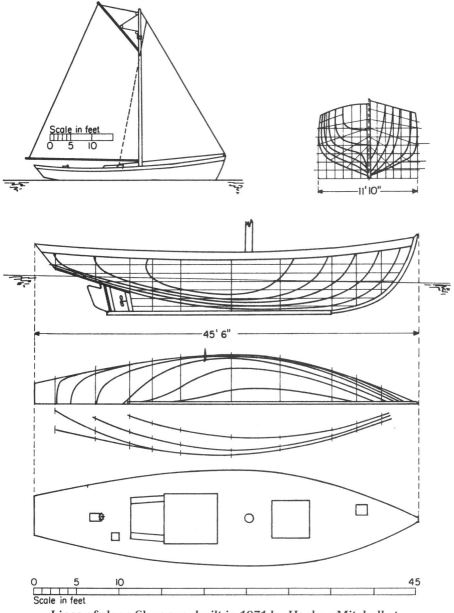

Lines of sloop Skywave, *built in 1971 by Haakon Mitchell at Friendship Bay, Bequia. Taken off July 1971.*

This remark, besides its importance in pointing to Nova Scotia as a design influence in West Indian sailing craft, was the first reference to his father I had heard Haakon make. Once, Uncle Nappy mentioned that Oily Cot had been owned by Haakon's father, Uncle Harry Mitchell, who bought it for its stands of cedar. Further questioning turned up the very interesting facts: first, that Uncle Harry had been a schooner builder and a landowner; and second, that he had also been the father of Reg Mitchell, builder of the huge three-masted schooner *Gloria Colita*. Under the circumstances, it seemed odd that Haakon should have been so poor and so isolated in the community. Out of friendship and respect, I never pursued the question further.

By midsummer it was apparent, despite the speed with which the planking and decking had been done, that the vessel would not be ready for the Regatta in August. No acknowledgment of this fact was made, nor was there any expression of disappointment. Still, the rhythm of the work slackened perceptibly. Haakon spent several days helping Winnie work the ground below and to the side of the house for planting of provisions. Corn and pigeon peas must be in the ground by late July in order to benefit from the rains that typically come when the trade winds lessen in August and September, the hurricane season. Orbin was sewing a new jib for *Cedar Blossom* so he could enter the Regatta. That left Earlin and me to continue alone on the vessel, setting nails and filling the holes with a mixture of paint and Portland cement.

As Regatta time drew near, Haakon suggested I take Earlin with me to Carriacou, then afterward go on to Grenada to pick up some further items of gear for the new vessel. I was ready for a break and agreed.

When Earlin and I returned to Bequia after our trip, Herbie and Luke Olliverre had already caulked the vessel's topsides and begun work on the bottom. Earlin immediately fell in behind them, filling the caulked seams with paint and Portland cement. I worked on top with Haakon, making sleeping shelves in the cabin and fitting the chainplates, crafted from heavy pieces of mangrove root.

When Herbie Olliverre didn't show up for two days running, Mitchell said, with much sucking of teeth, "Is spree he going. He won't fit to work for a week now. You knowing anything about caulking, Douggie?"

I didn't, but with coaching I learned to hold the iron, feed the cotton wick, and swing the mallet. Before long my seams were tight and even, though I was painfully slow in doing them. By early afternoon my arms were so tired that I had to stop. My efforts and limited success seemed to have broken some sort of spell, because as soon as I laid down the tools Earlin seized them and had a try. By quitting time he was already better than I was, and we had more caulkers than tools. From that day Haakon dispensed with paid labor.

For the Mitchell family, it was the planking that made the vessel a reality. For the community of La Pompe across the bay, it was the hollow booming of the caulking mallets that announced that Haakon was going to succeed.

"You know, Douggie," Haakon confided to me one evening after he had been to La Pompe on an errand, "when I did start, all is discourage me. They is tell me I will not succeed. Now is like they all want to be captain."

When the caulking was completed, we turned our attention to shaping the spars and fitting hardware. Work was even begun on the engine beds. Then one afternoon, Haakon announced that he had some men coming after work to help us roll a cannon down from the old fort at the top of Point Hilary, to lay out as a mooring for the new vessel.

My spirit recoiled from this desecration. My heart ached as I imagined the little fort restored, picturesque and romantic, on the rocky hilltop with its breathtaking view of the Grenadines to the south. As we climbed the hill, I raked my memory for some heavy object that could be substituted for the doomed relic. Nothing came to mind, and I couldn't find the words to speak to Haakon of civic duty and historic preservation.

When we reached the crumbling stone foundations of the small fort, I felt a surge of hope as I saw how heavy the half-buried cannon was. But five pairs of arms, conditioned to hard physical labor from early youth, made quick work of that. We lifted the muzzle and toppled the cannon toward the brow of the hill, then with one last heave sent it rolling and lurching down the hillside toward the bay. The others rushed after it, shouting and shoving when it slowed.

A realization came to me. Yes, the rusty old cannon was a relic, but a relic of plantations and exploitation, slavery and oppression. Except perhaps to have warded off the odd incursion of pirates, it had probably never done an honest day's work. Now it was being recalled from oblivion and given a useful function. It was going to be sunk to the bottom of the bay to provide a secure mooring for a vessel that was the key to a better future for a poor and struggling family. By the time we reached the shore I was yelling as loudly as anyone.

In early November Earlin asked me, in the offhand manner that I had finally learned meant something of importance was afoot, what I thought of the name *Skywave*. I replied that it had a nice sound and asked where he had gotten the idea. He said he had seen it on a passing yacht and asked my help in painting a name board, since this was to be the name of the new sloop.

Word was sent out on the coconut telegraph that the launching of *Skywave* would be on the second-to-last Sunday of November. Haakon, although not a church-goer, was careful to observe all the conventions and arranged with Father Adams, the Anglican priest in Port Elizabeth, to bless the new vessel on the Saturday before launching. On Friday, Haakon explained to me that a vessel must have godparents, and asked me if I would "stand" godfather. I was deeply gratified, and accepted gladly.

On Saturday afternoon, Father Adams came as far as possible in a Land Rover, then walked down the hill accompanied by two acolytes who carried a small cross, a vessel of holy water, and an altar cloth. The Mitchells, a few close friends, and I climbed to the deck of the vessel, where we stood while the blessing was taking place. An altar was arranged on the main hatch; the priest read from the Book of Common Prayer, then sprinkled holy water over the bows. One of the younger boys unfurled the name banner and the new vessel officially became *Skywave*.

After the ceremony, I approached Father Adams, eager to learn my duties and responsibilities as godfather.

"Very simple," he replied cheerfully, "if the vessel sinks, you must raise her."

There were other duties as well, however, as Haakon informed me later that evening when he handed me several banknotes and said, "After the cutting down in the morning, Douggie, you must put some money in the purse [suspended from the sternpost] to encourage the others to give a little offering. They might be 'shamed, but if they is see you going, they would be encourage."

I laughed. "You mean you want me to prime the pump?"

"That is it, that is it," he agreed. "You must use politics with some of these people. You know how."

Early on the big day, the first ones stirring were Winnie and her helpers, who were making final preparations to feed the expected crowd. Soon after, Haakon and his sons were busy tending to last-minute chores—laying out the kedge anchors, stropping the hull with a heavy cable, and smearing antifouling paint on spots where the shores had been.

By midmorning, enough people had arrived that the cutting down could begin. In fact, there was no cutting involved. Instead, a dozen men set their shoulders under the starboard bilge and held the weight of the vessel while the last of the shores were removed. Then the vessel was leaned gently onto sand-filled burlap bags that had been placed amidships on the starboard side. These, in turn, were slashed and the sand raked out until the vessel had come to rest on the rollers. In these and the subsequent proceedings, it was Athneal Olliverre the whaler who by common consent took charge, he being the person most likely to turn a gang of merry-makers into an effective labor force.

Skywave had been built on a low bank a few feet above the level of the water, so the launching was more a matter of controlling and restraining the weight of the vessel than actually moving it. Getting the hull to the water's edge was simply a question of easing the check lines running from the sternpost to trees on the hillside. There was one anxious moment, when someone on the check line slipped and the vessel lurched sideways, nearly sliding off the rollers, but when rollers had been shifted the hull was in an even better position.

As the bows reached the waters of the bay, the excitement of the crowd mounted to a frenzy. Rollers were heaved down the slope to be placed under the bows, men splashed and yelled in the shallows, and screaming children swarmed everywhere. Finally the vessel began to stir with her own buoyancy, then rolled slowly and heavily to port before floating free.

*Skywave, **hauling into the shallows. November 1971.***

A crowd of children swam out and swarmed aboard, while the older boys began to come and go in rowboats, carrying ballast stones. Back ashore, the remainder of the day's activities were being organized. First, the success of the new vessel was drunk in the prescribed manner: A tray with bottles of whiskey and rum, a glass, and a pitcher of water is presented to each guest in turn, who pours his own measure, tosses it off, and then pours the chaser, rinsing glass and mouth in one economical operation before the tray is offered to the next person.

Meanwhile, Winnie and her helpers had arrived with three dishpans of food to begin the "sharing out." One pan was heaped high with mutton, brown and pungent, the second held rice with pigeon peas, and the third was filled with boiled tania. Plates were served and carried to the little groups that had formed where there was shade. The men were served first, and the women came later to serve themselves. As plates were emptied, they were rinsed in the sea and returned to service. Later in the afternoon, the mast was floated out to be stepped, using the leverage of mast and halyards of another sloop brought from across the bay.

Floating there on the sparkling waters of Friendship Bay, newly rigged and ballasted to her waterline, *Skywave* must have been the realization of Haakon's every dream. And yet he was very subdued in his hour of triumph, simply commenting, "It true, you know, what they say: And a man have friends, he ain need money."

EIGHT

Blows!

After *Skywave* was launched, my official pretext for remaining in Bequia disappeared, and by rights I should have been on my way. But there was always something new and interesting to do, and I lingered for another four months. I helped rig the new sloop and get her sailing, hunted wild sheep on Oily Cot, gathered birds' eggs on Savanne, and simply shared the routines of daily life with people whom I had come to admire intensely.

If it had been only these idyllic pursuits, my conscience would have prevailed; it was Athneal Oliverre's invitation to go whaling that held me. The original invitation had been made in the convivial atmosphere of the La Pompe National Bar the preceding Easter. Once, too late in the season to have much chance of even sighting a whale, I did go out just to get a feel for the sailing performance of the whaleboats: seven nautical miles in forty-five minutes, or 9.4 knots, in an open boat with a waterline length of twenty-six feet, yields a startling speed coefficient of k = 1.8.

It seemed unlikely that Oliverre had really meant to set out in pursuit of the largest animal in the seas with a greenhorn in the boat. However, at the launching of *Skywave* in November he repeated his invitation for the season beginning in February, and I decided that if the whalers could take that risk, I could too. Even so, my courage was at a low ebb that late-February morning as I made my way down the beach toward La Pompe in the predawn darkness.

Early as it was, preparations on the two whaleboats were already well along. The canvas cover was off the tub amidships where a hundred fathoms of heavy rope lay neatly coiled. The first harpoon was in its chock, its canvas-sheathed toggle jutting forward over the bow. The other harpoon and three lances were tied along the starboard gunwale. Spars, sails, and stays were bundled together and laid across the thwarts. Lard pails with tight-fitting lids, containing food and fresh water, were stowed here and there in the bottom of the boat.

Athneal Olliverre greeted me matter-of-factly, then turned back to supervising the stowage of gear. When all was ready, both crews laid hold of the first boat. With arms and backs straight, we lifted, then heaved, at the grunted command. And again, until the slender double-ended boat slid down the beach and into the bay.

The steersman boarded and shipped the long steering oar, sculling to keep the bow into the waves while both crews returned to launch the other boat. Then we began wading back and forth in the water, trundling out ballast stones. Olliverre motioned me to a place on the port side of his boat *Dart* and with a shove we were away, tumbling quickly aboard to run out the long sweeps.

The man behind me indicated a seat and an oar, and I realized for the first time that I was not just along for the ride. I lodged my oar between wooden thole pins and seized the handle. Again there was a grunted command, and we began to pull away from the drag of the breaking waves and out into the bay. It took a couple of strokes for me to adjust to the slight hesitation that occurred as the oar slid, then thudded against the thole pin at the beginning of the stroke and again at the release. But the adjustment came quickly, and for the first time since college I was grateful for the long hours I had spent at crew practice on the Charles River.

When we had pulled far enough offshore to have sailing room, there was another grunted command and the oars were quickly unshipped and stowed. One man steadied and guided the butt of the mast while the others lifted from astern. When stepped, the mast was first secured at the bow by the forestay to which the jib was sewn, then on each side by the shrouds. The mainsail, already lashed to the mast, was knotted to the boom and run out, while the peak was hoisted on the sprit. The lower end of the sprit was fitted into a short piece of rope, the "snotter," which was looped around the mast, and the sail was stretched into an efficient airfoil by two men thrusting the sprit upward while a third slipped the snotter up the mast to hold tension.

The steersman, Joseph Ford, an elder given the honorific "Uncle Joseph," fitted the rudder onto the stern's pintles, slipped the tiller into its slot, and reached for the mainsheet. The jib was sheeted and in less time than it takes to tell, *Dart* was sailing. A few yards away, *Trio* (pronounced "try-oh") was carrying out the same transformation. The early morning breeze filled our sails, and the bows rose to the first Atlantic swell. The crew shifted their weight to the weather gunwale as spray began to splash back over the bow. I checked the plastic bag covering my camera and wondered again if I had been wise to come.

"Give she a touch more board," Uncle Joseph said. The man nearest the centerboard case shoved on an iron lever until he got a nod from the steersman.

On the lookout for whales; Athneal Olliverre on the right. March 1972.

As soon as we had cleared the headlands, Olliverre climbed onto a gunwale, using a shroud for balance, and began to scan the gray surface of the sea. We were sailing on a close reach out toward Mustique on the Grenadines Bank, seven miles to the southeast.

The humpback whales that Bequia whalers hunt calve somewhere in the South Atlantic in December and begin to appear in the Grenadines in small family groups in February. They remain in the vicinity until the latter half of April, feeding, resting, and tending their young. It is this sojourn that makes possible a shore-based whale fishery like that in Bequia.

This much Athneal had already explained to me, and it seemed logical that we should be out sailing where the whales might be expected to appear. So it came as a surprise when we anchored in a small cove on the lee side of Mustique and climbed past a small collection of houses to the top of the island. From the summit there was a commanding view of the sea for miles in all directions, and I began to understand the plan of action.

One of the younger men climbed to a fork in the lone tree on the scrub-covered hill and scanned the sea with a pair of binoculars. Meanwhile, a fire was started and a coffee pot produced from some hiding place in the rocks. Soon all of us were lounged around the hilltop, letting the sun and the coffee chase the chill of our pre-dawn sail. Someone passed around one of the lard pails, and we each helped ourselves to a handful of farine, a coarse meal made by grating and parching the cassava root.

"Look me hey!" Uncle Joseph shouted, gesturing in the direction of Bequia. "Someone cutting glass. Look away, over Kenneth's."

There it was, on the hillside above La Pompe, a waver, then a flash as someone held a mirror to the sun and moved it until the beam caught us.

"Yes, yes," Athneal replied excitedly. "Kenneth cutting glass." He hurriedly began to unfold the oilcloth wrappings of a parcel he had carried up from the boats, revealing a walkie-talkie that I later learned had been the gift of an American well-wisher.

What followed was a garbled interchange carried out in shrill West Indian dialect shot through with the usual squeals and crackles of the air waves and punctuated by sudden silences as the operator on the other end pushed and released the "transmit" switch in a purely random manner. I couldn't understand a single word of it, and apparently neither could Athneal as he fired off questions, instructions, and finally invective in a voice that rose steadily in both pitch and volume.

"Wait," one of the men exclaimed. "Look me, hey! Glass cutting down Moonhole. Must be whale in the Channel."

"Let we go then, boys," Athneal shouted, wrapping up the walkie-talkie and starting for the boats.

We scrambled down the hill as fast as the rocky path, lunch buckets, and other gear permitted. Inside five minutes we were back in the boats and under sail, on a broad reach and making our best speed for the southwestern tip of Bequia.

"Clean, sweet wind, man!" Uncle Joseph sang out exultantly. "Clean, sweet wind!"

The two boats were fairly evenly matched, and *Dart* was only some fifty yards ahead of *Trio* by the time we had sailed the ten miles to the West Cays. As we approached the narrow pass, a man scrambled onto a wave-splashed rock and stood waiting.

"Not far, not far," he shouted, with a sweeping, back-handed gesture toward the channel, nine miles wide, that separates Bequia from St. Vincent to the north.

We swept through the cut and hardened in the sails. Someone hammered down the centerboard as we came on the wind and drove into the first head sea. No one spoke now as we pounded through the steep waves, each man hoping to be the first to spot the tiny puff of gray-white vapor that betrays the whale. The man tailing the jib sheet played it in and out as the bows rose and

In hot pursuit off Bequia; whaleboat Trio *in background. March 1972.*

fell. The man opposite me in the stern worked steadily with a gourd, bailing the water that was coming constantly into the boat.

We stood north on the starboard tack until we had a clear view past North Point and up the channel. Then Athneal swung his arm back, palm down. Uncle Joseph leaned on the tiller and *Dart* came up into the wind. With the jib bundled around the forestay and the mainsheet loosed, we lay hove-to, riding the waves easily without splashing. A few yards to leeward, *Trio* did the same.

Athneal slipped the canvas sheath from the gleaming bronze barb of his harpoon and motioned for the line. From the tub amidships, the line was handed aft and taken once around our snubbing post next to the steersman's knee before it was passed forward to the deep, lead-lined notch in the stem head. Athneal shoved in a wooden pin to prevent the line from jumping out of the notch, then knotted the line solidly to the short nylon strop of the harpoon iron. With all preparations made, the waiting began.

"Blows! Blows!" The eerie cry, almost a howl, came from the other boat. The wisp of vapor hung over the sea surface long enough to see that we had overstood. The whale was astern and farther out in the channel. Quickly

Athneal handed back the jib sheet; Uncle Joseph was already overhauling the mainsheet with great sweeps of his arm. We bore away on the other tack.

The whale spouted again, and this time everyone saw it—more gray than white, but easily lost among the breaking wavetops. Twice more we saw spouts as we neared the whale. As Athneal wedged his knee into the harpooner's chock and groped for the harpoon, the whale's flukes appeared, lifted into the air, and then slipped massively down into the deep.

"Clean flukes!" someone intoned on a mournful note.

"Is a yearling only," Athneal said. "But plenty fat. Let we go back, Joseph. He going up with the tide."

We went onto the starboard tack and began beating our way into the east, trying to gauge where the whale would surface after its twenty-minute dive. The seas were becoming higher and steeper now as we worked our way into the tidal stream that sweeps along Bequia's north shore.

"Blows!" I sang out, and pointed to a spot well out ahead, earning a nod of approval from Athneal. We continued to sail since we were too far away for an approach. The whale spouted five times before sounding, and we now had a better idea of its direction and rate of travel as it fed in the ocean depths.

Again we beat into the wind, this time for about ten minutes, before Athneal gave the signal to heave-to. Tension mounted as the long minutes of the dive stretched on. Then a slick appeared on the water's surface forty yards off the starboard bow. This time the vapor cloud was accompanied by an explosive *whoosh*. There was no hail from any of us in recognition of the whale's presence; we were too close. By good luck, the whale lay with its massive head toward us. A boat approaching from either side is easily seen by a whale; a boat approaching from astern risks injury from the powerful flukes.

Softly, almost gingerly, each man went about his job. Any bump or scrape, magnified through the bottom of the boat, could send the whale sounding to safety. The sheets were lightly held, just enough to keep the boat gliding toward the shiny black mass. Athneal wedged his knee and tested the weight of the harpoon to loosen his arms.

Whoosh. This time we were so close that we could smell the warm, stale air expelled from the whale's lungs. Softly, Uncle Joseph slid the long steering oar into place. The oar is more effective in close quarters, where it may be necessary to turn the boat half around with a single stroke to avoid the dangerous flukes. Three other men had quietly gotten out paddles and were moving us slowly closer.

With one smooth, unhurried motion, Athneal lifted his right arm and surged forward with his whole body, arching the heavy harpoon up and over the back of the whale. It struck and buried itself to the wooden haft.

Suddenly, everyone was in motion. A broad sweep of the steering oar turned the boat to the side, out of immediate danger. The shrouds were hurriedly loosed, and the mast and sails thrown in a heap back along the thwarts. Uncle Joseph, with a quick tug, lifted the rudder off the pintles and left it floating at the end of a short lanyard.

From the whale, nothing . . . A long moment of empty time while an animal weighing thirty tons gathered the strength to struggle for its life. Then the dark shape of the tail began to move and a slick formed at the surface of the water. The flukes lifted clear and the heavy body of the animal began to slide downward into the sea. Deep, deep into the sea to escape, down until the choking need for air should force it back to the perilous surface.

While the others worked to prepare the boat for the battle, Athneal moved rapidly to clear the line and make sure there would be no fouling. As the dive began, the men crouched in the bottom of the boat to protect themselves from the smoking, hissing rope following the whale down into the sea. Abruptly, water began to rush in over the bows and the stern lifted sharply. The line was not running free and the whale was dragging us with it.

"Slack, Joseph, slack!" Athneal screamed.

Uncle Joseph grabbed for the bailing gourd and, in the nick of time, splashed water on the snubbing post, cooling the line and easing its run.

After a seemingly endless few minutes, the line slowed and we could sense that the whale had stopped sounding. As the strain lessened and then disappeared, line was taken in to be piled loosely in the bottom of the boat. The whale could not sound that deeply again.

When the whale blew and sounded next, line was paid out very slowly, most of the strain being eased by the boat moving across the surface of the water. After sounding three times, each for a shorter interval, the whale became winded and simply swam over the surface of the sea, towing us behind it, betraying its failing strength by smaller and more rapid spouts. Now the men began to overhaul the line in earnest, drawing us closer and closer to the whale.

Athneal slid one of the lances out and took up his station in the bow. The whale was almost still in the water, breathing heavily, and Athneal motioned us to paddle near. A pause, an adjustment of his position, and he lunged with his whole weight, driving the lance into the whale's side just behind the left flipper.

The whale responded by thrashing wildly. Athneal, still gripping the lance, was lifted clear of the boat and tossed into the sea. Uncle Joseph's quick action with the steering oar saved the boat, and Athneal scrambled back aboard.

Twice more he lanced the whale, until all three lances were in it, still without bringing on its death spasm.

"The bomb lance," one man suggested. "Use the bomb lance." Others nodded in agreement. They wanted to end the struggle quickly with the old brass blunderbuss and its exploding projectile.

"Lance going to get him, boys," Athneal laughed. "Is only a small one. Let we save bomb lance for big one."

He lifted his left foot onto the stemhead and motioned us close to the whale again. I was puzzled. What did he intend to do without a lance?

Then, with a single flowing movement, Athneal rose to balance for an instant on the gunwales before leaping toward the whale. He landed with both feet on the glistening back and hurled himself onto the last lance, driving it full into the whale with all his weight.

The whale made a convulsive dive, and Athneal was left swimming again. But this time the line stayed slack, and the whale floated slowly back to the surface, all life gone. The third lance had been well placed but had not gone deep enough. When he drove it in, Athneal was counting on cutting the spinal cord and paralyzing the whale.

Everyone was shouting at once as they helped Athneal back aboard, relieving the tension that had been building since early morning. Then, as the excitement died, *Trio* came along on the other side of the whale, and preparations began for getting the whale back to the tryworks on the small island of Petit Nevis, located a few hundred yards away from the houses of La Pompe.

First, a cut was made in the floor of the mouth and a rope passed through to lash the long, heavy lower jaw closed. Otherwise it might hang open, increasing drag as the whale was towed and causing the whale to fill with water and sink.

It had been exhausting to have to beat while chasing the whale, but now we were in the fortunate position of lying to windward of the tryworks, permitting us to sail home rather than having to row with the whale in tow. Since the whale was relatively small, it was simply lashed alongside *Dart* for the trip. Two hours brought us into the lee of Petit Nevis, where the whale was hauled onto a rocky ledge just below the level of the water.

A large, noisy crowd had already gathered, coming and going in a fleet of fishing boats. The cutting up began immediately with the standard instructions, advice, counteradvice, and incessant bickering over precedence and perquisites. The blubber was cut into large sheets and pulled ashore with ropes, and then butchering began with a surprising degree of excitement.

My notion of whaling, principally gleaned from the study of *Moby-Dick,* was that the value of a whale lay in the oil and in the bony plates that line the mouth of baleen whales such as our little humpback. Not so on Bequia, where no one wears corsets and no one uses whale oil lamps. Some oil is rendered in the large iron pots housed under a nearby shed, but the only market in recent years has been the Lever Brothers soap works in Trinidad, where the price is no more than that paid for coconut oil and thus not worth the trip.

The principal value of the whale in Bequia lies in the meat. Whaling is just another form of fishing, with a bigger hook and a longer line. The meat itself is red and somewhat coarse grained, without a trace of fat or gristle. It looks like the largest, most sumptuous beefsteak ever seen. The first time I had whale steak I went about preparing it just as I would beef, pan broiling an enormous, thick piece in a lightly greased skillet while rubbing my hands together and chortling in anticipation. The first bite was heaven, rich and delicious, almost sweet. The second bite was less to my taste, and after a third bite I ate no more of it.

It was the Mitchells who showed me how to cook whale meat. It must be cut into small chunks, fried in a generous amount of the rendered oil, and then added to a pot of rice and pigeon peas. In this combination it is delicious. However, tastes in meat are largely cultural, and any wholesome meat comes to have a value in a protein-poor economy such as the Grenadines.

As our whale was cut up, the meat was brought ashore and arranged in piles of about five pounds each. It was sold more or less continuously for the remainder of the day. Some people bought meat for their own uses, to be cooked and eaten fresh or to be preserved by covering the cooked meat with freshly rendered whale oil, in which condition it will keep for three to four months. Others bought larger quantities to dry on their roofs and sell for a small profit in St. Vincent.

The twelve whalers shared equally in the profits from the whale, while Athneal Olliverre and his two brothers each had an additional share as owners of the boats and the tryworks. The season is short, and in no year were more than four or five whales taken. It was difficult to dispose of whale meat profitably since there were no cold storage facilities in either Bequia or St. Vincent, meaning that the entire carcass, which might yield as much as twenty tons of meat, had to be sold in just a few hours. In fact, many of the customers simply waited for the end of the day and counted on pilfering what they needed as the whalers grew weary of waiting.

Financial rewards for whaling were thus not substantial, and all the whalers had other occupations during the off-season. Still they set out day after day when the whales were running, buffeted by wind and waves, blistered by the sun, sitting cramped on a hard wooden seat for up to eight hours at a stretch. The motive behind whaling may have been the experience itself, more than anything else: Bequia is consummately a seafaring island, and whaling is the greatest contest of the seas.

Tortola, and the "Next Fella"

~ ~ ~

When at last I renounced the gentle rhythm of life in Bequia, I resumed my journey north and homeward in a relaxed mood. I called on friends here, added a boat photograph there, but did nothing in the least energetic since, save for the simple chore of writing up my results, my casual research project had been completed with the launching of *Skywave*.

There was only one small inquiry that remained to be made, a simple detail, easily dealt with. Since it had been a Tortola-built boat, *Flame,* that had first aroused my interest in West Indian boatbuilding, it was simply a matter of thoroughness to make a stopover in Tortola. That it would be a short stopover there was no doubt. I knew from excursions to the British Virgin Islands, where Tortola is the principal island, that boatbuilding there was already a thing of the past. The most I could look forward to was a nostalgic conversation or two with former builders.

I knew the name of the man in the village of West End who had owned *Flame* before she came to St. Croix. He in turn was able to direct me to the builder, who had weathered the end of Tortola boatbuilding by turning importer and wholesale grocer, an important and profitable function on an island that currently produced nothing.

I found the establishment of Leo Smith on the main street of Roadtown, Tortola's only town. Business was slow in the middle of the afternoon, and Smith, a clear-complexioned man of uncertain age, readily fell into conversation. To my preliminary overtures about boatbuilding he gave a rueful shake of his head and replied, "Them days is gone, gone forever." We thereupon had a round of crocodile tears, mine because it meant that there was nothing further for me to do on my project, his because, I suspect, he was just as glad to be earning his living less strenuously now.

With unswerving devotion to duty, I nevertheless began to question Smith about those points of design and construction that I had come to regard as important: the proportions of length to beam; how he had learned his trade; where the traditions of boat carpentry had originated.

As he pondered my questions, a faraway look came into his pale blue eyes. "You know," he said, "it have a next fella come here some time ago asking all them same question." He rubbed his chin slowly and consideringly. "Then he go 'way and write a book."

My heart stopped, then raced. All I could hear was the pounding of blood in my ears. Had I really been so dumb? Had I spent nearly two *years* reinventing the wheel?

I had run a quick check of the maritime literature at the University of Puerto Rico before setting out on my researches. Their library collection, however, was sketchy, and I had done the search in great haste, simply assuming that my inquiry was original because it *felt* original. Now my house of cards—very dear to me, however flimsy—appeared to be falling in.

Evidently my chagrin was effectively masked by shock, because Smith cheerfully went on to tell me about "that next fella" and how he had measured and photographed, blithely driving the stake ever deeper into my scarcely beating heart. When Smith paused in his discourse, I collected myself enough to ask if he remembered the fella's name.

"Oh, yes," replied Smith. "He send me the book. Let we see and I can find it."

Whereupon he drove me to his house, beautifully sited halfway up the steep slope of the mountain overlooking Road Harbor. I could see that he was quietly pleased to share with me the affluence of his present circumstances and enjoying his worldliness in having overseas friends who wrote books. While he searched his cupboards, I sat on the verandah, consoling myself with the enchantment of a tropical perspective of sunlight, sea, and islands.

All too soon he returned, triumphantly waving my nemesis in its plain brown wrapper.

"Edwin B. Doran, Jr.," I read. *"The Tortola Boat: Characteristics, Origin, Demise."* A scholarly monograph published as a supplement to a journal entitled *The Mariner's Mirror.*

My heart sank even further at the crisp title and no-nonsense format. Here was obviously a scholarly work, not, as I had fleetingly hoped, a potpourri of sentiment and folklore put together for the tourist trade. Smith was obviously much attached to his memento, and so, with solemn pledges to return it soon, I crept back aboard *Eider* to read and lick my wounds, intrigued in spite of my disappointment.

The author, a geography professor at Texas A & M University, had visited

Tortola for several weeks in 1966, taking off lines, making photographs, and talking with builders at a time when there was still some active boatbuilding on the island. In addition to the fieldwork done here, he had extensively researched the historical aspects of the Tortola boat type. His work was detailed and precise, and with quickening attention I came to the short section on origins, which concluded:

> Once we have reached this point little more, unfortunately, can be said about the origin of the Tortola boat. Our basic problem here is the lack of knowledge about other West Indian boat types. Essentially no other lines plans of West Indian craft have been published and our ignorance of their detailed characteristics is almost complete.

My spirits rose now as rapidly as they had sunk before. Professor Doran had gotten to the islands first, but had *not* found all the answers! Not only did the Tortola boat monograph provide me with the lines of vessels no longer available for measuring, I had made the exciting discovery that I was doing exactly what a professional scholar in the field would consider a necessary next step.

That very afternoon I wrote to Professor Doran about my project and how I happened to learn of his work. He replied at once and was vastly encouraging. After his sojourn in Tortola, he wrote, his main focus of research had shifted to the watercraft of the Pacific basin. He had never followed up the direction of his research begun in the British Virgin Islands. Not only was I exploring frontier territory, I was not even encroaching on someone else's research domain.

As it happened I was intending to visit my mother in Oklahoma, conveniently close to Texas. This gave me the opportunity to meet Professor Doran at his home a few weeks following my discovery of his monograph.

Until this time I had planned simply to submit my drawings with brief notes to some learned journal devoted to Caribbean studies. After two days of conversations with Professor Doran, it emerged that the material thus far collected could form the basis for a broader treatment in a field—new to me—called marine anthropology. Thus far, I had concerned myself with only a few representative sloops and schooners. What was needed was information on *all* the watercraft of the Lesser Antilles, along with performance data and historical information where available.

Not only did Professor Doran encourage me to pursue the topic, he also kindly put at my disposal copies of his monograph, photographic negatives, related reprints, and bibliographic materials on the subject. And he pointed out to me an important historical resource that had been right under my nose, the registers of shipping kept in the harbor master's office of all former British colonial ports.

The realization that much remained to be done had the unusual effect of producing in me a further sense of elation rather than depression. After all, *Eider* was still in the Antilles and there are many things worse than sailing from island to island in quest of boat types and historical records—especially since I now had the assurance that my inquiries were not mere personal eccentricity but could be considered, at least in some circles, a useful sort of enterprise.

From Professor Doran's monograph I have included two sets of lines that seem best to typify traditional boat construction in Tortola. The first is from the sloop *Yolanda,* built about 1930 by Leo Smith, my friendly informant in Roadtown. The lines were taken from the builder's half model. This vessel is similar to both *Skywave* and *Mermaid* in length-to-beam ratio, in the sharp floors of the midsection, in the overhanging stern, and in the moderate drag to the keel. There are individual differences in the shape of the stem and transom, but it is clear at a glance that all three belong to the same family of inter-island sloops, a type that is remarkably constant over a considerable span of time and distance.

By contrast, *Sea Queen* has markedly different characteristics: a length-to-beam ratio of three-to-one, a rounded midsection, noticeable hollow in the lower waterlines, no overhanging stern, extreme drag to the keel, pronounced

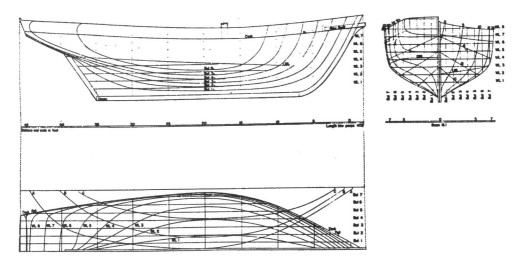

Lines of sloop Yolanda, *built in 1930 by Leopold Smith at Roadtown, Tortola. Taken off 1966 by Edwin M. Doran, Jr.*

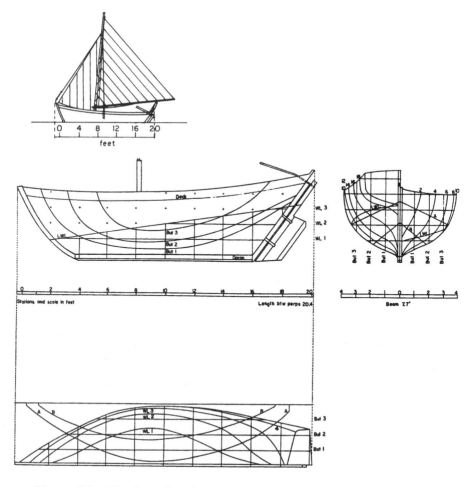

Lines of Tortola sloop Sea Queen, *built in 1959 by Osmond Davies at East End, Tortola. Taken off 1966 by Edwin M. Doran, Jr.*

or "moon" sheer, and a leg-of-mutton mainsail instead of the gaff or sprit rig found elsewhere. Taken all together, it is these traits that characterize the type known as the Tortola sloop. The transom stern and the moon sheer of the Antigua fishing boats, which I later discovered, are recent copies.

The distinctiveness of the Tortola boat type gave me my first taste of the joys of life as a marine anthropologist. Inter-island trading vessels, which had occupied my attention up to this point, show such similar characteristics that a common ancestor or design influence is easily inferred. Not so for smaller and purely local watercraft, which are usually unique to an island or group of islands and with recognizable ties. Finding some clue to the origins of these purely local types became one of my preoccupations during the second phase of my inquiry.

The sixty-eight–foot schooner *Pride of Tortola,* represented in the Doran

Sea Queen *on the hard at Roadtown, Tortola, 1966.*
(Photo by Edwin M. Doran, Jr.)

monograph, deserves comment even without her lines being reproduced here. Though built in Tortola for a Tortola owner, this schooner was actually built by MacDuff Richardson of Anguilla, whom I met on my first trip there. As a matter of fact, it was while working in the Virgin Islands that Richardson received the blow to his head that was said to account for his unconventional views on current affairs and a certain unreliability in professional capacities. In any case, the exchange of boatbuilders between island communities does give a clue as to why inter-island trading vessels should be broadly similar, while smaller craft retain their distinctive local traits.

~ ~ ~

As *Eider* and I lay at anchor in Tortola following my conversations with Professor Doran, I began to consider in a new light observations that had previously seemed unrelated and without meaning. For instance, I had been vaguely aware even before leaving St. Croix that there was no evidence of any indigenous boatbuilding activity in the U.S. Virgin Islands. My initial reaction had been a shrug of the shoulders. Only now that I had seen similar patterns of one island having builders while the island next door did not did I start thinking about the quirks of history that might underlie parts of the emerging story.

St. Croix, a relatively small island with no near neighbors, once had a pure plantation economy. Manufactured goods arrived and sugar left in ships belonging to the Danish West India Company. There was simply no employment for locally built watercraft, and none were made. The situation in St. Thomas was similar, although there the economic fortunes of the island turned after t he late nineteenth century on its free port status and its functions as a transshipment point and coaling station. For both islands, European vessels dominated shipping. The very limited local commerce—largely exports of produce and barnyard animals—was carried on from Tortola in vessels built in Tortola.

The Lesser Antilles constitute a cultural mosaic of bewildering complexity. There are, of course, the obvious differences produced by colonial acquisition and administration, as well as differences in climate and economics engendered by different rainfall patterns. Other differences are not so easily explained. On some islands—Carriacou, for example—there is an awareness of African descent that extends to a detailed knowledge of tribal origins. On others, such as Martinique, many of the people are fiercely Europeanized, to the extent that can only occur in a post-colonial society. In some communities in sight of the sea, most people do not swim and are afraid of the water. In others, all ages swim and watersports are popular. On some islands, political administration is malicious, lackadaisical, or both; on others, government functions remarkably well.

Boatbuilding shows in the islands the same mosaic quality and is similarly unyielding to analysis. On some islands like Anguilla, with few natural resources, there has been continuous and conspicuous boatbuilding. A few miles away in St. Martin, advantages abound but no established tradition ever existed. As my interests broadened to include the origins and design influences in boatbuilding traditions, it became almost as important to know where building had *not* taken place. This would mean looking through all the islands, even when I was reasonably certain that I already knew the answer.

The Beach Boats of St. Martin

~ ~ ~

S
t. Martin lies south of Anguilla across a channel only four miles wide, yet the contrast between the two islands could scarcely be more marked. Anguilla is low, flat, and isolated; it has no all-weather harbors and no stands of trees suitable for boat timbers. St. Martin has a backbone of rugged volcanic crests, a number of protected harbors, timber resources, a long-standing tourist industry. That both islands are dry is about their only shared condition.

The southern half is officially Sint Maarten, administered in Dutch by Dutch civil servants with the advice of a locally elected council. The northern half is St. Martin, administered in French by French bureaucrats with the advice of no one. Meanwhile, the daily life of the whole island is carried on in English with little regard for the niceties of administration or frontiers and few objections or difficulties from government, however constituted. The low level of official interference may simply be because there are few taxes to be wrung from a dry island outside the tourist areas.

On one of my early visits to Anguilla I heard of a fishing boat regatta held in St. Martin's Marigot Bay every year on Bastille Day, July 14. That summer I made shift to celebrate the first assault upon France's *ancien régime* as it should be done, namely on French soil with French bread and red wine, if available. This would provide, I thought, an excellent opportunity to measure the boats gathered for the regatta.

On the evening of July 13, I anchored close to the long, curving beach that stretches westward from the little town of Marigot and scanned the shoreline for boats. It proved easy to select the boat that would represent the island in my study, for there was only one boat in view. This was clearly a racing boat; a group of men was gathered around it, rigging and trimming the freshly painted hull.

I rowed over to make acquaintance and ask permission to take off the lines, finding to my surprise a friend in the group. NoNo Richardson, whom I had known in St. Croix, had come back to St. Martin to race his cousin's boat in the regatta.

NoNo was something of a sensation in St. Croix yacht racing circles. He skippered a small yacht of no special distinction yet managed invariably to outfoot and outpoint all competitors large and small. If you can do that consistently, you can bring home a lot of silver. NoNo regularly did this, frequently

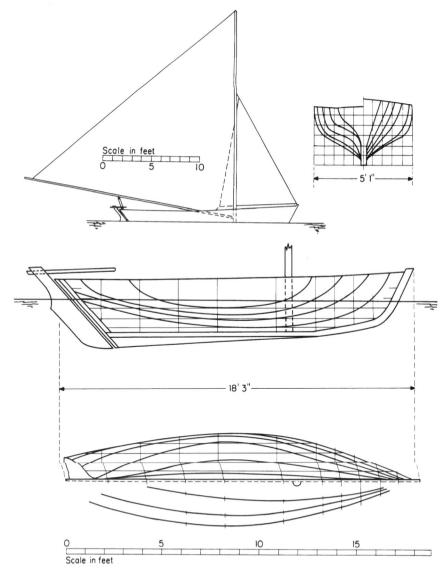

Lines of fishing boat **Alma Gloria,** *built by Philbert Richardson at Marigot Bay, St. Martin. Taken off July 1974.*

being the only dark face at the after-race award dinner. NoNo's presence in St. Martin meant that I was assured of getting lines and performance data.

The lines of *Alma Gloria* show a close resemblance to the Anguilla beach boats in the strongly curved forefoot, fine entry, marked drag to the keel, sharp floors, and the easy run carried onto the transom stern. The rig also is similar, with its leg-of-mutton mainsail and jib hoist at two-thirds of the mast.

The next morning, NoNo was out to tune the boat and came alongside *Eider* to pick me up. The breeze was very light in the confines of the bay, too light for *Alma Gloria* to develop her full potential. Nevertheless, as we tacked back and forth I found that the boat would still reach speeds of up to almost six knots close to the wind. As NoNo put *Alma Gloria* through her paces, I noticed that he was carrying bags of sand for ballast instead of stones. When I asked about this variance from convention, he grinned and explained that on the downwind leg he planned to leave the sand dry and keep the boat light. On the beat back to the finish line he would wet the sand and increase the ballast according to wind conditions prevailing at the time.

By the time we finished our performance trial, the rest of the contestants had arrived. No one else was surprised to learn that the whole lot had sailed in from Anguilla, and that in fact NoNo would be the sole representative of the host island.

A crowd had begun to gather along the sea wall in front of the town, and the race committee, meeting in a dockside grog shop, disposed of the ever-troublesome issue of handicapping by assigning all entrants either to the eighteen-foot or the twenty-four–foot class.

Soon the smaller boats were ready for the start, arrayed along the sea wall with sails set, crew in place, and stern held by the skipper, standing waist deep in water. At the starting gun, the skipper and as many well-wishers as cared to get wet pushed, swam, splashed, and shouted the boats into motion, each seeking to be the first to clear the sea wall and get clean wind.

The afternoon was bright and hot, and the breeze continued very light. The boats were still closely grouped as they passed among the anchored yachts, but racing downwind in light airs never settles anything. The race would be decided on the long beat back from the leeward mark, and it was then that I expected to see NoNo show his stuff.

When the smaller boats were all down the bay, the larger class was started. After they passed through the anchorage there was nothing to watch, so I began idly to compose a paean of praise for NoNo, nautical terror of St. Croix and now the scourge of St. Martin as well.

Using my field glasses, I scanned seaward. The small boats were rounding the leeward mark, and I could just make out a change in the shape of their sails

NoNo Richardson skippers the Alma Gloria *(foreground) in the Bastille Day Regatta, Marigot Bay, St. Martin.*

as, one by one, they came close-hauled. Now the tiny white triangles began to glide effortlessly back and forth across the smooth expanse of bay, slowly drawing closer. I strained to pick out *Alma Gloria,* but it was impossible to distinguish one white hull from another against the sea's shimmering surface.

The boats were well up among the anchored yachts again before I could be sure that NoNo was not among them. After half a minute of anxious searching, I located *Alma Gloria* close under the shore as NoNo had planned, but completely out of the race.

As I pondered the implications of this for yacht racing in St. Croix (what if the Anguillans came to try their skills where NoNo was already unbeatable?), the leaders in the class were nearing the finish, designed to avoid any possibility of argument over first place. A stake boat had been anchored off the sea wall where the race started. Affixed to the stem of the stake boat was a small Tricolor, waving merrily in the breeze. As the two leading boats closed with the stake boat, a crew member lay in the bows of each, held by the ankles and stretched to his full length. Amid a crescendo of shouts from the shore, the boats feinted, then one edged inside the other and *Quick Step* of Anguilla snatched the flag. There being no second flag, there was no second place. Winner take all.

The larger class was won by *Saga Boy,* owned by Emile Gumbs of Anguilla but built in St. Kitts.

In the past, the inhabitants of St. Martin supported themselves in part by killing wild cattle that roamed the island and preserving the meat with salt produced in the shallow lagoons on the southern, Dutch side of the island. Salt and bully beef were then sold to passing ships, many of them fishing schooners from New England and Nova Scotia. I can only suppose, when remembering those steep hillsides covered in dry, thorny scrub, that the purchasers of this bully beef must have had very keen appetites and even better teeth.

What mainly interested me when I learned about this trade was that local boatbuilders would have had ample opportunity to see and emulate the visiting schooners. This influence, coupled with natural harbors and the timber resources of St. Martin, might have fostered a maritime industry at some point in the past, even if there was none at present. With this in mind, I tackled both French and Dutch administrations in search of ship registrations.

My inquiries produced brows knit in concentration, shaken heads, and shrugs, but no vessel registrations. I did happen onto a man named Williams whose father had built fishing vessels some thirty years earlier, and a young woman whose father had told her of two schooners, named *Anna* and *Leontine,* which were built at the beginning of World War I by John Connor Vlaun. It was only later, when examining the registry of shipping in St. Christopher (St. Kitts to the islanders), that I began to have a clearer picture of what this meant.

Over the years since 1838, as slavery ended, inter-island trading increased, and when the St. Kitts register was begun, there were scattered entries for vessels built in St. Martin, Saba, St. Eustatius, and St. Barthélemy and then brought to St. Kitts to be registered. I expect this was the practice because Basseterre, St. Kitts, was the only town in the vicinity with the necessary maritime services. Those vessels registered from St. Martin were either built by Anguillans for Anguillans or, if the residence of the builder was given as St. Martin, by someone with an Anguillan name such as those the reader has already noted: Richardson, Connor, and Williams.

My initial conclusion was that these were actually Anguillan vessels, but built in and cleared from St. Martin for access to materials. And further, I suspected that the scarcity of boatbuilding in St. Martin resulted largely from having a near neighbor where a thriving maritime industry already existed.

ELEVEN

The Mystery of Saba

~ ~ ~

Ⅰn my earliest conversations about boatbuilding, I heard references to the island of Saba made often and in tones of awe. This awe was explained by my first glimpse of the single volcanic cone that forms the island, rising from two thousand feet under the sea to soar another three thousand feet into the atmosphere. The shoreline is everywhere steep-to, and there are no anchorages. At one spot on the southern side of the island, the pilot book grudgingly concedes, "landing may be effected by small craft, with local knowledge, in fair weather."

Cloud-obscured summit of Saba. March 1970.

No anchorages? A difficult landing? Then why, or even how, could boat-building have been part of Saba's history? Yet it was, if the rumors amounted to anything. Boats and schooners had been built in Saba. In defiance of all common sense, it was asserted that vessels had been built high on the side of the volcano and lowered down the face of the cliff for launching.

My research concerning Saba was going to be second hand as long as getting there required landing as prescribed by the pilot book. Fortunately, in St. Martin I discovered a perfectly acceptable way to visit the island. An enterprising Saban had found a shoulder of nearly level ground on the windward side of the mountain and had boasted that he could build an airstrip if only he had a bulldozer. The Dutch administration of Saba rose to the challenge, somehow putting a small bulldozer ashore at South Side Landing, whereupon the aforesaid Saban gouged a road across the island and proceeded to keep his end of the bargain.

All very well, but a sizable hurdle still remained since, for all the ingenuity in the world, the landing strip thus devised was almighty short. In fact, a new type of aircraft, designated the Short Take-Off and Landing, had to be developed by DeHaviland in the early 1970s before the Sabans could achieve air contact with the outside world. This approach to Saba seemed in every way preferable to the terrors of anchoring my lovely *Eider* in fifty fathoms of poor holding on the rocky, wave-pounded flank of a volcano, even an extinct one.

As we banked in a stiff crosswind for our landing, I spied the landing strip below looking about as big as a tennis court and reconsidered my decision on the safest mode of transport. I am well aware that appearances may be deceiving to the inexperienced eye, but in sober truth the wheels jarred onto the tarmac while I, seated just behind the wing, was still staring down into the foaming sea below.

After deplaning, I stood beside the strip and watched as the airplane taxied to the end of the runway, lifted off like a kite, and struck out for St. Eustatius, the next stop on the circuit. I stood for a time pondering the ingenuity of mankind in its quest for mobility, then set forth to retrace the historic route of the bulldozer, puffing up the steep side of the volcano over switchback after switchback. Soon I was hiking through swirling mists. Above me loomed the unseen summit, hidden in the wind-driven clouds.

The contrast with St. Martin was a little unsettling. A few minutes earlier I had been sweating in the sun while around me people bustled and traffic snarled. Now I climbed the middle of a steep roadway, made clammy by the mists and the hidden sun, and there was no one to be seen—no cars, no people, not even any telephone poles by the roadside for company. I went up the main thoroughfare of Saba in lonely splendor, climbing up toward the

Community of Windward, Saba. March 1970.

little collection of houses known as Hellsgate. There people stood in their doorways smiling and speaking to me, helping to restore a sense of reality.

At another group of houses called Windward, the road stopped climbing and began to circle, following the side of the mountain for a distance before dropping down into the crater where lay the main settlement of the island, called, with commendable economy, The Bottom. At the near edge of the settled area, a young man lounged in the doorway of a small, neat house exactly resembling all the other small, neat houses in sight. I had been lucky enough, he informed me, to locate on my very first try the Old Inn Club.

I entered his establishment, asking for and getting in the following order: a cold bottle of beer, a meal (plain but filling), and information on Saba boat-building. The beer and food came from a small room at the back of the house and were served to me in a small room at the front of the house. The information on boatbuilding came from a small house across the road wherein dwelt the publican's father, Bertil Chance, a shipwright and carpenter.

Chance, then already in his eighties, was born in St. Martin and had lived for many years in St. Bart's before coming to Saba thirty-six years earlier. He told me of vessels built in Saba, and when I asked how they were launched he replied that the lower ends of the ways along one side of the completed hull were sharpened so that they drove slowly into the sand, bringing the hull gently to rest on a bed of planks and rollers. Then a tackle was rigged from a kedge anchor to lower the vessel into the water.

From these recollections he drifted into tales of hurricanes and other extraordinary happenings, mostly centering on the occasion when high winds swept his privy into a field two hundred yards away. After the eye of the hurricane passed, the winds changed direction and the privy was picked up and returned to its foundation. During the following hour, my repeated attempts to return to the subject of boatbuilding failed, although I became something of an expert on the aerodynamics of the West Indian backhouse.

After saying goodbye to Chance, I walked down the steep, winding road to South Side Landing, where a strip of rocky shingle fifty feet long and ten feet wide was tucked into a fold in the volcanic cliffs. There was no sand. At one end, a tiny customs house had been built, just in case. Nearby, two rugged surf boats were pulled up beyond the reach of the waves. It was apparent that there was absolutely no room here to build anything larger than a rowboat, much less to launch in the manner described by Chance. I could only conclude that the passage of time had telescoped his experiences of launchings elsewhere, probably St. Barts, onto his memories of Saba. In any case, the rumors about Saba had all agreed that launching took place by lowering the vessels down the cliffs.

As I weighed these thoughts, a small freighter put a line onto the Texaco mooring buoy and began preparations to discharge cargo. A Land Rover was swayed up and over the side, then lowered onto a small raft made of empty oil drums and rough lumber. One man sat at the wheel of the Land Rover; another waited at the tiller of an outboard-powered surf boat.

Pushed by the surf boat, the raft left the side of the freighter and moved sluggishly toward the shore, pausing just beyond the point where the incoming waves began to crest. Several waves passed under the motionless raft while the man in the Land Rover waited. When he saw his opening, he yelled to the boatman, who stirred the outboard to maximum effort and brought the raft onto a cresting wave. The wave gathered power, and suddenly the raft was rushing forward, pulling the surf boat behind it. As the raft grated onto the rocky beach, the driver gunned the engine and the Land Rover surged off the raft, all four wheels spinning and fighting for purchase on the slippery stones. For an anxious moment, the pull of the receding wave held the struggling vehicle. Then the front wheels gathered traction, pulling vehicle and driver up the beach just ahead of the next wave.

Through the whole sequence I stood dumbfounded. Seeing is believing, but somehow my imagination would not stretch far enough to encompass a charging bulldozer accomplishing the same feat.

Long after my visit to Saba, as I tried to add historical depth to my inquiries, I found references to Saba in a couple of traveler's accounts. Charles

Stoddard, writing in 1895 in *Cruising Among the Caribees,* represents the earliest reference I could locate of Saban vessels being built and lowered into the sea. However, neither Stoddard nor the others did anything more exacting than view the island from the deck of a passing cruise ship; their accounts merely establish that the hearsay evidence of boatbuilding in Saba is of greater antiquity than I had come to suppose.

As a matter of fact, the sole hard evidence ever found for the legend was Professor Doran's discovery of a single entry in the Tortola shipping registers, mentioning that in 1859 the schooner *Augusta* of sixty-six–foot length overall and forty-nine tons was built in Saba by Benjamin Horton and brought to Tortola to be registered. There were other vessels *registered* to a Saban owner and built elsewhere, but of all the entries I surveyed throughout the islands, no other vessel was actually attributed to construction in Saba.

I surmise that the folk history of boatbuilding in Saba developed in the following manner. Benjamin Horton, an unusually determined individual (possibly an intrepid ancestor of the daring Land Rover driver and/or airport-making bulldozer operator), against all advice and common sense built a schooner in The Bottom and lowered it, not over the cliffs but down the steep valley now followed by the roadway. At South Side Landing it was launched in some way. Even in this attenuated form, Horton's accomplishment was so memorable that it quickly became enshrined in the folklore of the island. With the passage of time and frequent retelling, this singular event became pluralized until finally whole fleets of vessels were popularly supposed to have been built and lowered over Saba's cliffs into the foaming sea below. This, at least, is the version I favor.

In the matter of seafaring itself, the Sabans are secure from all corrosive skepticism. Beyond any doubt, they *are* seamen. Employment on Saba is minimal, and most Sabans who leave the island follow the sea as a matter of course. No doubt they would have built boats if only circumstances were a little more favorable. In the meantime, the island forms another curious fragment of the Caribbean maritime culture: an island of seafarers who do not build boats.

TWELVE

The Quiet of St. Eustatius

~ ~ ~

The twin peaks of St. Eustatius (Statia) are easily visible from Saba or Sint Maarten, and the three islands together form the northernmost part of the Netherlands Antilles. Between the gently sloping volcanic cones of Statia lies a saddle of nearly level land, eight square miles in all, which forms in its lee a large and well-sheltered roadstead. The foreshore of this anchorage is edged with the ruined shells of buildings whose size and grandeur seem out of character with the peaceful, unfrequented roadstead of such a small and arid island. Above, on the bluff a few dozen feet up, is the small town of Oranjestad under the wings of a small comic opera fort.

View of the roadstead at Oranjestad, St. Eustatius. November 1970.

The overall impression is that a once large and prosperous island has sunk into the sea, leaving a fringe of its former glory at the water's edge while the ruined inhabitants, having fled to higher ground, are reestablished in dramatically lessened circumstances. Actually, reality is more political and meteorological, but no less bizarre. During the eighteenth century, as England and France grappled for primacy in Europe and the New World, the American colonies of both were obliged under severe penalties to trade only and directly with the mother country. Since the economic interests of the colonies did not always coincide with those of the mother country, trade among the colonies flourished in defiance of regulations. To give legitimacy to this intercolony trade, sugar and rum from Martinique, for example, were shipped to Statia where they were "purchased" by neutral Dutch entrepreneurs, warehoused briefly ashore, and then sold to a merchant vessel, perhaps from New York or Boston, that had sailed to Statia carrying lumber or salt cod. It was the little fort on the bluff that first saluted the new Stars and Stripes ensign flown by an arriving American merchant ship, constituting the first official recognition of the new revolutionary experiment in North America.

The convenience of Statia for business had, of course, monetary value. Statia waxed prosperous wildly beyond its resources or its size. The Dutch middlemen were neither the first nor the last in the Lesser Antilles to prosper as neutrals. At one time Statia was one of the busiest and most prosperous ports in the Antilles. This changed after the late 1790s, when the Netherlands became a satellite state successively of the French republic and then Napoleon's empire. To fund the infrastructure, excesses, and military adventures of the period, the French imposed merciless taxation, including transshipment enterprises such as those that were the life blood of Statia. Statia was buffeted also by free port competition from Gustavia in St. Barts and Charlotte Amalie in St. Thomas, and in the more literal sense when severe hurricanes scattered shipping and badly damaged the Lower Town.

Statia's high point of population was reached in 1790 at over 8,000; by the end of the Napoleonic era in 1815 it had collapsed to around 2,500, and today it hovers at around 1,500. The mercantilist fixations of British and French economic theorists were replaced in the 1800s by a century of burgeoning free trade and a near absence of warfare between the former enemies. The vagaries of European economics and politics account for the creation and destruction of the docks and warehouses of Oranjestad's Lower Town.

After visiting the fort and walking around the little town a while, I stopped for refreshment in Charlie's Bar, located in the lobby of the once-a-week movie house in the heart of Oranjestad. It seemed as good a place as any to make inquiries about a maritime past. In fact, it was exactly the right place, since old Charlie himself had once sailed aboard a whaling vessel. In April 1917, he told me, at the height of World War I the *B.S. Woodruff* of New Bedford, Massachusetts, had called in Statia and taken on crew before sailing after sperm whales to a whaling area called the Western Ground. The threat of U-boats cut short the voyage, since the United States entered the war in that month, and the crewmen were returned to Statia in September.

It is always fascinating to reach into the past through some personal contact, and in this case unusually so, since I was actively looking for contacts that might have influenced the design of West Indian sailing craft. And here was such a contact, dropped into my lap, wrapped up and tied with a pretty ribbon.

Later I was able to verify old Charlie's story. When I visited the Whaling Museum in New Bedford, Massachusetts, hoping to learn what type of vessel the *Woodruff* had been, I was directed to a bound register of all known American whaling vessels. To my disappointment, my search through the W's produced nothing even faintly resembling "Woodruff." Then I was informed that ships are always indexed alphabetically using the first letter of the registered name, so I turned to the B's. Still no luck. I stood quietly riffling the pages of the register, absorbing the loss of such a promising lead. Something caught my eye, and turning back three pages I discovered an entry for *Arthur V.S. Woodruff* of New Bedford, 105 feet overall, 155 tons; built in 1888 and rigged as a tern schooner; J.A. Tilden, master and owner.

I thought back to the cool, dark interior of Charlie's Bar. There had been no mention of "Arthur," but it was not unusual for crew to abbreviate long names. As for the "B" instead of a "V," better ears than mine have confounded the two in the soft West Indian dialect. In other respects, the discovered vessel fit nicely the specifications of a whaler in the closing days of the Atlantic fishery. And a tern schooner with three masts, designed to run best across the wind or into it, was just the type of design suited to alternative work in the islands. It might have been copied by a local builder or returned sailor.

Presumably the reserves of indigenous Statian timber, still on occasion exploited by Anguillans in search of frames, had existed more robustly in earlier times. The potential for construction of inter-island trading vessels should have been apparent on an island where commerce had once been so profitable. However, no such thing occurred. Apparently some necessary element escaped being integrated on Statia, and there was never anything more than very occasional boatbuilding activity there. After talking with old Charlie, I looked around for other signs of marine architectural activity and, finding none, soon went aboard *Eider* and made preparations to leave the next morning.

THIRTEEN

The Lighters of Nevis and St. Kitts

~ ~ ~

The eccentric and uncomfortable motion of a small yacht at sea is a nuisance I learned to tolerate in order to enjoy the convenience of traveling without leaving home. Rolling at anchor, however, has generally seemed beyond the call of duty, so on my earlier trips through the Leeward Islands I had bypassed Nevis and St. Kitts, where the pilot book noted that "neither island has a protected harbor, and a swell frequently sets into the roadsteads of both." Only after my metamorphosis into a marine anthropologist did my zeal drive me to call in Nevis and then in St. Kitts—and to discover how much I had been missing.

Both Nevis and St. Kitts are picturesque and inhabited by gentle people; both harbored significant maritime lore. Nevis had a series of *Registers of Shipping* dating back to 1838, the earliest and most complete set I found in all

Sailing lighter at anchor off Charlestown, Nevis. April 1975.

the Lesser Antilles. In addition, both are classic examples of volcanically formed islands. Nevis, in particular, rises to a single perfect cone whose summit, often robed in clouds, appeared to Columbus to be snow covered and inspired the island's original Spanish name of *Nieves*.

Nevis's lower slopes are wrapped about with the glossy, swaying green of coconut palms except where the stone buildings of Charlestown peek shyly out onto the roadstead. Charlestown is the port, administrative center, and sole emporium for the island, as well as the beginning and ending of the single encircling road. I was told that the island could be circumambulated in a day, and by way of introduction I set out to do it.

The fresh coolness of early morning lasted as far as the Nisbet Plantation, once the abode of Frances Nisbet. The parish register of the nearby church records that in 1787 Frances Nisbet, widow, married Horatio Nelson, then Captain in His Britannic Majesty's Navy, stationed at the time at English Harbour, Antigua, just over the horizon to the east.

On the next leg of my walk, which was hot and dry, I fell in with a Nevisian whose son worked as a gardener in St. Croix. When we reached his home he invited me in, refreshed me with cool water, and filled my arms with mangoes and bananas as I was leaving. I thanked him for his warm hospitality.

"Oh, that is nothing." He smiled. "If I coming to your country, is be just the same, won't it?"

I doubted that it would, and to cover my embarrassment offered to take a message to his son in St. Croix, where I would be stopping in a few days.

"You tell him 'plenty howdy' from all he folks in Nevis," my host called.

Soon afterward I reached the windward side of the island and was in the shadow of the cone during the long, hot hours of the afternoon. Late in the day I stopped at a small guest house on the northeast coast for further refreshment. Falling into conversation, I talked until twilight, then accepted a jeep ride for the few remaining miles to Charlestown.

The following morning I began my day by measuring one of the sailing lighters built in Nevis. A lighter is a barge used to load and unload deep-draft vessels in shallow harbors. These, crewed by Nevisians, operated in the roadstead at Basseterre on nearby St. Kitts, which had no deep-water pier. Some of the lighters were simple barges towed in strings by a tug belonging to one or another of the commercial establishments of the island. Others, however, worked under sail. Some plied between freighters and pier during the week, then returned home to Nevis for the weekend. I was told that under the best conditions, lighters could cover the eleven nautical miles between Charlestown and Basseterre in under an hour, sailing a broad reach.

Of the four fifty-foot sailing lighters still in service, one, *Victoria*, was

Nevis sailing lighter headed home on a Saturday afternoon
off Basseterre, St. Kitts. April 1975.

hauled ashore for repairs, enabling me to take lines off this interesting and unique type. The lines reveal a harmony and gracefulness that is not evident in the utilitarian construction of these vessels. A length-to-beam ratio of 2.5:1 is adequate testimony to their carrying capacities; nevertheless, the entry is fine and the run aft is smoothly developed, demonstrating that beaminess does not in itself preclude good lines.

The sailing lighters were, of course, undecked for ease in cargo handling. They carried only a single, fixed deck beam where the mast was set; a removable one was lashed into position to provide strength for the hull during longer trips. *Victoria* was not rigged the day I examined her, so I drew a rigging plan from photographs of the boats under way. The plan is essentially like the local beach boats: a small jib and a large leg-o-mutton mainsail with a gunter pole—a cross between a gaff and a headboard—seized to the head of the sail.

Although waves were breaking over the Charlestown pier, the roadstead was comfortable, and I set sail for St. Kitts hoping the cruising guides were unduly pessimistic. Sailing conditions could not have been better. Fresh breezes and a close reach in sheltered waters brought me to Basseterre in a buoyant

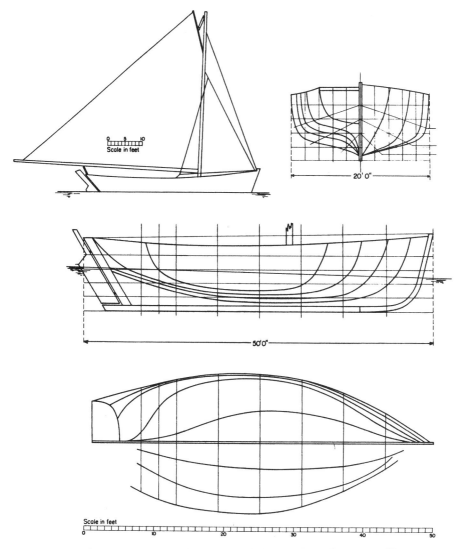

Lines of sailing lighter Victoria, *built in 1951 by George Mills at Charlestown, Nevis. Taken off April 1975.*

frame of mind. This lasted until I set the anchor, when *Eider* began to roll heavily, and I quickly decided to do some late-afternoon sightseeing ashore.

The town of Basseterre retains in some quarters a sense of its Georgian prosperity, particularly around the small square in the oldest part of town. Elsewhere, it is pretty typically West Indian—unglazed windows, sheet metal roofs—and definitely on the quiet side. The bar and restaurant that I scouted out with some care, planning to make a long evening of it for comfort's sake, began trying to close as soon as the sun was decently behind the mountain. The rest of the town was already shuttered and dark, so there was nothing to do but return aboard and grind my teeth in accompaniment to the many-throated serenade of a rolling yacht.

The following morning, desperate for something to do ashore, I acted on a suggestion of Professor Doran's and went to the harbor master's office to see about ship registrations. The dusty office was on the second floor of a nondescript building that stood at the head of the pier, its shuttered windows opening on to the waterfront below. I presented myself and stated my business, and the harbor master waved me cordially toward a large volume lying on a small table at the back of the office.

It was titled *Register of Seamen and Shipping,* and a quick glance disclosed that it recorded on double pages of heavy velum the detailed particulars of all vessels that had been brought to Basseterre to claim the privilege of sailing under British colors. The earliest entry in the volume was 1929, but when my interest became clear, the harbor official indicated a stack of similar volumes, dusty like everything else in the office, lying on the lower shelf of a small book case. With increasing excitement I lifted two more heavy volumes onto a work table and discovered that the record of ship registrations was complete back to 1876, while a smaller volume with a disintegrating binding held abbreviated entries back to 1838! The record began just as slavery was ending, when inter-island work boats began to be built.

The long night tossing back and forth in my bunk was suddenly worth it. Here in these heavy volumes was a comprehensive record of the boatbuilding activity of St. Kitts and its dependencies, Nevis and Anguilla, for a century and a half, as well as occasional entries mentioning vessels from more distant islands. As I turned the thick pages, the dry bureaucratic forms began to stir with the romance of colorful names: *Telephone R, Try Again John, Widow's Mite, Windrush.* And behind the hope, pride, whimsy, and defiance of the names lay a wealth of detail: builder's and owner's names, date and place of building, full measurements for computing tonnage, rig and structural details for identification. And on the right-hand pages, scrawled diagonally across the lower half of the sheet, the date and the reason for closing the registration. Lost in the gale of 1922 at Basseterre. Sold at auction for £22.18.12. Foundered at Montserrat in 1926. Sold Dutch 1909. Wrecked at Dieppe Bay 1912 . . .

Never could I have anticipated that the tedious alluvium of official thoroughness could be so absorbing. I was breathless with excitement, and in the thrill of the moment it seemed that the value of these data made it somehow likely that they would be denied to me. Speed must be of the essence, so I got permission to photograph the pages. It was then a matter of focus, snap, turn the page, and do it all again as quickly as possible before anything could intervene.

I must emphasize that in this instance, the harbor master was truly delighted to have in his possession something that was of interest to me. Elsewhere in the islands this was not always the case. In some offices my advent was greeted with everything from suspicion to indifference, and nowhere were the records so extensive or complete as in St. Kitts. In fact, it was fortunate that my first contact with the registers occurred there, where a slight effort was so richly repaid. If I had made my first try where the records were sketchy or begrudged, I would very likely have concluded out of indolence that the *Registers* were not worth consulting. As it turned out, they came to be one of my major preoccupations during my remaining time in the islands.

Apart from the registers, there was very little marine anthropology that needed doing in St. Kitts. No large vessels had been built on the island for

St. Kitts fishing boats off Basseterre. April 1975.

many years, nor have they been recently except, I hear, for a series of non-traditional, extremely expensive custom multihull yachts made in a boatyard catering to expatriates. There were, however, fishing boats that operated under sail as there had been in Nevis.

I had already measured a good example of a St. Kitts boat during the

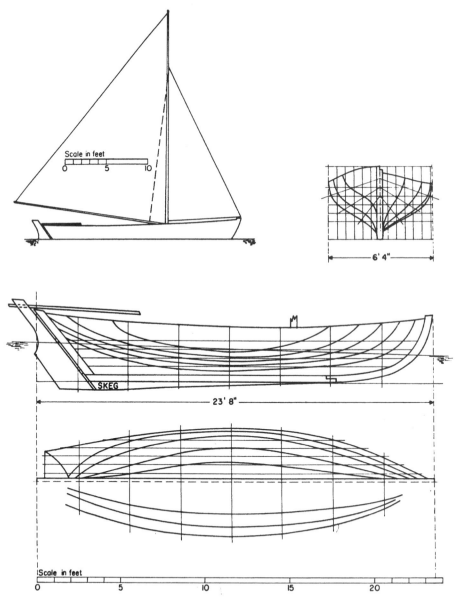

Lines of beach boat Saga Boy, *built around 1966 at Basseterre, St. Kitts. Taken off January 1971.*

Saga Boy in foreground; Bluebird at right rear. January 1971.

Bastille Day festivities in St. Martin: Emile Gumbs's *Saga Boy*. The lines and rig show the same characteristics as *Alma Gloria* (St. Martin) and *Bluebird* (Anguilla). Sharp floors are complemented with lots of deadrise, pronounced drag to the keel, a fine entry, a length-to-beam ratio of four-to-one, and a leg-of-mutton sail. There are, of course, slight variations, but it is clear that these craft are of the same basic type. The type is found throughout the northern Leeward Islands and can be consigned to a group called the Leeward Island Beach Boat.

My stopover in Nevis and St. Kitts provided important information, but one night of rolling was about all that seemed necessary. As soon as I had collected my precious registry data, I returned aboard *Eider* and considered my next move. The November day had gone cloudy, and the freshening trade winds had backed a point into the northeast. My next stop was St. Barts, but an immediate departure would have brought me to an unfamiliar landfall on what was likely to be a very dark night. The best course was to sail northwest along the south shore of St. Kitts to anchor in the security of Pump Bay, where the yacht might lie more quietly than at Basseterre.

After an exhilarating sail in strong, gusting winds over flat water, I rounded to at my destination and dropped anchor. Gray clouds swirled over the volcanic summit, partly obscuring the carefully tended, lush sugarcane fields. Overlooking Pump Bay stood the once formidable citadel of Brimstone Hill, which I visited in a drizzling rain.

During the night the wind moved still farther into the northeast and Pump Bay began to roll. Clearing off in the dark with strong winds and in unfamiliar waters didn't seem wise, so I clung to my berth and beguiled the dragging hours with visions of tomorrow's weatherly passage to St. Barts.

FOURTEEN

Deceptive St. Barts

St. Barthélemy, more commonly known as St. Barts, was mentioned frequently by my new acquaintances as an island with a significant sailing tradition, and Gustavia was said to have been an important schooner port. It was hard to believe at first. The tiny, landlocked harbor appeared saturated with the easy indolence of the tropics. And really, there was no apparent reason not to take things easy. An island of nine arid square miles and 2,500 inhabitants could scarcely produce or consume enough to generate even a modest amount of trade.

Two days at anchor in the placid inner harbor were enough to persuade me that under the air of nonchalance lay an almost feverish (for the West Indies) level of activity. Sloops and schooners came and went, but stayed so briefly that there seemed to be almost no commerce. Small trucks and hand carts ranged among the shuttered stone buildings surrounding the inner harbor. The focal point of this antlike trundling was the small wharf at the harbor entrance where an odd assortment of vessels made brief appearances.

The small shops of the town displayed an unexpected array of luxury goods. I marveled at perfumes, cameras, electronic devices, cigarettes of every conceivable brand, and liquors of all descriptions at prices so low they made me dizzy. Had I known at the outset what later unfolded of the island's past, I might have been spared much fruitless foraging for evidence of boatbuilding.

The first permanent settlement on St. Barts was made in 1658 by several families of Norman French. Their descendants eked out a living as subsistence farmers, unnoticed until 1740 when the English raided the island and dispersed the 660 inhabitants. Most, if not all, the Bartsians found their way to St. Thomas, where they founded the section of Charlotte Amalie still known today as Frenchtown. In 1763, St. Barts was returned to France during deliberations concluding the Seven Years War with England, upon which some of the former inhabitants and their children took up residence on the island again.

In 1784 the island and its 739 inhabitants were traded to Sweden in ex-

Trading sloop loading in Gustavia harbor,
St. Barts. May 1975.

change for a French trading base on the Baltic island of Goteborg. The Swedes founded Gustavia, made it into a free port like St. Eustatia, and were able to operate it in the same way for a time with similar profits. While the Norman French tended their provision gardens and chased goats, some six thousand Swedish entrepreneurs arrived to operate the port.

This was the golden age of St. Barts, when as many as two thousand vessels a year arrived and departed. Goods came in from all over the world, were landed in the warehouses that sprang up around the Inner Harbor, and later were reshipped with a new and unexceptionable bill of lading. The end of the Napoleonic Wars and new political and trade perspectives brought things to an end here as they were ending in Statia. The Swedes went home, and the warehouses, empty and ruined, crumbled in the tropical sun.

In the flush economic times France enjoyed in the early 1870s, that country bought back the island when the Swedish government decided there was no solid rationale for keeping a distant chip of real estate with its 792 Norman French aboard. The Bartsians were glad to be again within the French realm, and soon discovered that the old notion of a free port might be made profitable once more, albeit now without the background of continuous European rivalry and warfare.

Whiskey from Scotland, cognac and wine from France, rum from Barbados and Trinidad, bourbon and cigarettes from the United States were conveyed by steamer to St. Kitts, then in sloops and schooners to St. Barts. From the shuttered, half-ruined buildings along the waterfront these goods eventually wandered to small, out-of-the-way bays and landing places up and down the island chain. Cattle, as many as eighteen thousand annually, were brought on the decks of schooners from Tortola, St. Croix, and Puerto Rico to pass the night ashore in Gustavia before being reloaded and sailed to Guadeloupe and Martinique where they landed as French cattle, hence duty free.

Gustavia eventually became home to the largest schooner fleet in the Antilles. Former captains and owners with whom I talked in the shops and cafes around the port could remember as many as twenty schooners and unnumbered sloops. Memories were still fresh of the stars of the fleet: *Cachelot,* built in Florida; *Nina,* in Anguilla; *Ruth,* in Bonaire; *Ruby,* in Carriacou.

Of all the vessels that figured in this folk history, only two were actually built in St. Barts, however: *Islena* in 1910 by Romney and *Inez* by Romney and Ledee. Romney is a common name in Anguilla, whereas family names in St. Barts are Norman French, leading me to speculate that these vessels were built with imported skills. Here again was a seafaring island without a boat-building tradition.

Whatever its source of vessels, St. Barts flourished. It witnessed if not a second golden age at least a silver age that continued until after World War II. Then, in 1950, it was discovered accidentally that Gustavia was not hurricane safe. A tremendous storm demolished about half the fleet on that occasion; a second hurricane destroyed most of the remainder in 1960.

In neither case were replacements bought or built, effectively ending the age of sail here, although vessels from other Antillean islands continued to frequent the port. The reasons for this collapse were twofold. On the one hand, the French authorities, understandably annoyed at the size of the fiscal leak created by these enterprising folk, began to impose industrial standards of maritime construction and safety that were impossible for sailing vessels to meet. In the meantime these beached sailors had, with the faultless intuition of true entrepreneurs, discovered the advantages and enjoyments of small aircraft. Out with the boats, in with the Cessnas.

In light of these facts, the extraordinary busyness of the little port becomes less perplexing and the folklore surrounding this *bobol* (illicit) trade acquires a distinctly Caribbean flavor. Consider, for example, that the inhabitants of St. Barts, putatively fishermen and subsistence farmers, today have the highest per-capita income in the Antilles, judging both from tax records and from the pleasant dwellings in which they live, not to mention the astounding restaurant prices and nightlife. And they have something even better: net worth.

In 1955, when Charles DeGaulle devalued the franc, returning one nouveau franc for each one hundred anciens francs, the Treasurer of the Departement de la Guadeloupe visited St. Martin, which had no bank in those days, to carry out this exchange. The sum of seventy million old francs was turned in by a population of around seven thousand. Based on this, the official then visited St. Barts prepared to exchange in as many as twenty-five million old francs, judging that estimate reasonable for a small, dry island with two thousand inhabitants. Within fifteen minutes of opening for business, his stock of new francs was exhausted. By the time the exchange was completed, with several retreats to Guadeloupe for fiscal reinforcements, the island of St. Barts had coughed up nearly one and a quarter *billion* old francs.

At about this point the French policies concerning record keeping and official supervision began to change. No one in the revenue offices back in Paris had dreamed that so much money was moving around in St. Barts. Free port status for the island, which in 1874 must have seemed an easy and inexpensive way to provide for the island and its stone-poor people, required adjustment. By the 1970s, the phrase "in perpetuity" in the original guarantee was declared to mean "one hundred years." A customs agent was installed in Gustavia and began quietly but pointedly issuing clearance papers to all vessels leaving the port. Another official began prowling the highways and byways of the island, making cryptic notations in chalk on houses and outbuildings, presumably so taxation upon assessed value could begin.

Boatbuilding is slow, heavy work that must be done in the heat of the tropic sun. It is work done by poor people and people forced by economic circumstances to provide their own employment. It is not work done by people with capital. Such people are consumers of vessels, not their builders. Although St. Barts had little to contribute directly to my knowledge of boatbuilding, it did provide one profound insight into human economic behavior: Prosperity has an inhibitory effect on the sweat glands of the human brow.

For that reason I was obliged to extrapolate what once was the traditional

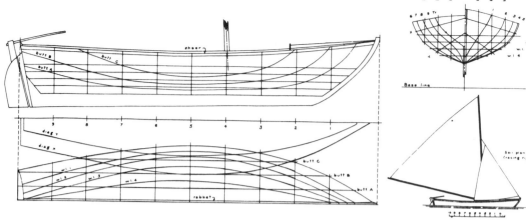

Lines of St. Thomas fishing boat Glève, built in 1950 by V. Tacklin at
Frenchtown, St. Thomas. Taken off by John Kochiss in 1963.

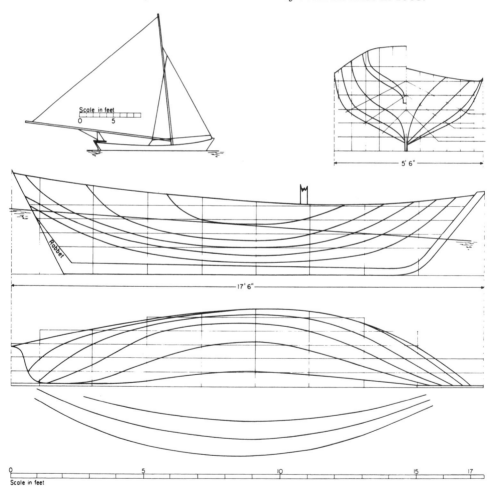

Lines of Patsi, built by Bernardin Palmier at
Pointe-à-Pitre. Taken off May 1975.

Fishing boat Patsi, *Gustavia,*
St. Barts. May 1975.

watercraft of the Bartsian Norman French. Neither of the two small water-craft whose lines I collected for St. Barts was actually built there.

The features of this type are beaminess, full and flaring bows, some drag to the keel, and the leg-of-mutton mainsail. In 1963, John Kochiss took the lines of *Glève,* a fourteen-foot dinghy being used in St. Thomas among the descendants of the Bartsian French. Even then, traditional watercraft in St. Thomas were fast disappearing under the spread of tourism, and I count my-self lucky to have found the Kochiss data. Since the people of Frenchtown have maintained their cultural integrity for many years, there is every reason to suppose that this design was brought with them from St. Barts.

As she lay tied to the quay in Gustavia, seventeen-foot *Patsi* was the pret-tiest and most carefully built of the small craft I found in the Lesser Antilles. Although built in Pointe-a-Pitre, Guadeloupe, by Bernardin Palmier and

Patsi running into Gustavia. May 1975.

referred to by her Bartsian owner as a *canot saintois,* her lines so resemble those of *Glève* that the two taken together establish by projection what the older boat type of St. Barts may have been.

Since *Patsi* was primarily employed as a pleasure craft, the owner readily agreed to a sailing trial in exchange for a photographic portrait of his boat. The winds were very light and the sea calm in Gustavia's Outer Harbor and roadstead, making an easy and pleasant job of collecting the data but limiting the speeds obtained. Nevertheless, *Patsi* showed a good turn of speed and was a delight to sail. We made over five knots with the wind on the beam; close-hauled she still made nearly three.

There were many small seafaring communities that I visited in the West Indies whose cultural integrity was precarious and whose future was uncertain. St. Barts was not one of them, despite the now frequent visits by tour ships and a string of resorts on the north coast. Former schooner owners and captains have become wholesalers and Cessna jockeys. Since there was never a great investment in traditional skills, the passing of the old order was undoubtedly rendered easier, occurring as it did without great loss of pride or integrity.

FIFTEEN

Tranquil Montserrat

~ ~ ~

Many of the islands of the Antilles had seafaring reputations that reached me long before I visited them. As has already been made clear, some were active boatbuilding centers, some had been active in the past, still others were seafaring but did no building.

And then there were some islands, such as Montserrat, that were never mentioned at all.

My first visit to the island was pretty brief, the occasion being a passage from Martinique to St. Martin. Conditions got me to Montserrat at first light after sailing 144 miles in twenty hours, an average speed of seven knots—not very fast by the standards of the space age, but seven knots is *Eider*'s hull speed, the fastest she can go. I made the passage under double-reefed main and the smallest jib aboard. The sky was overcast, but the conditions were not by any means stormy. It was simply the trade winds at full force—the Christmas winds, which blow from December into March. It was the fastest passage I ever made in *Eider,* and the only significance that Montserrat had for me at the time was the shelter it provided and few hours' sleep.

Later, when I was dividing the island chain into islands where vessels

Montserrat fishing boat.
April 1975.

were built and those where they weren't, I visited Montserrat again. Despite my high resolve and consuming interest, the second visit lasted little longer than the first. There was, in short, very little marine anthropology to be done in Montserrat.

A small, steel coastal freighter and an island sloop lay at anchor in the roadstead off the town of Plymouth. Just beyond the solitary jetty was a fish market where a few boats were drawn ashore. These boats no longer used sails, and their resemblance to the beach boats of the other Leeward Islands was so close that I took the easy course and left them dozing contentedly in the sun. On other islands where outboard motors had replaced sails, I noticed that newer boats were frequently given a broader stern to provide extra buoyancy for the weight and thrust of the outboard. Here, however, the outboards were of such low power that the boats had retained the narrow transom of the sailing model.

In the harbor master's office there was a single volume that contained all the vessels ever registered in Montserrat. The earliest was the sloop *Vigilante*, built in 1844 in Petit Martinique; the most recent was the steel freighter *Gefion*, built in 1952 in the Netherlands. Of seventy-three entries in the register, forty-six were vessels built in Montserrat, but none had been built there since the 1950s. Over the years the island had produced sixty-three percent of its own shipping capacity and thus deserves to be considered an island with a seafaring past. It was never important as a boatbuilding center and is not presently active, except for simple repairs to small watercraft.

The question of why this island developed so small a maritime heritage must remain speculation at the moment, but part of the reason may stem from the absence of a meaningful local fishing tradition, rumored to result from arsenic content in fish taken from the nearby offshore bank where undersea vents release volcanically charged waters. Also, Montserrat was too small and rocky to become an important plantation island, its most important export by the nineteenth century being lime juice to the British naval establishment nearby on Antigua at English Harbor. Without stimulation to build, or individualized family-level interest in marine architecture, Montserrat was bypassed in this area of West Indian life as it has been in so many others.

SIXTEEN

Nelson's Royal Navy, Antigua, and Barbuda

~ ~ ~

O n my first trip to Antigua, I approached the island from the south in company with the yacht *Lancer*. We both left Guadeloupe at the same time, both bound for English Harbour, so naturally an impromptu race developed. *Lancer* was ahead when we began in midafternoon to close with the line of rocky bluffs forming the southern coast of Antigua.

I searched with binoculars for the marks and alignments given in the sailing directions. Nothing was clear to me, but I pressed on the wake of *Lancer,* assuming that with their lead her captain and crew saw some landmark not yet visible to me. It was difficult to make out anything through the bouncing binoculars, but there seemed to be a line of breakers between *Lancer* and the shore. I took a quick glance at the chart; by the time I looked up again, *Lancer* had let fly sheets and was altering course drastically to port.

In a flash all was clear. *Lancer* had not made any better sense of the sailing directions than I and was shying away from the shoals while a better reading could be made. Since I now saw the marks, I was able to follow the serpentine entryway into the harbor to drop a victorious anchor in English Harbour.

Anyone who has made a landfall in English Harbour will affirm that blind faith in the sailing directions is necessary. You literally are within a stone's throw of the entrance before the break through the cliffs is discernible, and you come in close-hauled between the submerged rocks to starboard and the narrow spit of peninsula with old battlements peering down at you to port. I could only marvel at the luck or good management of the Royal Navy in making this the base for their West Indies Squadron. It was a haven secure from hurricanes and nearly impregnable from a sea attack. From here, the British had been in position to dominate the whole of the Leeward Islands.

With the passing of the sailing navy, the harbor and dockyard were abandoned and lay unused until after World War II, when an English yachtsman,

Fishing sloop nearing completion at
St. Johns, Antigua. April 1975.

Desmond Nicholson, and his family halted there on a round-the-world cruise. Settling in English Harbour, they gradually reconstructed what is now known as Nelson's Dockyard, and visiting yachtsmen find the place a peaceful, picturesque haven for rest and resupply. The stately old Georgian military buildings are now first-rate hotel and restaurant facilities, and one houses a small museum. The Dockyard is so pleasant that there is ordinarily little incentive to visit the rest of the island.

But I had examined the *Mercantile Navy Lists,* published annually by the Registrar General of Seamen and Shipping for the British Empire, and I knew that Antigua had been a center of schooner building from the 1840s onward. This is no surprise, since the naval facility in English Harbour must have required the training and employment of local shipwrights and carpenters. In an effort to substantiate this influence, on my third visit to Antigua I ventured for the first time beyond the brown sandstone landward gateposts of the dockyard.

Outside the comfortable little enclave of English Harbour, the island was dry and desolate. Antigua, although not as flat as Anguilla, does nevertheless lack the mountainous heights that coax the trade winds to rise, cool, condense, and let fall a little rain. Aridity I anticipated; what first surprised and then depressed me was the clutter and dilapidation of the landscape.

It might be that I am obsessively litter conscious, but that seems unlikely. It is hard to remain for several years on a small sailing yacht without developing a working tolerance for clutter. But in Antigua the wasted land and gaunt buildings seemed to be choking under a shroud of junk: empty bottles, cans, and plastic wrappers, discarded appliances, abandoned buildings and vehicles. It was insult heaped upon injury, and yet I found it hard to feel sympathy. Here was a tremendous debt in floors unswept, chores not done, and repairs not made, a daunting backlog of unkept promises needing to be discharged before development could even be attempted.

It was a distinct relief when my bus reached St. Johns, the capital. It's nothing to write home about but not actively depressing. Here as elsewhere I relied mostly upon random inquiry to locate vessels under construction. I quickly got directions to the workshop of Vincent Simon on the far side of the harbor.

Simon was easy to find but hard to draw into conversation. On the bare ground between his shop and an open-sided school were two vessels in

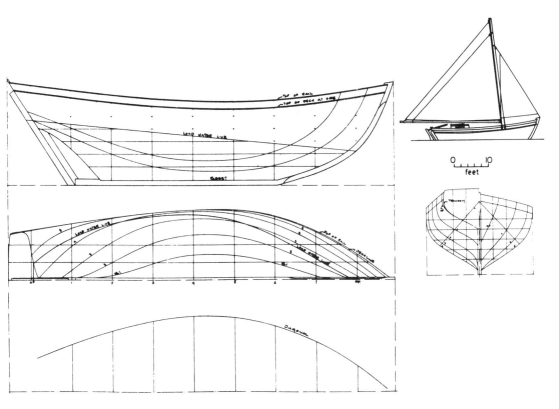

Lines of Antigua fishing sloop, built in 1961 by Vincent Simon at St. Johns, Antigua. Taken off in 1961 by Jan Olaf Truang.

frames, and on the other side of the shop another vessel of the same type was nearing completion. Simon was directing and coordinating the efforts of a number of workers at what was almost breakneck speed. It was a new experience for me to find a boatbuilder too busy to lay aside tools and talk indefinitely.

While waiting for this opportunity, I wandered around and confirmed that the vessels under construction were being built to essentially the same lines as a twenty-eight–foot Antiguan fishing sloop measured by Jan Olaf Truang in 1961, a copy of whose specifications I had already obtained. This confirmed a similarity I had detected connecting Antigua to Tortola: a length-to-beam ratio of three-to-one, "moon" shear, pronounced drag to the keel, and a relatively large leg-of-mutton mainsail.

By this time Simon was able to chat with me for a few minutes and related the following. The present flurry of activity was the result of a subsidy program that loaned money to fishermen for the construction of vessels. It had also provided the means for his shop to obtain a band saw, table saw, and some handheld power tools such as drills. Yes, the present generation of fishing vessels was much influenced by the Tortola sloop. Schooners had not been built on the island in his memory. Lastly, there was no timber and no boatbuilding whatsoever on neighboring flat Barbuda. This was the most welcome news of all, since I had not been looking forward to a thirty-mile beat through reef-encumbered waters to find out for myself.

When looking at a hull nearing completion, I noticed a detail in the garboard plank that I had not seen on any other island. The line of the keel rabbet, cut to receive the garboard, was curved and carried back across the deadwood onto the sternpost. Elsewhere, the practice had been simply to fasten the butt of the garboard directly onto the sternpost without preparing a fit for it. When asked about this, Simon replied that if a vessel took the ground there was frequently trouble with leaking at this point, and that the curved rabbet avoided the difficulty. He was unable to say if this technique had been worked out in Antigua or was copied from elsewhere.

In the matter of small sailing craft, Simon corroborated my observation at the fish market. No small, open fishing craft were in use, all fishing now being carried out in motorized sloops of the type he was building.

By the time of my final visit to Antigua I had become fully aware of the importance of the registers of shipping, so after talking with Simon the next item on my agenda was some historical delving. As in other places, I went to the harbor master's office, located in this case on the new deep-water pier outside town. Here I found the current volume of the register, beginning in 1946 and containing twenty-odd entries. For the earlier volumes I was referred to the old office, which had stood on a now decayed section of waterfront at the shallow head of the harbor. I found the old building but was informed by an onlooker that it had been vacant since the earthquake of 1974. He directed me to the present customs office in a nondescript government building, where a series of mildly interested functionaries showed me a mildly interesting series of closets overflowing with boxes and folders of yellowing papers waiting quietly to crumble into dust. The registers were not to be found among this debris.

Then someone remembered that Mr. Darwin Flax, a retired civil servant, had once been interested in the preservation of government records. So I made another trek down a sun-scalded street, this time to a pleasant house on a quiet residential lane. There I learned that Mr. Flax had once participated in a project to unify all the records of the then West Indies Federation. He was also a member of a boatbuilding family that had come to Antigua from Tortola a generation earlier. But he was unable to help, since the project for archiving had gone aground along with the Federation.

Inquiry at the local library and two more government departments entirely satisfied my yearning for dusty streets and stifling offices. The search officially ended at Brother John's with a bottle of Schooner beer, the registers still missing in action. I would have to extract the necessary historical data at a later date from the annual issues of the *Mercantile Navy List*, a dull and laborious process.

The pattern that emerged from the *List* was one Antigua shared with other plantation islands. While sugar prospered after slavery ended, vessels were built. As sugar became unprofitable in the latter half of the nineteenth century, boatbuilding slowed and finally almost stopped. A brief flurry of activity occurred at the time of World War II, and any subsequent activity has been associated with subsidized efforts such as the one in which Mr. Simon was working.

Having made these determinations, I was happy to escape back into English Harbour's parallel world of tidiness and hopes for the future. Antigua proper has not seen my return.

Guadeloupe, The Saintes, and *Le Canot Saintois*

~ ~ ~

W hen talking with builders and others in the islands, I was frequently asked where I was born. Initially I answered with the simple, unvarnished truth: "In Oklahoma." Blank stares were my
usual reward in those benighted regions where the work of Rogers and Ham-
merstein is unknown, so I learned to add in the same breath: ". . . that's near
Texas."

The case of the Saintes is a similar matter. On a map with scale sufficient
to show the Caribbean in relation to North and South America, Guadeloupe is
an island that can be found, being the largest of the Lesser Antilles, while the
Isles des Saintes are among the smallest.

The Saintes are another of those tiny enclaves that are interesting far out
of proportion to actual size. The four settled islands of the group are rocky,
dry, sparsely inhabited, and located on the edge of a fishing bank. Guadeloupe is high, verdant, densely packed with people, and short on protein. And
there you have it—*la raison d'être des Saintes*. They are nicely positioned for a
local fishing industry, rather like Bequia in relation to St. Vincent or Carriacou in relation to Grenada. And like these two, the Saintes have their characteristic boat, called *le canot saintois*.

When anchoring for the first time in the little harbor at Bourg des Saintes,
I had a fleeting impression that I had somehow made some fantastic error in
navigation. The little town with its prosperous, plastered houses and air of
quiet repose seemed more Mediterranean than Antillean. The streets were
paved with cut stones and free of litter, both conditions not seen even in the
larger towns of the Commonwealth islands. At the head of the ferry dock was
a small hotel complete with terrace and parasols. The main street was a boule-
vard shaded by lovely chestnut trees.

Along the sand beach in front of the town the boats of the fishing fleet were
drawn up in orderly array. All were *le type saintois*: nineteen to twenty-one feet

long, with hollow, flaring bows, and extremely well finished. They were driven by one or two outboard motors on the stern, and there wasn't a mast or sail in the lot. A single glance established that the days of sail were over in the Saintes. Government loans to fishermen for the purchase of outboard motors had converted the fleet to mechanical power, modifying in the process the design of the stern. The fine entry and flaring bows were well suited to a power-driven boat, but the stern was broadened for buoyancy and the "tuck" was decreased, being no longer necessary to provide lateral resistance when sailing.

Older boats of the sailing model were easy to spot because of this difference in the stern. Fishermen readily boasted of the sailing abilities of this one or that, seeming to regret the passing of sail. But nowhere could I find a boat that still had sails actually in use, so that a performance trial might be made or a sail plan drawn.

For lines I chose *France-Lise,* built by Georges Cassin in 1965 and reputed to be a fast sailor. Throughout the islands, reputations for fast sailing are made by sailing a particular passage, distance unknown, in a certain time that is easily and accurately compared with the average. When necessary, I used the local yardstick of performance, converting it to knots by laying off the passage on a chart and dividing in the time.

For the Saintes, the standard for performance is reckoned on the passage from Bourg des Saintes to Trois Rivières, seven and a half nautical miles due north to Guadeloupe on a broad reach. *France-Lise* had made this distance regularly in under an hour; thus her hull speed is 7.5 knots. Her lines show very clearly her kinship to *Patsi* on St. Barts in the fine entry and hollow, flaring bow, deep tuck, and appreciable drag to the keel.

François Bocage was one of three builders then active in Bourg des Saintes. From him I gathered the following information on materials and methods.

The stem, sternpost, and frames were shaped from *poirier* (white cedar, the same wood favored in the British islands), formerly cut on the islands but now in Guadeloupe. The keel was made from *bois du nord* (pitch pine or Douglas fir), and the planking was *acajou* (mahogany). The *acajou* planks were ripped with a chainsaw and planed by hand. The main frames, called *les gabarits,* were set up at one-third and two-thirds along the keel, then ribbands called *les lisses* were bent around and nailed to the stem and the transom. The remaining frames were shaped and fitted inside this framework. Bocage learned his trade from his father and was teaching it to his son.

In all essentials, the traditions and methods of boatbuilding were the same in this French-speaking community as those prevailing in the English-speaking islands. The major differences were in design and in finish. *Le canot saintois* was the most highly finished boat type I encountered in the Lesser Antilles. The frames and other members were shaped and planed on all faces, not just on the nailing faces as was the practice elsewhere. In addition, scantlings were adequate but not exaggerated, as by some builders who sometimes substituted excess of bulk for careful workmanship.

As we talked of changes in design brought about by the outboard motor, Bocage remarked that fishermen used about twenty-five gallons of gasoline a day and bought a new motor every year. Even with gasoline as cheap as it was, it seemed an expensive way to go fishing. Since that time, fluctuations in petroleum prices have undoubtedly made some fishermen wonder about the wisdom of motorized fishing. If fuel costs rise much, a transition back to sail is still possible, for the technology is certainly not yet lost. Bocage was able to give me, without pausing for reflection, the dimensions of spars, rigging, and sails.

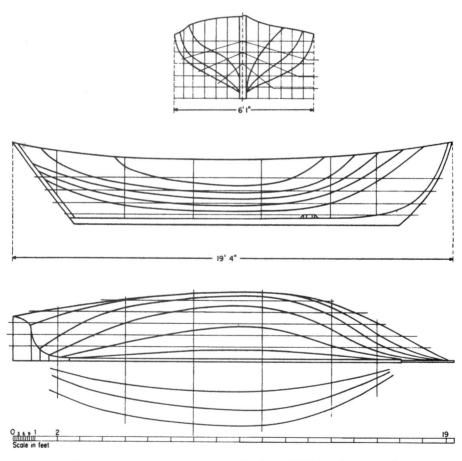

Lines of canot saintois France-Lise, *built in 1965 by Georges Cassin at Bourg des Saintes. Taken off in 1971 at Iles des Saintes.*

Schooner model at Mairie,
Bourg des Saintes. April 1975.

It was evident from the moment of anchoring off Bourg des Saintes that sloops and schooners no longer played any part in the commercial life of the island. The ferry made several runs daily to Pointe-à-Pitre, Guadeloupe, carrying all supplies and passengers. However, the traditions of boat carpentry were so well established that it seemed worth inquiring whether there had been any schooner building in the past. On my first visit, inquiry about schooners yielded nothing. Something must have been wrong with the way I asked, because I discovered on a visit several years later that there had been a shipyard organized enough to have a formal name, *le Chantier de Coquelette,* where sailing vessels were built as recently as the early 1950s.

Thus encouraged, I went to the *Mairie* to see if any records had been kept of this activity. No such luck, but there was by pure coincidence a schooner model in the antechamber built by Théodore Samson. A simple model would not ordinarily have stirred me to great exertion, but Théodore Samson turned

Semi-automated boat measuring at
Bourg des Saintes. April 1975.

out to have been the owner of *le Chantier de Coquelette,* and that cast an entirely different light on the model.

Samson died in 1960, and it was from his sister and a former employee
that I pieced together a reasonably complete account of such schooner building as had occurred. Both sources agreed that the first person to build
schooners at Bourg des Saintes had been Bernard Agincourt, who took as a
younger partner Léon Samson, in time the father of Théodore Samson. The
earliest vessel that could be called to mind was a ninety-one–foot cutter built
by Agincourt for the customs service about 1885 and lost in 1928. Agincourt
and the two Samsons were natives of the Saintes, and the elder two men had
no formal training. Théodore Samson, on the other hand, served an apprenticeship in a shipyard somewhere in France and learned to read plans and
take lines off a half model. In his lifetime, he built about twenty vessels including those serving Marie Galante, an island to the windward of Guade-

loupe. Samson's last construction, a motor vessel, was launched in 1960, the year he died.

In addition to his other creations, Samson the Younger had laid his hand to the model of *L'Étoile des Marins,* thereby giving it more than the usual significance. For taking off the lines, I had by this time moved even further down the road toward fully automated marine anthropology. This method requires only a short piece of electrical cable, a camera, a carpenter's rule, and an assistant. The wire, held by the assistant, is bent to conform to the hull at selected stations, then photographed with the carpenter's rule in the field of

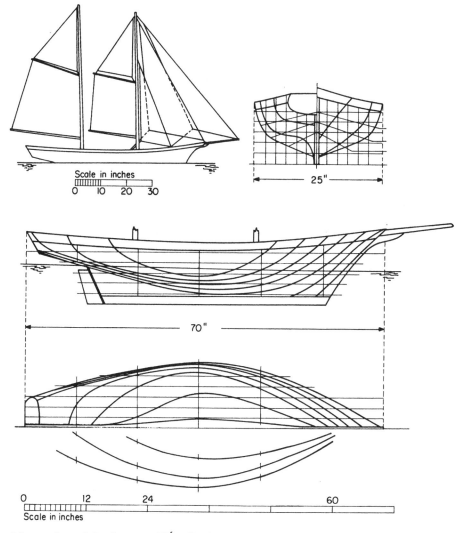

Lines of model schooner L'Étoile des Marins, *built about 1959 by Théodore Samson at Bourg des Saintes, Iles des Saintes. Taken off April 1975.*

vision for scale. Later the negative can be projected onto graph paper with the enlargement adjusted to make the ruler conform to the scale chosen, and the curve delineated by the wire is traced onto the paper, where it constitutes one of the sections of the body plan. The sheer line of the hull is similarly traced from a side view, and the deck plan is drawn from widths measured and recorded at the selected stations.

This method worked well, and the lines thus obtained fitted together with ease. No scale was given on the model, but it was probably around ninety feet long, a common size for vessels built at *le Chantier de Coquelette.*

If it is assumed that Théodore Samson, who could read plans and take lines off a half model, was engaged in making a faithful copy of a representative schooner, then the following may be remarked: In overall appearance, schooners built at Bourg des Saintes were similar to the general run of West Indian and North American schooners, though somewhat beamier than elsewhere and having a flaring bow as a purely local trait.

In terms of boatbuilding, Guadeloupe, though the larger island, stands decidedly in the shadow of the smaller. In short, nothing much was going on in Guadeloupe, where I tried both in Basse-Terre and Pointe-à-Pitre to find records of vessel registrations such as were routinely kept by the British colonial administrations. For my trouble I got that peculiarly Gallic shrug of the shoulders that is somehow discernible even over the telephone. Local boatbuilding seems never to have attracted the attention of French officialdom except in its relation, real or imagined, to the nuisance of smuggling.

As for small craft, I found only rough versions of *le canot saintois.* These had recently replaced the *gommier,* or dugout canoe, according to anthropologist Jean Archambault of the University of Montreal. Therefore the principal importance of Guadeloupe in the present narrative is that it provided my first introduction to two matters of increasing importance as I proceeded southward through the islands: official French indifference to local maritime enterprises; and the persistence in French-speaking communities, into the present or recent past, of the original type of Caribbean small watercraft—the dugout canoe.

EIGHTEEN

A Familiar Pattern in Dominica

~ ~ ~

Dominica is a high, rugged island whose darkly forested volcanic backbone thrusts abruptly out of the sea to summits almost a mile above sea level within five miles of shore. Here and there plumes of smoke ascend slowly from the flanks of the ridges where charcoal burners are at work. Somehow this island always seemed mysterious and brooding to me. I felt, or perhaps merely imagined, an undercurrent of hostility on the few occasions when I went ashore. I was warned against going alone into the countryside. As a consequence, I know less about Dominica than any other island

Gommiers at Portsmouth, Dominica. April 1975.

I visited, and less than seems desirable, especially about the *gommiers*, built on the windward coast.

The Carib Indians, who originated on the mainland of South America in the Orinoco Basin, were spreading rapidly northward and had occupied the islands as far as Guadeloupe at the time Columbus arrived in the New World. They used large dugout canoes up to sixty feet long, carrying several dozen paddlers and capable of speeds up to eighteen knots. By all accounts the Caribs were as bloodthirsty a folk as ever munched the *boucan* (a dried piece of a former enemy boiled up and chewed on the eve of a raid to put the warriors into the proper frame of mind). They continued to raid and harass even such colonial strongholds as Antigua until well into the eighteenth century. The last stronghold of the Caribs was in the rugged fastness of Dominica, where there is still a reservation for their descendants and where small dugouts are still made.

The hull of a dugout is made from the trunk of the tree *Dacryodes excelsa,* called *gommier* in Dominica and the other islands where a French Creole dialect is spoken. The tree is still plentiful in Dominica, but scarce in Martinique and Guadeloupe since the turn of this century.

After a suitable tree has been felled and flattened on one side with ax or adz (iron tools being the only difference between modern and primitive methods), coals are heaped on the flattened surface, left to char, the char is scraped away, and the process repeated until the hollow nears the desired depth. Then several holes are drilled along the centerline of the bottom, so the thickness of the hull may be accurately gauged. The hull is then worked to a final thickness of three inches in the bottom and one inch along the gunwales, the bow is sharpened, and the stern is cut square.

Next the hull is "opened," transforming in the process from a simple pointed cylinder into a complex shape of astonishing hydrodynamic efficiency: The hollow is filled with water and heated by dropping in hot rocks. As the wood softens, the hull is opened by wedging temporary thwarts between the gunwales until the water cools and the wood sets to its new shape. This process is repeated, using longer and longer thwarts, until the final shape of the hull is achieved.

In this unfinished state, hulls are often towed to Martinique and sold. The new owner then completes the hulls, adding one or two raising strakes, which are edge-nailed to the gunwales and braced by widely spaced frames.

~ ~ ~

Roseau, capital of the island, has a poorly sheltered harbor with foul bottom and poor holding. On occasion I have seen waves breaking full over the concrete jetty. There was little to recommend such a place to boatbuilder or yachtsman, especially when a few miles northward lies Prince Rupert Bay, one of the most beautiful stretches of sheltered water in the islands. Protected by the green heights of Morne Diablotin, this grand expanse of perfect calm stretches from Rollo Head in the south to Prince Rupert Bluff in the north. Lying in the northeast corner of the bay is the little town of Portsmouth, slumbering now but once so lively that an American consul was stationed there.

In 1913, when Robert Cushman Murphy called there aboard the whaling brig *Daisy,* there were thirty-eight whaling vessels lying in Prince Rupert Bay.

Romulus St. Clair (Jack) Mitchell, seated at left.
(Photo property of Conrad Mitchell.)

According to Murphy, vessels of the New Bedford whaling fleet frequently trans-shipped their oil from Barbados, then sailed to Dominica to rest and refit. Apparently Prince Rupert Bay was chosen because there was little likelihood that crewmen would jump ship in a place where only other whaling vessels called. Also, it may be that there were fewer restrictions on how the resting whalers acted when ashore in such an out-of-the-way spot. There were, in any case, numerous conflicts and complaints, and the primary assignment of the American consul was to smooth over these difficulties.

Portsmouth had pretty well quieted down by 1970. As soon as the anchor bit, I sat down and stared into the distance, fascinated by an antlike chain of workers, each with a stalk of bananas on his head, who emerged from a shed, walked the length of a long jetty and up a steep gangplank, and disappeared into the side of a gleaming white freighter, then emerging from another door, bananaless. I don't know how long they had been at work when I arrived in midafternoon, but they continued until the freighter departed at four o'clock the following morning.

On the beach south of Portsmouth there was a small vessel in frames which I learned in town was being built by George Noel of Petit Martinique. It was hardly surprising that, since that island is just to windward of Carriacou, the vessel should closely resemble the Carriacou sloops. The register of shipping in Roseau confirmed what I suspected: Relatively few of the vessels registered in Dominica were built there. Of those that were, most were constructed by builders from Bequia, Carriacou, Petit Martinique, and in one instance, surprisingly, Montserrat. Presumably these builders were drawn here by the abundance of timber available in Dominica.

Almost all the boatbuilding carried out by a builder whose residence was given as Dominica was done by Romulus St. Clair Mitchell. "Jack" Mitchell came to the island from Bequia (no surprise in this) and built some seventeen vessels between 1916 and 1948. In the next generation, Jack's son Conrad had built three vessels, including the *PM Bill*.

Here again is the anomaly of an island that should have had some boatbuilding history, but never did. The rugged terrain of Dominica makes coastwise commerce a convenience if not an acute necessity. There are timber resources in abundance, and at the turn of this century there was ample opportunity and inspiration for any local person interested in the ancient and honorable trade of boat carpentry. Yet the builders originated elsewhere, and all but Jack Mitchell left when the job was done.

NINETEEN

The *Gommiers* and *Yoles* of Martinique

~ ~ ~

Martinique, with its cultivated landscape and civilized air, forms a marked contrast to the unsettled ruggedness of Dominica. Although volcanic and mountainous, Martinique has rolling lower elevations that are gardened or grazed, while the uplands are planted in bananas, pineapples, or coffee. Dotting this Mediterranean countryside are tiled and stuccoed dwellings, appropriately called "villas."

In Fort-de-France, shiny Pugeots, Citroens, Mercedes, and Fiats ply the streets. Elegant shops display perfume, crystal, and the latest Parisian fashions. Outdoor markets overflow with tropical abundance, while supermarket shelves are lined with French gastronomic delights. And threading its way in affluent haste through these symbols of the good life is a bustling population with the clothes, grooming, and carriage of European urbanites.

Yoles racing in Fort Royal Bay, Martinique. July 1974.

In the aftermath of World War II, as European colonialism was phased out around the world, the British chose divestiture and proceeded to grant constitutions and internal self-government to their Antillean possessions. The French, moving in the opposite direction, absorbed Martinique, Guadeloupe, and French Guiana into the Republic as full-fledged offshore *départements*.

And bang in the middle of the glamour and glitter of aggressively modern Martinique, the original watercraft of the Antilles were still in extensive everyday use. The *gommier* and its close relative, the *yole*, direct descendents of the aboriginal dugout canoe, formed the basis of the most intensive local fishing industry in the Lesser Antilles. In 1972 there were over two thousand of these craft registered in Martinique. Low-interest government loans for the purchase of outboard motors have completely mechanized the fleet, but all fishermen still carry spars and sails in case of engine failure.

During part of my time in Martinique, I anchored near the fishing village of Vauclin on the windward coast. Daily at sunrise, the fleet set forth in groups

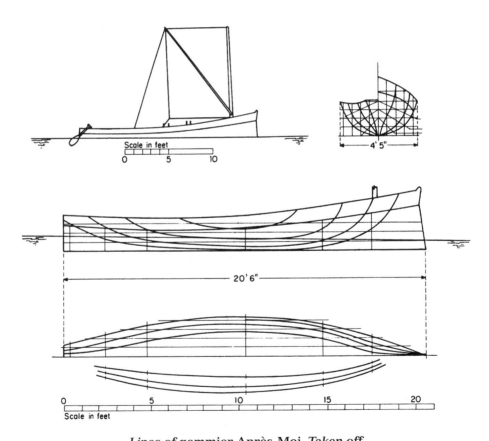

Lines of gommier Après-Moi. *Taken off at Vauclin, Martinique, January 1975.*

---

of two and three, the front half of each hull thrust cleanly out of the water by the fifty- or sixty-horsepower motor, reminding me of those aquatic birds that skim the water's surface before launching into flight. All were heading for the banks lying ten miles to windward, where they spent the day trolling and handlining. In the afternoon they returned to sell their catch either directly to householders on the beach or to jobbers in small vans who carted the fish across the mountains to eager appetites in Fort-de-France.

For measurement I chose *Aprés-Moi,* a three-person fishing *gommier* based at Vauclin. The lines are simple in the extreme: The midsection was nearly a perfect semicircle and the bow and stern sections were nearly symmetrical. The lower waterlines were hollow both in bow and stern, resulting in a highly efficient fusiform shape. The emergency sailing rig consisted of an unstayed mast, a bamboo sprit, and a rectangular sail, all very simple to set, stow, and sew.

The hull form was so streamlined that high speed and efficiency were hardly astonishing. What did come as a surprise was the seaworthiness of these craft. Not only did they fish offshore in almost all weather, they also had a staggering carrying capacity. When I went to the customs house in Dominica to check ship registrations, I had to step carefully past the sticky rivulets oozing from a heap of bagged sugar that half-filled the outer office. The customs officer, wrinkling his nose in distaste, told me the sugar had been impounded because duty was not paid on it. (Duty on sugar soaked with sea water?) This sodden mass, a ton even before waterlogging, had been brought from Martinique in a *gommier* the preceding day. That was twenty-five miles across an open channel on a day when I had made the passage with double-reefed main.

The true dugout, hollowed from the trunk of the *gommier* tree, was still preferred by fishermen. However, as suitable large trees had disappeared from Martinique and became scarcer in Dominica, the cost of *gommiers* had risen and a new type of craft, the *yole,* had developed. The *yole* had the dimensions and lines of a *gommier* but was built from keel, frames, and planks in the conventional European manner.

At Trinité, a few miles north of Vauclin, I watched Alphonse Renoverre replace a plank in the bottom of a *yole.* The tools and skill he used in spiling a plank were the same as those used in Bequia, Carriacou, and Anguilla. If nothing else, this matter of retaining shape while substituting new materials stimulates the speculative mind to wonder if the same sort of thing occurred in the dawn of boat carpentry thousands of years ago.

Alphonse Renoverre replacing a plank in a yole
at Robert, Martinique. January 1975.

When seen from a distance, only the shape of the stem distinguishes *yole* from *gommier*. In order to verify this judgment, I measured the racing *yole Goodyear,* which I found in the village of Robert. The lines are virtually the same as those of the *gommier*—the same round midsection, fore-and-aft symmetry, and hollow waterlines and fusiform shape. The most striking difference lies in the sail plan: In addition to the *mizaine* set forward, there is a *grand voile* stepped a little forward of midship. The difference here, however, is not between *yoles* and *gommiers,* but between a boat built for racing and one built for work.

Sailing traditions in Martinique have been preserved in a manner typical of many societies in a period of rapid technological advance: Skills no longer in functional demand are enshrined in the form of sport. Some years ago, an association of sailing enthusiasts was formed that has developed a calendar of some twenty races a year, generally coupled with the *fête patronale* of a

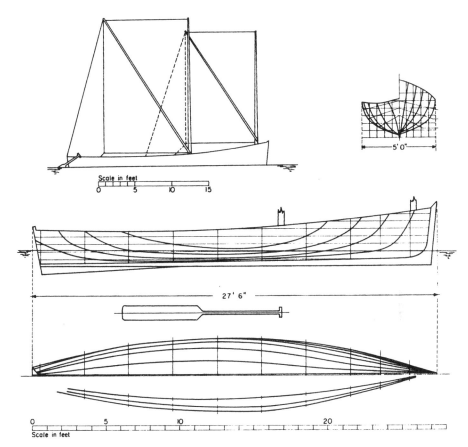

Lines of racing yole *Goodyear, built in 1974 by Michel Meongyen at François, Martinique. Taken off September 1974.*

given village. These are occasions of general merriment designed to bring folks into town to consume popcorn, peanuts, and whatever else isn't selling well. For the purpose of drawing a crowd, what could be better than a fleet of white-winged *yoles* and *gommiers* lined up to race?

To gather performance data on a racing *yole* was no easy thing. These craft do not sail except in races, when they take a crew of eleven to fifteen men and cannot welcome visitors. My good friend Raymond Asselin, however, was acquainted with the owner of a racing *yole* and was able to arrange for me to sail aboard it one afternoon. Raymond had asked me to stop and see him before keeping my rendezvous, and when I arrived he quietly gave me to understand that the opportunity to sail in *Vini Oué Ça* was a bit of a conces- sion since it usually was brought out only on race days. He gave me cash to buy a round of drinks, an amount that seemed excessive until I reached the shed on the outskirts of Vauclin where the *yole* was sheltered.

Gathered on the beach, engaged in the multitude of chores necessary to launch the sleek hull, was a squad of perhaps thirty men and boys of all ages. First the sails and spars were brought out, laid on the sand, and knotted together. Then about half the men laid hold of the hull, turned it over, and carried it into the sea where they remained, holding it. The remainder began to step the *mizaine* and *grande voile,* carrying the spars and sails as a unit and setting them into the canoe. Naturally this increased by a good amount the difficulties of holding upright the unballasted hull, and I was beginning to see the purpose of Raymond's pocketful of francs.

When all was ready, the crew scrambled aboard and we were pushed into deeper water as the sails were sheeted and the *patron* began to scull with the steering oar to carry us off the shore. There were eleven of us in all: three men forward on trapeze lines (there were no stays on either mast), four men with hiking poles, one man amidship to bail and handle the clew of the *mizaine,* another aft on the clew of the *grande voile,* the *patron,* and I. For sails we had set the lightweather mainsail of 380 square feet and the *mizaine* sail of 190 square feet, a total of 570 square feet of sail on an unballasted canoe with five feet of beam! For comparison, *Eider* at nine tons' displacement sports only 560 square feet of canvas with all sails set.

As the breeze began to fill the sails, the *patron* leaned into the big steering paddle and brought the head farther off the wind. The crew scrambled to their positions and continued for the entire time we sailed to shift in and out on their poles and trapezes, compensating automatically for even the slightest change in course or wind. The *patron,* in addition to steering with the big paddle, actually sculled more or less full time—three or four strokes to pull the head off the wind, then a brief rest while the *yole* surged up into the wind. This pumping action had the effect of countering leeway so well that we made no more of it than three degrees despite having nothing at all under the hull to counter slipping. This practice makes the *patron*'s seat the warmest in the *yole,* and in a long race the place is rotated among the senior members of the crew.

To measure wind speed, I used a hand-held anemometer with a small red ball for an indicator. After watching me hold the device up to the wind and squint at the bouncing ball, the *patron* asked me if he could get "one of those things to take the temperature of the wind." For speed through the water I used a simple Pitot tube with a top measure of seven knots, completely adequate until that day. However, in the puffs of wind, which never exceeded twelve knots, the indicator in the Pitot tube slammed up to the top of the tube and water squirted well over my head. The breeze was very light and we never even came close to the hull speed of *Vini Oué Ça;* though I would have had no way to measure it if we had.

After I had made a series of measurements while beating, the *patron* motioned for me to lend a hand at steering. I grinned and accepted readily this evidence that things were thawing out after a certain initial coolness the crew had shown me.

"*Vas-y, blanc,*" several of the men called as I took up the position and leaned into the steering. The *yole* surged in response. It was for all the world like twisting the throttle of a powerful motorcycle. There were cheers of encouragement from the crew.

"*Encore, blanc, encore!*"

Whom the gods would destroy, they first make mad. Again I leaned into the paddle, intoxicated by the double dose of power and approval. I was instantly in trouble.

Too late, the *patron* shouted at me to ease up. Already the speed and the increased angle of heel had brought water rushing in over the lee bow, and we rushed upon our fate. Suddenly it was all over, and there we were—eleven men, 570 feet of wet canvas, several hiking poles, paddles, bailing gourds, my camera, instruments, and notes—all swirling and bobbing in the sea.

I didn't know whether to dive for the bottom or strike out for shore, but the crew were shouting and laughing their heads off. In some odd way, the ice had been broken and it was all right. One man swam over with my camera looped around his neck; another waved the Pitot tube aloft. The *patron* swam up to assure me that even after forty years of experience he sometimes capsized a *yole*.

In theory, it is possible to right a capsized *yole*, since the unstayed masts come out of the steps and float clear. Then the hull is easily righted and the crew clings along the gunwales scooping water out until the smallest man or boy can crawl in and continue bailing. As the canoe floats higher, more men crawl aboard and at last the hull is baled dry. Then the sails are hauled aboard, and with a little balancing and a lot of luck the masts are restepped, sails set, and off they go again.

In practice, with a fluky breeze and a short chop, we were too near shore to bother with the process. An outboard-powered *gommier* came out and towed us back to Vauclin, and as we came in the day's diversion was already on the way to becoming a village event. Subsequently on a number of occasions when walking in Vauclin I was stopped by strangers and asked if I was the man who had sailed the *Vini Oué Ça* under.

The francs, wet but still negotiable, bought a round of *petit ponch* for the crew and their friends and relations. I shrugged off solicitous inquiries about my watch and the camera and expressed as my only regret that I had not gotten data for the downwind performance of the *yole*. The owner of *Vini Oué Ça*, who had joined us at the bar after watching the performance from the comfort and security of shore, suggested that I accompany him in the committee launch the following Sunday to collect additional data.

On Sunday afternoon, I drove down to Robert with the owner and crew of *Vini Oué Ça,* unsure how accurately I could estimate the performance of the *yole* from a distance. The regattas that I had seen elsewhere were invariably started downwind to the leeward mark, then beat home, displaying only two points of sailing too far away to benefit the spectators. At Robert, however, the course was laid out in such a way that there was a beat, a run, two reaching legs, another beat, and a run for the finish line, most of it in full view of the cheering crowd on shore. In consequence I did not lack for opportunity to collect data, especially since the committee launch followed the canoes very closely.

As race time drew near the wind seemed to be increasing, so the crew, after some discussion, decided to set the smaller of the two *grandes voiles.* The freshening breeze proved to be temporary and *Vini Oué Ça* thus was badly undercanvassed. She finished only sixth, first place going to *Goodyear.* After the *yoles* there was a race along the same course for the heavier *gommiers.* In the final event the *yoles* set their largest sails as *mizaines* and raced

Yole *racing with* mizaine *only at François,*
Martinique. January 1975.

under it alone. In this event, *Vini Oué Ça* ran much better and was leading until she hit a buoy on the reaching leg and was disqualified.

Under the standard racing rig of two sails, *yoles* produced (at least) 7.5 knots close-hauled in a wind of 12 knots; off the wind speeds decline to 5.5 knots for a run. Under one sail, close-hauled speeds are around 5 knots and runs are up to 6.5 knots.

These ranges of performance put the *yoles* in the same league as other types of small craft in the Antilles, but there is a difference in the much higher speeds of which the *yole* is capable. I was not equipped to measure their peak performance, but on two occasions I saw *yoles* sailing at speeds that I estimated to be in excess of twelve, perhaps as high as fourteen knots. The *yole* was without question the swiftest boat type I encountered in the islands.

One way or another, I spent a good bit of time in Martinique and never saw a sloop or schooner. Inter-island trading vessels no longer played any part in the economic life of the island since commercial relations were exclusively with metropolitan France, which supplies manufactured goods and buys bananas, pineapples, and other tropical produce.

It was always possible, however, that boatbuilding had gone on at some earlier time, so I inquired about it. Nothing was available from official sources; the same indifference to the question of boats I had encountered in Guadeloupe prevailed here. I did finally stumble onto the carcass of a ruined schooner hauled ashore near an abandoned sugar factory at Cosmil, on the windward coast. It had been the property of the sugar factory and was used during the Allied blockade of World War II to carry sugar around to Fort-de-France and return with fertilizer.

It sounds a bit odd to take to the seas during a blockade, but wars produce unusual circumstances as well as strange bedfellows. When France was overrun by the German Army in the early months of World War II, the French fleet was scattered to a number of overseas locations, including Martinique. Some naval officers maintained an unbroken chain of command that wound tortuously upward toward Vichy; others "surrendered" and became Free French; some scuttled their ships. The commandant in Martinique was Vichy, as they say, and technically an enemy of the Allies. However, it was part of no one's plan to attack or to break out; everyone's interests were best served by a bloodless blockade, which unfortunately left the island without gasoline for road transport but did leave the sea lanes open for windpower.

The dimensions, clunky lines, and shoddy construction details of the ruined schooner at Cosmil all suggested to me a temporary solution to a temporary problem rather than the outgrowth of a traditional culture. Aside from the situation created by the blockade, Martinique has probably never had any great need for sloops or schooners. There are no smaller, off-lying island dependencies that might trade with the main island. If there were trade with the nearby Commonwealth islands, it would undoubtedly be carried in vessels built there, while trade with France today goes by container ship.

Though indifferent to schooner building, French officialdom had shown a lot of interest lately in fishing craft. There was a program to develop and diffuse a new type of fishing vessel to be called the *yole amélioré*. The name suggests "modified" or "improved," and a number of interesting possibilities flitted through my mind on the way to the yard where a prototype was being built.

What I saw fell sadly short of my imaginings: All I found was a little Mediterranean putt-putt—a small, decked, diesel-powered, three-person launch able to spend two or three days at sea and costing more than an individual fisherman could ever afford. When I sought by questioning to understand the wisdom and necessity of this development, it emerged that official concern centered upon something other than the practical economics of marine architecture and fisheries management.

With the present arrangement of *gommiers* and *yoles*, constructed locally and cheaply, the fishermen could run ashore anywhere and sell all their catch with no records kept and little or no taxes paid. Naturally, this informal arrangement worried the government no end. Larger and more expensive vessels would mean the fishermen would have to organize into co-ops or, more likely, work for an owner/capitalist. Larger catches would have to be landed at government-operated fish markets, where records are kept and taxes paid. I am gratified to report that the new type of boat did not catch on, and that the fishermen continued to prefer their traditional watercraft.

TWENTY

The Secrets of St. Lucia

~ ~ ~

Early in my island-hopping days, someone advised me that channel crossing from one island to the next was best done by holding up close under the lee of the first island, even tacking if necessary to work as far to windward as possible before entering the rougher waters and stronger currents of the open channel.

It was implementation of this strategy that took me early one March morning into the dark calm of Chateau Belair Bay, lying in the lee of the Soufrière, St. Vincent's once and future volcano. The surface of the bay was smooth, but masses of cloud boiled and surged past the top of the volcano. In the steep valleys that scored the sides of the cone, the silver flash of falling water here and there streaked the dark, glossy green. Occasionally a small patch of coconut palms marked a human habitation—one or two thatched huts in a small area of cleared ground.

The fishing fleet from Chateau Belair—small two-bow boats of the Bequia model—was spread across the bay, tacking slowly back and forth, so dwarfed by the volcano's mass that they seemed to change position without moving. There was dreamlike immobility to the whole tableau, which was soon left behind as we changed course and let go for St. Lucia.

The wind that had been pushing the clouds around overhead was now at wave-top height. The strategy of working to windward had been successful, however, and even in the steep seas of the channel *Eider*'s course was free enough that little water came aboard.

We were nearing midchannel when something in the animated monotony of the waves caught my attention—a flash that was not a whitecap, a motion not part of the heaving sea. A few minutes later, there was another visual disturbance, this time from a different quarter altogether. As the disturbances became more frequent, they also drew closer, slowly revealing themselves as human figures clad in yellow oilskins and topped by straw hats with fantastic high peaks. The figures seems to skim the surface of the water at high speed, darting this way and that like disembodied spirits.

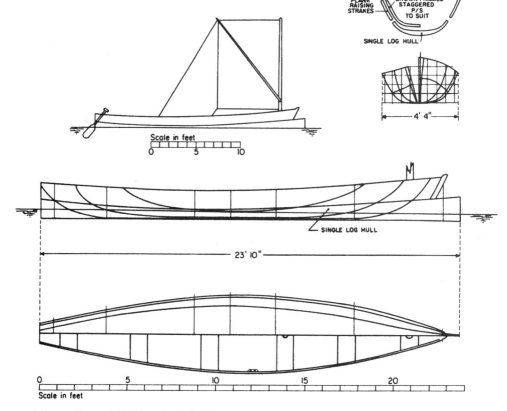

PLANK RAISING STRAKES

GROWN FRAMES STAGGERED P/S TO SUIT

SINGLE LOG HULL

4' 4"

Scale in feet
0   5   10

23' 10"

SINGLE LOG HULL

0   5   10   15   20

Scale in feet

Lines of canot St. Bénédic, *built by Joseph Hendricks, Soufrière, St. Lucia. Taken off at Carriacou, August 1970.*

When the full reality was finally disclosed, the figures were seated by threes, one behind another in a canoe so narrow and so low in the water as to be invisible at a very short distance. The figure in the stern was steering with the outboard motor; the one in the middle was bailing. In the bow, lifted completely clear of the water by the thrust of the motor, the third figure peered forward and gestured from time to time, sending the whole rig swerving this way and that.

This was my first encounter with a St. Lucia *canot*. Several years later I had an opportunity to measure one when a pair of them appeared at the Carriacou Regatta to compete in the newly created "engine boat" class. These two craft, originally from St. Lucia, had been fishing for a couple years out of Kingstown, St. Vincent, which is how their owners learned of the regatta.

The basis of the *canot*, as with its counterpart the *gommier*, is a log, hollowed and opened, with a raising strake added atop the gunwale. The *canot*, however, is easily distinguishable from the *gommier* by the striking extension of the dugout forward into a sort of cutwater. There are other, less evident differences that emerge from an examination of the lines of the *St. Bénédic*. The midsection is not so nearly round, the beam is relatively narrower, the length at the waterline is longer, there is less freeboard in the bow, and the waterlines show less hollow and are less streamlined.

On a later trip to St. Lucia in search of schooners, I made for the major port of Castries, entering after dark but with no anxiety since the harbor is deep and well buoyed with a straightforward entrance. I followed the leading lights and proceeded to the quarantine anchorage as designated in the *West Indies Pilot* because I had been told the authorities were strict about that sort of thing. After anchoring and stowing the sails, I turned in for what was left of the night, tranquil in the knowledge that Castries is the safest harbor in the islands. Just before dawn, the heavens quietly opened and water began to pour from the sky.

There may be better music than rain on the deck heard from a dry bunk, but not wishing to be hasty in my conclusions I lay abed until after nine o'clock to consider the matter. When at last I emerged into the sunlit cockpit to get my bearings and plan the day's activities, I was dismayed to discover that in the dark *Eider* had been anchored much closer to shore than was necessary or in fact safe. The anchor could scarcely have dragged in the windless night, and the directions for anchoring had been carefully followed. As I mulled the matter, the shoreline came even closer. When the first flies began to buzz around my ears, a great light dawned. What had appeared to be the shoreline was, in fact, a great raft of garbage that had floated off the town's harborside dump and was drifting gently down the harbor.

Undaunted by this inauspicious beginning, I gathered my notebooks and set out to get clearance papers and, I hoped, information on schooner building. A bracing row through the garbage brought me to the customs house, glumly situated on the dilapidated waterfront whence came the debris. Here I learned that clearance papers were now issued at the deep-water pier across the harbor. I made my dogged way back to the dinghy and turned out a crowd of urchins merrily engaged in determining how many undernourished bodies it takes to sink such a craft. Ignoring their good-natured shower of rocks, I set off for the deep-water pier and clambered gaily up an oily piling, no ladder being available.

When I finally presented myself at the harbor office I was hot and disheveled but I pluckily filled out the required forms in triplicate, without carbon paper, stating draft forward and aft, what mails carried, and how many cannon mounted.

St. Lucia fishing boat; detail of sail plan.

"How long do you intend to stay?" demanded the officer as I turned in the forms with the harbor dues.

"Uh, well . . . I don't know," I mumbled. I had no exact schedule and the question had caught me off guard.

"Aha!" the officer said. "You don't know how long you are staying? Very suspicious, Mr. Pyle. That makes me very suspicious."

Suddenly it was all a bit more than I had bargained for, and I interpreted all the signs as an augury that little good could come of my stay in St. Lucia. I therefore chose to make outboard clearance on the same forms with which I was entering, a convenience permitted if the vessel departs within seventy-two hours. That left exactly seventy-one and a half hours to copy the register of shipping, talk to any builders still around, interview the widow of the legendary Reg Mitchell, and take lines off any fishing boats I could find.

I recount all these grim hardships only to explain why I was in a crashing hurry two mornings later as I rowed to the head of the harbor where the fishing boats were drawn ashore.

I found *Merci-Dieu* by herself at the end of the rank, just like all the others but looking a little unused. Ordinarily I would have made inquiries and sought out the owner before setting to work compiling lines data, but on this occasion my haste and general sense of ill-usage overcame better judgment. I was down to the last two stations when the challenge came.

"Who say you come messin' bout de boat?"

The irate voice belonged to a man with the short pants of a fisherman and the indignant air of a boatowner whose boat is being closely handled without his consent. My luck was definitely out in St. Lucia.

"I was just making a few notes because this boat has the best lines . . ." I began—you never know until you've tried.

"Humph," the man said. "Is a very technical thing, a mold and all. And you takin' a man mold, you must pay."

I groaned inwardly, apologized, explained what I was doing, then apologized some more; and to my surprise, the man became genuinely interested. Eventually he softened, told me his name was Joseph Evans, explained about the two types of small craft used in St. Lucia, and finally asked if I would like to take his picture beside another of the small string of fishing craft that he owned.

The lines and construction of *Merci-Dieu* show a generic relationship to the other beach boats of the English-speaking islands northward along the Lesser Antilles: sharp floors, moderate deadrise, transom stern, and slight

Builder Joseph Evans with canot Saint Peter at
Castries, St. Lucia. April 1975.

drag to the keel. The unique feature of the St. Lucia variation was the hybrid rig: The proportions of the spritsail are the same as for a *canot,* but the mast is stepped farther aft, permitting a small jib to be set. As Evans so concisely put it, "In St. Lucia, it havin' two kind of boat: *canot* and boat."

That these two divergent types occur on the same island, and that the boat itself is a sort of hybrid, undoubtedly results from the peculiar convergence of French and British influences that occurred here. During the seventeenth and eighteenth centuries, as Britain and France staked out and then sought to maintain and enlarge their claims in the New World, St. Lucia had the distinction of being one of the most-traded islands in the West Indies, changing hands some fourteen times before winding up on the British side of the board. It is hardly surprising therefore that a form of dugout canoe exists side by side with a beach boat derived from another tradition entirely.

St. Lucia was another of the islands never mentioned when schooners

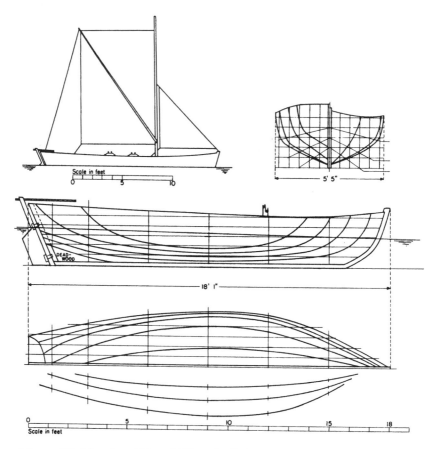

Lines of fishing boat Merci-Dieu, *built by Joseph Evans at Castries, St. Lucia. Taken off April 1975.*

and schooner building were discussed. Nevertheless, on the chance that there might have been some activity in the past, I wanted to check the local register of shipping. The personnel in the harbor master's office were cordial and helpful, but even so there was a fundamental obstacle: The whole town of Castries burned to the ground in 1948. I began to understand why the town had such a drab appearance. And of course this meant the records available for perusal began only from the date of the great fire.

Since the fire there had been a certain amount of boatbuilding centered in Castries, and the name of Malings Compton appeared frequently, first as builder and later as owner. The officials told me that Compton was still alive and could be found at his store a few blocks from the harbor.

Malings Compton was born in 1898 on the island of Canouan in the northern Grenadines, and there learned boat carpentry from his father before emigrating to St. Lucia in 1916. In all, Compton built eight vessels between 1920 and 1952, the largest of which was the 110-foot *Albertha Compton*, finished in 1937. The methods he described for the proportioning and setting up of vessels corresponded precisely with those used throughout the Grenadines. He did not, he told me, read plans; but Lewis Magras from St. Barts, the other major builder in Castries, could.

The pattern of activity in St. Lucia was therefore already familiar to me, since I had seen it in Dominica, Montserrat, Grenada, St. Kitts, St. Barts, and St. Martin. There had been sporadic boatbuilding as local economic conditions dictated, with the builders themselves coming from either Anguilla or the Grenadines.

As our conversation drew to a close, I asked Compton about the origins of boat carpentry in the islands. This was the question that had drawn shrugs, blank stares, and the odd fantastic answer from one end of the island chain to the other. By now my asking it was purely perfunctory. Compton's answer, however, was anything but perfunctory.

"Well," he said, leaning back reflectively. "This is the way it came about. In 1838, when Sir William Snagg came out to take charge of the island of Canouan . . ."

His information was so detailed and unhesitating, so concise and specific, that I instantly felt his account was significant. Later, in the most unexpected way, his account fitted together with official records and other information from widely different sources to provide the key to the puzzle of boatbuilding in the Lesser Antilles. It forms the basis of Chapter 25 on the culture history of island boatbuilding, a chapter that, until that point, I had not known it was possible to write. Meanwhile, there were three islands left before I could conclude my survey.

TWENTY-ONE

Investigating St. Vincent

~ ~ ~

uring the time *Skywave* was being built in Bequia by Haakon Mitchell and his sons, I occasionally had errands to run in nearby St. Vincent. If the errand was brief, the most convenient method of conducting business was to rise before dawn, walk the three miles up and over from Friendship Bay to Port Elizabeth, and recline in luxurious ease on the deck of the mail schooner for an hour and a half while she thrashed her way northward across the nine-mile channel to St. Vincent. The mail contract was held by *Friendship Rose,* which left Bequia at six o'clock and reached Kingstown on the south coast of St. Vincent with the sun still behind the mountain.

Schooner wharf, Kingstown,
St. Vincent. March 1975.

This trip grew to be a great favorite of mine because it entailed, among other things, a belated breakfast at a little planks-and-tin snack shop that huddled just outside the gates to the dockyard. My unvarying choice was a mango, a fried egg sandwich, and a large mug of coffee sweetened with condensed milk—simple enough but a gastronomic delight after the pre-dawn hike and a lively sail in the early morning chill of the trades.

St. Vincent is a lush volcanic island with a primarily agricultural economy based upon the production of bananas and arrowroot flour. Recently efforts have been made to develop Caribbean markets for the island's abundant supplies of those tropical root crops known locally as "ground provisions": tanias, dasheens, yams, edoes, sweet potatoes, and cassava. In addition, St. Vincent is the administrative and commercial center for all of the northern Grenadines, and Kingstown harbor was still much frequented by wooden sailing vessels. This being the case, it seemed a good idea to inquire along the waterfront about boatbuilding.

"Oh, yes," came the reply. "It have a big vessel building over Indian Bay. Plenty big."

When I got to Indian Bay, sure enough, there was a large vessel on stocks. Not only was this vessel large at ninety feet overall, it had some other unusual features as well. The bow was high and flaring in a way that I had never seen in a schooner before. An even closer inspection revealed that there was no sternpost; instead there was an enormous deadwood of timbers laid on top of the keel.

One of the shipwrights was from Bequia (naturally) and was glad to explain the unorthodox construction to me. The vessel was to be an "engine boat" fitted with twin engines and twin propeller shafts on either side of the deadwood. There would be a cargo mast but no sails, making this actually a derrick, and the high bow was for punching head-on into seas, something a sailing vessel is neither able nor expected to do. Since the vessel was not intended for sailing and was far too large to be measured for mere curiosity's sake, I moved on.

St. Vincent's steep volcanic top is mirrored below the sea by an equally steep base. I learned that it has no submerged shelf to speak of and consequently no onshore fishing grounds. What fishing there is in St. Vincent was carried out in small two-bow boats of the Bequia model. Recently, *canots* from St. Lucia had begun to appear in St. Vincent. With their greater speed and range, they were able to go after the pelagic species such as bonito, dorado, mackerel, and various billfishes. The sum and substance of it, then, is that St.

Detail of construction on a trading vessel at Indian Bay. October 1970.

Vincent did not have any distinctive indigenous type of small watercraft.

This had not always been the case. Stedman Wallace, a knowledgeable Bequian, told me that until the 1940s passengers and mail were carried daily between Georgetown and Kingstown in a forty-foot dugout canoe that was paddled, not sailed. The twenty-four mile trip was made in about two hours. It is recorded that there was a group of people called Yellow Caribs living in the northeast part of the island in the early part of this century. One can infer a connection, but there was nothing left to measure, nothing to photograph.

In the course of my inquiries up and down the island arc, I became familiar with particular islands roughly in proportion to how much boatbuilding activity there was. The exception was St. Vincent, which became very familiar to me as the "big town" for Bequia, but where there were no new types of watercraft and little boatbuilding. The explanation was, by this time, rather obvious. To an even greater extent than Grenada, St. Vincent was eclipsed in maritime affairs by the neighboring Grenadines.

TWENTY-TWO

Trading with *Rosarene*

~ ~ ~

The quiet of a tropical morning had already been swallowed by the dusty cacophony of the dockyard as I picked my way through backing trucks, stationary handcarts, swaying cargo slings, and shuffling dockers. I was in Kingstown, St. Vincent, seeking passage south to Trinidad.

The customs guard at the gate to the dockyard pointed out the captain of *Rosarene,* a slender man wearing an unlikely felt snapbrim. As I approached, Captain Hazell dismissed one man with a nod and set another to work with a pointed finger.

"I would like to get a passage to Trinidad, please," I began. "Haakon said to tell you . . ."

"You must see the agent for that," the captain cut in with the harassed air of a man who doesn't intend to be bothered. "Is nothing to do with me."

Something was wrong. Haakon had said to mention his name and that there would be no problem—probably not even a passage to pay. As I tried to explain further, Captain Hazell stepped onto the rail of the schooner and began to shout instructions to one of the men stowing cargo below decks. He didn't even give me the chance to ask who the agent was.

I was determined to make the trip, so I went and asked the customs guard again. He directed me to a dusty office on a side street a block away, where I repeated my request to a man behind the counter. He gave me a puzzled look, plainly wondering why a white man would want to book passage on a schooner. Even West Indians didn't travel by schooner any more, once inter-island air service had become an integral part of island life. It seemed only polite to offer an explanation, but I was afraid my real purpose would sound romantic or eccentric. For practical reasons I had no wish to be regarded as either.

"I need copper paint for my yacht, and it is too heavy to carry on an airplane," I offered, and in fact this was true. Also, I wanted to see Trinidad without having to take *Eider* into a large commercial port said to be hot and uncomfortable. But the real reason I wanted to book passage was to sample life aboard one of these fascinating schooners.

Whether convinced or not, the agent began to write out my passage. The basic rate was augmented by double the amount in bond—against my jumping ship in Trinidad, he explained apologetically.

Hoping Captain Hazell might thaw a bit at my perseverance, I returned to the dock, showed him my passage, and asked when *Rosarene* would be sailing. He appeared to like the new state of affairs even less than the other, and told me grudgingly that when the schooner was loaded she would return to Bequia for the night and sail for Trinidad sometime the following morning. With that I had to be content, and I promised myself to be aboard very early since it was evident that the captain had little inclination to delay his departure for the likes of me.

For my purposes, avowed and unavowed, *Rosarene* was ideal, being very typical of the larger schooners still trading in the islands. She was built in 1946 by Armand and Samuel Hazell, who still owned her; the captain was a cousin. The vessel measured 86.5 feet overall, had a 22-foot beam, and was listed at 60.28 registered tons. She had worked under sail alone until a Kelvin-Hughes diesel was fitted in 1971, and most of her career involved carrying rice from Guyana to Barbados and general cargo between St. Vincent, Trinidad, and

Schooner Rosarene *near Mustique, bound for Trinidad. February 1971.*

Barbados. She had also held the mail contract, off and on, for the northern Grenadines. At the time I made my trip she was under charter to the St. Vincent Marketing Board to carry fresh produce to Trinidad twice a month. In fact it was this produce that was being loaded that morning in Kingstown: 1,150 bags of sweet potatoes in the hold and 460 bags of carrots on deck, about 120 tons in all.

Wishing to take no chances with what I interpreted as a highly flexible departure time, I was on the dock in Bequia very early the following morning. As it turned out, there was still cargo going aboard. Ahead of the foremast, a rough pen had been nailed together, and nine sheep, one very large hog, and five smaller hogs were relaxing therein. One of my only disappointments during the whole trip was that I was not present when the large hog was loaded.

In addition to the livestock, there were the "traffickers" to be loaded and accommodated. These were seven people who paid round-trip passage and carried small consignments of goods to be sold in Trinidad, where they bought other goods to be sold in Bequia. These seven, the eight crew members, the captain, mate, supercargo, and another passenger were all as busy as ants, moving back and forth between bundles of belongings on the dock and the deckhouse at the stern, stowing parcels and contriving little nests for themselves for the voyage.

My position aboard was a little too ambiguous to engage in the predictable territorial encounters, so I perched on top of the deckhouse and watched the show while one of the traffickers, Lozina Kidd, told me of her father, a whaler man. When the owner came aboard I helped him repair a chafed place in the mainsail and seize on some reefing ties. Eventually there was a crescendo of shouting, an acceleration in the bustling, and the engine roared into life. A little after nine o'clock we backed away from the dock through a blue-black cloud of exhaust smoke and were under way.

As we motored down Admiralty Bay toward the West Cays, the crew went unhurriedly about their work, setting first the stem staysail, then the foresail, the jib, and finally the big mainsail, all while proceeding *downwind,* which you can do when you have gaff-rigged sails on hoops circling the mast rather than on slides in a track. When we rounded the Cays, the sheets were hardened in a bit and we began to thread our way across the Grenadines Bank toward Sail Rock, which lies on the eastern edge.

The long roll period and easy motion of the heavily laden schooner came as a pleasant surprise. The decks stayed dry even though we were pitching slightly into the seas, which build up rapidly over the Grenadines Bank. In fact, there was nothing to spoil a perfect day in the trades except the guttural drone of the engine. However, as I have already mentioned, to have an engine

Detail of rigging on schooner **Rosarene.**
February 1975.

in a commercial vessel is to create a compelling reason to use it, and more-over the breeze was so light that we would scarcely have moved without me-chanical power. As it was, we were proving another time an important theorem in the engineering of auxiliary sailing vessels: The whole (speed through the water) is frequently greater than the sum of the parts (speed under sail + speed under power). This is because powered motion creates apparent wind, making the sails work even in light airs.

As we passed Sail Rock shortly after noon, the captain dived into his cabin and brought up a small wooden box containing the compass, which he set on a small shelf by the companionway. Port and starboard watches were set—four men for the captain, four for the mate. A bell also appeared and was set on the wheel box, where it was struck by the helmsman on the half hour, somewhat erratically at the beginning of the watch but with increasing precision as eight bells drew nigh, ending his time at the wheel.

There was little to do but watch the swaying gaff or ogle the sheep, one of whom—presumably male—was mounting the others, male and female indifferently, at the rate of one about every five minutes. He had been doing this before we left Bequia and was still doing it when we reached Trinidad. Even the crew, vastly amused at first, finally wearied of the sheep's machismo and began to throw things whenever he made another assault. I was dividing my attention between this sideshow and the green heights of Grenada, which were slipping past well down to leeward when the captain appeared at my elbow.

"I ain't know if you does eat our food, but the cook have a little something for you."

Since I had never thought to provide food for my journey, I replied gratefully that I had often eaten Bequian food when I was working with Haakon Mitchell.

"Oh, is you then?" the captain exclaimed. "Is you that helping Haakon with the little sloop? If I did know that, we ain't worry with agent and passage and all. I putting you on the crew list and done."

He seemed genuinely embarrassed that in his preoccupation with loading he had let a friend of Haakon's pay passage. He anxiously shepherded me back to get a plate of rice with a rosette of canned pilchards arrayed on top. He asked if I used pepper sauce, then dived into his cabin again and brought up his own private stock for my use. Apparently, only a real greenhorn goes to sea in the West Indies without an assured supply of this vital condiment.

At sundown we had a meal of "cocoa tea" ("in Bequia, it have three kinda tea: coffee tea, cocoa tea, and tea tea") and a soup of pigeon peas with boiled plantains. Afterwards, the cook filled the running lights from a tin of kerosene and trimmed the wicks, upon which the mate fastened them in the rigging. The compass was moved to a small shelf just above the captain's bunk, where it was also visible to the helmsman through a small port cut in the cabin trunk.

Darkness soon mantled the schooner. The other passengers began to settle into the nests they had prepared for themselves along the lee side of the deckhouse. My place on the bench to windward, comfortable enough during daylight hours, was heeled just enough that I couldn't lie down or recline. As the hours wore on, my night became a kaleidoscope of shadowy images: the helmsman, face dimly lit by the glow of the compass light, leaning forward to peer into the dark; the captain disappearing into his cabin after prowling restlessly around the darkened decks; a sailor balancing on the lee rail, hand on the shroud while he emptied his bladder; a groggy passenger, dislodged by a lurch of the vessel, grumbling and worrying at a small parcel; the flare of a match mating with the glow of a cigarette. Thus the hours passed. The striking of the bell seemed at times to hasten the passage of the hours, at others to impede it.

At 1:30 A.M. the helmsman grunted something through the window and the captain roused himself to peer forward into the night. The Bocas Light, a ten-second flasher, had come up right on course, and Captain Hazell was noticeably easier. At 5:00 A.M. we reached the entrance to the Gulf of Paria, having sailed 140 miles in nineteen and a quarter hours, averaging 7.3 knots. We entered the narrow channel between Trinidad and Monos Island, the captain perched on the weather rail just outside the deckhouse and shouting piloting commands to the helm.

"Steady now, steady so."

"Down, go down now. Keep she down."

There is another channel, Boca Grande, wider and easier to navigate, on the other side of Monos Island, but it is much trafficked by tankers and other heavy shipping. Schooners preferred the narrower pass even though the wind there is often fluky, as it was for us. The crew quickly got the sails down while the captain continued to relay his steering instructions.

Once in through the narrow channel, we motored east across the Gulf of Paria, which was glassy smooth and slightly obscured by early morning haze. Large numbers of tankers and other ships just visible lay at anchor. There was not a breath of air moving, and a sticky heat lay over the bay. Already the impression was forming that Trinidad is not, either geographically or economically, part of the Antilles.

Inside the deckhouse the captain, frequently licking the end of his pencil, was preparing crew and passenger lists. His nervous attention to this ordinarily routine chore reminded me of certain outraged talk back in Bequia about some schooner captain who had recently been jailed in Trinidad for a minor (at least in the Bequia version) irregularity in immigrations procedure and was still in prison.

When we tied up at the Quarantine Dock well outside Port-of-Spain, it became apparent that immigrations was no empty formality here, as in the islands to the north. First we were lined up and conducted to a bare room where we waited while the schooner was searched. Then one of the officers returned to go over the lists, each person stepping to the other side of a white line painted on the floor as his or her name was called. When I answered to my name, the officer glanced up quickly.

"What is the purpose of your visit?" he asked, scowling ferociously.

In my chattiest and most confiding tone, I replied that I had come to buy some bottom paint. This was the line, after all, that had worked in St. Vincent.

"It says here the purpose of your visit is tourism." The officer waved my landing card at me and scowled even more darkly.

"I . . . er . . . um," I stumbled and stopped. Alas, Captain Hazell and I had not consulted on this particular point, and there seemed little profit in trying to tell the officer that I was a friend of Haakon Mitchell's.

Trinidad has had a problem with illegal immigrants from poor islands, and to a certain extent I sympathize with this difficulty. However, I would be double-dipped and deep-fried before I ever thought of emigrating, legally or otherwise, to this country, which I was rapidly beginning to view in such terms as "smelly" and "squalid" and "jerkwater." Even so, there was little to gain by pointing this out to the man. I was having enough trouble as it was.

"You make me very suspicious, Mr. Pyle," he growled, doubtless imagining that this remark was new to me. "I shall record, 'Purpose of visit not clear.'" He scrawled in his ledger, scowled a scowl to end all scowls, then waved us all back to the schooner.

By the time we were under way again the sun was burning through a lens of humidity and it was breathlessly hot. We motored through the gray-brown water toward Queen's Wharf at the head of the harbor. There all the schooner traffic of the Windward Islands seemed to be seeking accommodation. The scene was nightmarish: nineteen schooners or equivalent-sized vessels

Queen's Wharf, Port-of-Spain,
Trinidad. February 1975.

crowded onto four hundred feet of dock. Other vessels were anchored off, others still circled, crews waving and screaming for space. Vessels on the inside cast off and fought their way out. Vessels on the outside immediately shoved bowsprit and bows into the tangle, trying frantically to shoehorn their way to a place on the wharf. All this frantic maneuvering went on in the sticky, choking heat. It looked as if it might be a good little while before we saw the clear waters and blue skies of Bequia again.

Rosarene circled a few times, the captain did a little screaming of his own, and a rift miraculously appeared in the wall of hulls, spars, and rigging. We nudged and edged, edged and nudged, trimming up the mainboom to clear the small steamer astern while jabbing our bowsprit past the boom of the vessel ahead. We finally came to a berth on the inside. I later learned that our apparent good fortune was owed to being a government charter. Otherwise it was not uncommon for a vessel to wait one, two, and even three weeks to get alongside for loading.

The crew immediately began preparations for unloading our cargo. As they threw back the tarps and started to work clearing the hatches, Captain Hazell drifted over to me.

"In Trinidad, they having all kinda people. They does tell you a thing, and then someone waiting to hold you. Is like a gang they having. Best you rest the nights 'board the vessel while we here."

I was touched by his concern and grateful for the hospitality, and I thanked him accordingly. But I had no intention of leaving the vessel and missing one minute of the dockside circus that was surging and swirling all around us.

The crew of *Rosarene* had already begun heaving our bags of carrots off the deck and laying them on the rail. There the bags were picked up by one or another of the oddest assortment of stevedores imaginable. All ages, sizes, races, and both sexes were represented. They came and went between the rail and waiting carts and trucks, seeming to work for no one and toward no particular end.

It took me half the afternoon to grasp the fundamentals of the system. These people who swarmed around the side of the vessel were not being paid. They were "helping" to unload us simply for the opportunity of being present if anything broke or spilled. From time to time someone would grab a handful from a bag not tightly tied. The captain and mate watched this but did not interfere unless the pilferage became too obvious. What the dockers could glean they immediately sold to one or another of the fraternity of small entrepreneurs who had set up shop as close as propriety permitted. With cash in hand, the workers then nipped smartly over to a grog shop conveniently situated on the dock, where they quickly invested their earnings in cigarettes (sold singly as well as by the pack) or in 140-proof rum (sold by the shot only). "Economic velocity," the rate at which money changes hands within a system, is regarded by some scholars as an indicator of economic well being. No great degree of well being seemed to arise from the dizzying economic velocity I witnessed on the Trinidad dock.

With the carrots out of the way, the hatch covers were taken up and the cargo gaff was hauled up the foremast. A diesel winch, called a "donkey," at the foot of the mast was started after a short session of grunt-and-tug, and the mate took his place on the tail of the line which ran up to the gaff and down into the hold. Three of the crew worked down there in a humid inferno, throwing 175-pound bags of sweet potatoes onto the cargo sling. When the sling was filled, the mate deftly threw four turns of rope onto the spinning drum of the donkey engine and tailed it. The sling rose squealing and swaying out of the hold until high enough to clear the rail. There the mate paused, holding just enough tension on the tail to keep the load aloft, while a man on the dock swung the gaff outboard by means of a vang attached aloft. The line was let run, and the load eased neatly onto the dock. In the whole sequence, the margin between success and catastrophe depended entirely on the mate's strength, timing, and experience. I would not have worked in the vicinity of that cargo sling for all the sweet potatoes and half the bananas in St. Vincent.

Luckily the crew were made of sterner stuff—much sterner, considering that they had not only loaded all that cargo the day before but had also stood watches during the night. By 7:30 P.M., when they knocked off, most of the 1,150 bags of potatoes were out of the hold. The job was completed the following morning in a couple of hours, the hatch covers replaced, and the decks washed down. The crew dived down the forward companionway and reappeared a short time later rigged out for a turn ashore, it now being early Friday afternoon. The captain and supercargo did some maintenance, including a little caulking from the inside to slow a leak that had appeared on the trip down. Then, after a further warning to me about the hazards of Port-of-Spain by night, the captain left in a taxi for a quiet weekend at the home of friends outside the city.

After two nights on the narrow wooden bench inside the deckhouse, with swarms of mosquitoes and sticky heat for my covers and the all-night blare of radios on the surrounding vessels for my lullaby, I got busy and located a hostel for foreign seamen operated by the Anglican Church. From this base, made bold by the twin luxuries of a cot and a shower, I ventured forth during the following days (daylight only) to find the evidence of boatbuilding described in the following chapter.

Ten days after arriving in Trinidad, on a Monday, I stopped by the schooner to see how loading was going. Nothing was happening. The captain told me that the agents were looking for the cargo. Not looking for *cargo,* looking for *the* cargo! The cargo for the return trip was already consigned and paid for, but the agents simply could not find it in the warehouses. So for two more days, while they scouted around, the schooner and her crew sweltered and other vessels waited for space at the dock.

By Wednesday I was feeling pretty bleak. What there was of boatbuilding in Trinidad I had seen, and my life of ease over at the Mariner's Club had begun to pall, particularly in view of my sundown curfew. Although I never confessed it to Captain Hazell, I did go out early one Sunday morning when there was no one in the streets except a dry and withered woman who offered to sell me the small baby she held in her arms. It was a nice little baby, as I recall, and the price quoted was not unreasonable. But the experience left me shaken and I yearned for Bequia.

Suddenly on Wednesday afternoon, with a rush and a roar, cargo began to appear and be loaded. We took on 500 sacks of cement, 200 oil drums, 1,500 clay building tiles, and 850 cartons of crackers. In all, forty tons of goods were loaded in about three hours and the schooner secured for sea. There remained only our outbound immigrations clearance and we would be gone.

Two officers came aboard, for this was no formality. One read our names from a master list while the other laid on hands and conducted each person individually across the deck. Guess whose name was *not* on the passenger list, presumably because "purpose of visit not clear"? There followed another round of fierce scowling and implied hindrance, ending, to all our relief, in our dismissal.

As we motored toward the Bocas, the reason for the crew's afternoon flurry of activity became apparent. The narrow pass used by the schooners is unlighted and very tricky by dark. We threaded our way through and out just before sunset and set a course for Point Saline Light on the southeast tip of Grenada. On the outbound trip we passed "over" (to windward of) Grenada, while on the return our course took us "under" the island and in the lee of the Grenadines. The trade winds are usually a little north of east, so the return course was intended to be an easier point of sailing.

On this occasion, the wind was south of east and we were able to sail through the night with sheets started. At one point I was awakened by the flapping of canvas and the sound of running feet on deck. The jib halyard had chafed through, dropping the sail unexpectedly, and had to be repaired the following morning while we were in the lee of Grenada.

The cement we carried was consigned to Union Island, so we held up

Schooner Rosarene; *aloft for repairs in the lee of Grenada. February 1975.*

close under Carriacou when making for Clifton, the reef harbor on the windward side of Union. The sea was calm and the mate was at the helm as we eased sheets and ran down toward the harbor mouth. At this point, Captain Hazell came out of his cabin, glanced around at what was going on, and burst into violent activity. He screamed at the helmsman to "bring she up, man," sent another hand running forward as lookout, and ran himself to cast off the peak halyard of the big mainsail. Only when the peak was broken down did the schooner answer the helm and swing up into the wind.

I never saw the shoal and have no idea how close to it we came, but it was not simple nervousness on the captain's part that galvanized him. I learned later that there is a shoal patch called Gran de Coi lying in the approach to Clifton harbor that breaks in blowing weather but is difficult to see otherwise. Formerly the patch was marked by a few timbers that remained after the schooner *Anne-Marie* struck and sank there, but these had disappeared, leaving the reef again unmarked.

At dock in Clifton the crew began unloading the cement, but there was no dockside circus and it seemed doubtful if they could finish before dark. When the mail schooner *Friendship Rose* came in I felt that Providence had smiled. I bid farewell to Captain Hazell, transferred my three gallons of copper paint (yes, I did buy bottom paint in Trinidad after all) to *Friendship Rose,* and was back in Bequia by dark.

TWENTY-THREE

The *Pirogues* of Trinidad

~ ~ ~

Trinidad is considered an island of the West Indies for historical and political reasons only. In geography and ecology, it is a shoulder of South America, separated from the mainland only by the Gulf of Paria, a part of the Orinoco River delta system. Owing to the presence of oil and asphalt, Trinidad has become the wealthiest and most extensively developed island of the southern Caribbean, widely known for steel pan bands, calypso music, and probably the most elaborate carnival in the Carribean. Although the islands to the north depend extensively on commerce carried to and from Trinidad in schooners, nothing I knew about the island itself inclined me to expect I would find much marine anthropology to be done there.

Then, what to my wondering eyes should appear—even before *Rosarene* docked—but a new and exotic boat type.

I soon discovered that this was a *pirogue,* and that all the *pirogues* in the

Trinidad pirogue, Port-of-Spain. February 1975.

north of Trinidad were built in a small shop on Sackville Street in Port-of-Spain. There I found a neatly lettered wooden sign designating the establishment of L. Taitt, Boatbuilder. Taitt, a quiet and unassuming individual, had been building *pirogues* for fifty years, the first twenty with his father, who in turn had built them for forty years prior to that. It was ninety years, he pointed out with quiet pride, that the same type had been built in the same location. The only change had been the late broadening of transoms to carry the weight of an outboard motor.

One *pirogue* was nearing completion at the front of the small, covered yard, while construction was just beginning on another at the back. I learned that the typical *pirogue* was completed in about two weeks. This rapid rate of work gave me the opportunity to measure a hull one afternoon and return the following day to see the next one built. The operative concept here is *built,* not *being built* or *under construction*. It was no small part of the fascination of this unique boat type that the hull took form in a single day.

Construction began with the shaping of the shell from a log of "red cedar" (probably *Guarea trichilioides,* a member of the mahogany family). The shaping was done in half a day by a man who came in once a week for this purpose only, working without molds or templates. Along the upper surface of this curious keel a trough was cut. In the completed *pirogue*, the trough functions as a waterway to keep the bilges dry, but provides in addition an important clue to the origins of this boat type. The waiting keel has the distinct appearance of a tiny dugout canoe.

In the next step, the stem and transom were fastened to the shell. The long stem was shaped from a single piece of "cypre" (*Cordia alliodora,* called "silver balli" in Bequia) and positioned by Taitt "according to taste." The transom was formed from wide planks of red cedar and held in place by a long knee. With the bow and stern thus fixed, Taitt and his helpers immediately began to plank with an ease and speed born of long practice.

The first plank, a ten-inch white pine board, was held along the shell and the rake of the stem transferred to the end of the plank. The plank was allowed to pivot until nearly horizontal, and a line was scribed onto the lower side by running a pencil alongside the shell. The board was then placed on a workbench and cut away to the two lines using drawknives.

Being used to the slower pace and solemn care with which cutting had been performed in Bequia, I was surprised and at first dismayed by the reckless abandon of the two men who hacked, split, and gouged their way down to the line, chips flying. After the initial cut, the plank was again laid alongside the hull and high spots marked for additional hacking. Without further ado the plank was nailed in place, first to the stem and then to the shell. Galvanized

Frames being added to a pirogue,
Port-of-Spain. February 1975.

nails were driven downward through the plank into the shell, the plank being twisted as it was fastened farther and farther aft. When in place, the upper edge of the plank was beveled, again with drawknives and again rapidly, the purpose being simply to knock off the edge so there would be no channel for water to lie in.

The subsequent planks were treated in the same manner, with the scribed line following the upper edge of the first plank. Only this time the nailing was done without even the benefit of a second shaping. The trick was that the second plank was lapped onto the outside of the first and the two nailed together surface to surface instead of edge to edge. Nails were driven from the outside and clinched. Thus the first plank was laid on in what is called carvel fashion, while the others are attached in the clinker fashion known primarily in northern Europe.

The men worked without talking and with such precision that the planking was finished well before the end of the day. Then the hull, formed but wobbly, was carried to the front of the shop and set on horses. There it was finished in the next few days by the addition of frames, stringers, wales, thwarts, and a small deck forward. The frames were sawed from natural crooks of "saman" (*Pithecellobium saman*) on a band saw, the only piece of power equipment in the shop.

The *pirogues* built by Taitt were so standardized that he had a pile of templates from which the frames were rough-shaped. Final cutting was done by hand. In addition to the two men in the shop, Taitt employed two others who worked in the bush, cutting logs for shells, frames, and other members.

The lines of a Taitt pirogue seem to confirm its hybrid ancestry. The waterlines forward showed much greater hollow than I found in any small craft other than the dugout *gommiers* and their derivatives, the *yoles*. Use of the shell as a keel points to a dugout origin here. The odd thing was that raising strakes should be lapped instead of fastened on edge as was done elsewhere with dugouts. I questioned Taitt about this matter, but he only replied with bland disinterest that he had no idea. Nor could he give me any help with a rigging plan.

Eventually I met Frank Delmas, who in his youth had been a *pirogue* racing enthusiast. He was happy to share his memories, filling in the gaps. He asserted without hesitation that the *pirogue* was of Amerindian origin, that raising strakes had been a development connected to diminishing availability of large tree trunks for dugout canoes. He surmised that the notion of lapping had been learned from the Royal Navy, whose launches and tenders were always clinker-built.

From Delmas I got the sketches for the rigging plan. I was openly skepti-

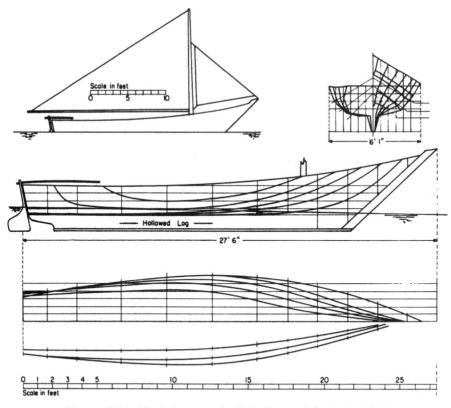

Lines of Trinidad **pirogue, built in Port-of-Spain in 1975
by L. Taitt. Taken off February 1975.**

cal, but he insisted that the peculiar low aspect ratio of the mainsails was accurate. Still doubtful, I made a concerted effort to find a photo of a rigged
pirogue, consulting museums, libraries, and especially the photo archives of
the *Trinidad Guardian*—all to no avail. Until further notice and better evidence,
the Trinidad *pirogue* was rigged as shown here.

Delmas's memories of *pirogue* racing were particularly interesting since
the sailing vocabulary for these craft was in patois, beginning with the word
pirogue itself. This is the French version of the Spanish *piragua,* reputedly
derived itself from the Carib Indians. When sailing close-hauled in a *pirogue*,
the command *jambez* was given, whereupon one of the crew wrapped the
shroud around his waist and hiked to weather with his feet on the gunwale,
like a contemporary crew of a racing catamaran using a trapeze. Sailing in
this attitude was called *contrepas,* incidentally. To sheet in was *halez,* to make
fast was *tenez.* The size of a *pirogue* was given as one *bordage,* two *bordage,*
and so on, according to the number of planks (from the French *bordé*) added
to the shell.

Here again I was encountering the curious association of a dugout with a French cultural heritage. The Trinidadian *pirogue* had evolved a long way from the Carib dugout, and the French cultural heritage had dwindled to a few words of patois largely fallen into disuse since pirogues stopped sailing. Nevertheless the association was there, and it continued to intrigue me.

In the matter of larger vessels, I came to Trinidad with a certain amount of information already in hand. While copying out the registers of shipping in Grenada and St. Vincent, I had found a few entries for vessels built in Trinidad in the late 1800s that had been transferred to St. George's or Kingstown by a later owner. Thus I knew that there had been at least some boatbuilding in the past.

But when I presented myself at the Port-of-Spain harbor master's office, I was told in a friendly but unequivocal manner that there were no registers older than the current one and that there had never been any boatbuilding in Trinidad. I knew otherwise but saw nothing to be gained by argument. A pretty thorough sweep through the ranks of historians, sailing buffs, and the coast guard commandant, followed by combing through such institutions as libraries, museums, and newspaper offices all availed nothing. The general feeling seemed to be that sailing vesesels were relics that were characteristic of the poorer islands to the north—that Trinidad looked inward toward its natural resources and had a continental rather than an insular destiny.

Twenty-Four

The Flying Fish Boats
and Speightstown Schooners
of Barbados

~ ~ ~

It is a natural consequence of sailing geography that my final island as a marine anthropologist should have been my first as a cruising yachtsman. Barbados, ninety miles east of the main arc of the Antilles, must be reached by beating into the trade winds unless, of course, you are crossing the Atlantic. In that case it is the first possible landfall. This is how it happened that I first strolled the waterfront of Bridgetown in Barbados, still riding the wave of well-being that comes from bringing landfall up dead ahead after twenty-seven days at sea. In this expansive mood I paused beside the schooner *Frances W. Smith,* 110 feet of decaying grandeur.

In the shade of an awning stretched over the stern, a white-haired captain seated in a captain's chair supervised his sweating crew as they swayed up bags of rice out of the hold. From time to time, when something didn't go to suit him, the captain leaned forward, spat tobacco juice over the rail, and lashed out with his booming voice. I stood hypnotized by this scene until the sound of my own voice brought me back to reality.

"You have a lovely schooner there," I said to the captain.

"Thirty thousand and she's yours," came the instant response, a reflex from frequent repetition.

"I'll be honest with you," he continued in the confiding tones of one who has no such intention. "She needs new sails and rigging."

My eye swept up the dark, oiled mainmast and back down the heavy iron rigging, sewn in sleeves of white-painted canvas, and seized around wooden deadeyes as big as ham steaks. Encouraged by this display of interest, the captain pursued his theme.

"You will need top hamper as well. No engine." He was apologetic. "She draws nine feet loaded and bumps coming in on a low tide."

He held me with his glittering eye, and my imagination raced—green islands in the calm of early morning, the sounds and smells of strange ports, the romance of life under sail in the eternal springtime of the tropics . . . Captain Ben Hassel, as he introduced himself, talked of this and that—of storms and calms, of freaks of weather and miraculous shoals of fish, of grounding and near catastrophe, of freight rates too low and canvas, wire, and crew too high. The steeper he pitched it, the better it sounded to me. It was a consummate job of salesmanship.

Luckily the price was well beyond my means, even with Eastern Caribbean dollars at fifty cents against the United States dollar. *Frances W. Smith* was safe from me and I was saved, though with regret, from her.

She was not of Antillean origins, having been built as a fishing schooner in Lunenburg, Nova Scotia. I later heard of how she came to her end not long after I listened to the wily enticements of Captain Hassel. She was bought by Albert Lake, who took her to Anguilla for refitting (where else?) and removed her foremast of Guyana greenhart to help rig the *New London* (see Chapter 5, page 44). The stripped hull was anchored in Road Bay, Anguilla, remaining there until a winter gale sank her. As I was leaving the islands, Anguilla was my last port of call, and I spent two ghostly hours diving over the sunken hull, hoping to find a builder's plaque or other memento. The vessel had a special significance to me, and her fate seems curiously symbolic of the decline of sail in the Caribbean and elsewhere.

Closer contacts with the realities of the schooner trade have dispelled many of my romantic notions about working sail or maritime hauling in any form. The prudence of middle age has tempered the enthusiasms of youth, but the yearning I felt that morning in Barbados has never entirely left me. If the world were a proper place, wooden vessels built with skill and respect would ever afterward sail seas unsullied by oil spills and castoff plastic, yielding an honest return to the owners and a decent living for the crew.

When I returned to Barbados six years later with measuring tape and camera, many of the larger schooners were already gone. In their places were small coastal freighters brought over from Europe. However, the warmth of the people and the easy charm of their manner had not altered with passing time.

On my earlier visit to Barbados, I went one morning to the open market near the harbor with a friend, another recent alumnus of the Atlantic passage. "How much are your mangos, Mistress?" asked my friend of one of the vendors.

The woman in the madras kerchief named her price. It wasn't much as I recall, but my friend offered her half because anyone who has read the guidebooks knows that a tourist who pays the asking price, however low, is regarded a fool.

"No, please, sir," she said, smilingly declining to dicker.

"How much are your limes, then?" countered my friend.

"White man," she replied sweetly and completely without malice, "you can't afford my limes."

We drifted on and got limes elsewhere. A few days later I was walking alone near the market when a huddled figure intercepted me, hand extended in the wordless entreaty of the beggar. It was the same woman.

"What happened?" I asked.

"Oh, sir," she answered, dejected but still without rancor. "Some bad boys shove me and hold me and steal my stock. Now I lost my capital and must go into the street."

I gave her twenty dollars, all that I had with me, hoping it would do something to replenish her capital. Even in the retelling, I still can't fully explain why this episode came to epitomize Barbados for me, somehow different from all the other islands.

Although most of the schooners in the Carenage were transients from the smaller islands to the west or imported from Nova Scotia, there was at least one Barbados-built schooner. That was enough to encourage me to seek out the harbor master's office and the now-familiar registry of shipping. The registry in use began in 1920, and as in Trinidad, older volumes could not be found. Of the eighty-five entries powered by sail, fifty-five were built in Nova Scotia, a dozen in the United States, mainly New England, and five in other islands of the Lesser Antilles. Nine sloops and schooners had been built in Barbados, all before World War II.

While searching I turned past a number of power vessels, at first with scarcely a glance, then, as the numbers grew, with quickening interest. Most of these vessels, built in Nova Scotia and registered *de novo* in Barbados, were under one hundred feet overall, rather a small size to come such a distance to be registered. I noticed that although most were transferred back to Nova Scotian ports after a few years, there were occasionally other reasons given for closing the registry: "Lost N. Atlantic, 1931"; "Lost 150 mi. E. of St. Pierre, 1932"; "Sold at Auction, Philadelphia, USA, 1934"; "Forfeited to U.S. Gov't., 1937"; and then the clincher, "Rammed and sunk by the U.S. Coast Guard, 1932."

Between 1931 and 1933, forty-eight Nova Scotia–built vessels between seventy and one hundred feet in length were registered in Barbados. All had a length-to-beam ratio of five-to-one or less, and none was deeper than nine feet from deck to keel. The corporate owners' names had an odd, impersonal ring about them: Associated Traders, Blue Line Traders, Bear Cove Fisheries, and so on. From the coincidence of dates and places, and their occasional fates, it would appear that these vessels were built specifically for and engaged in a final flurry of rum running to the United States before the repeal of prohibition made such activity unprofitable. Evidently it was expedient and possible to register these vessels in Barbados rather than nearer their sphere of action.

The activities of these enterprising Nova Scotians underlined the lesson depicted in the registry. At least for the period since 1920, it was easier and more economical to import trading vessels from elsewhere than to build them on the island. Thus I was unprepared when I learned that Barbados at one time had a well-established tradition of boat carpentry that produced two interesting and unique types of local watercraft.

The "flying fish boats" once formed the basis of Barbados's only commercial fishery. I had been told of these craft by Stedman Wallace of Bequia,

Barbados flying fish boat; detail of bow. (Photo by Barbados Government Information Service.)

who said admiringly that "they could really split the wind," meaning they could sail well to weather. This was strong praise from a Bequian, most of whom are generally grudging of kind words for any boats other than their own, and I therefore hoped to be lucky and find one. I didn't; they have been extinct since the 1930s, when they were replaced by small inboard launches. Not even a hulk remained from which I might make measurements.

Only by luck did I happen to meet Carlton Hackett of the Government Information Office, who remembered that at some time photographs had been made of the flying fish boats. He was clever enough actually to find the precious negatives and make prints for me. In lieu of lines drawings, let me only say that these images reveal an open boat of around twenty feet in length belonging to the same category of beach boats as still existed in Anguilla and other points in the English-speaking West Indies. Unique to the Barbados model were a recurved stem and decurved bowsprit, and I noticed at least one boat that seemed to have a very long gunter-staff fastened to the luff of the mainsail.

This was such an interesting type that I tried in all the obvious places to find additional information about them. I had no luck at all in my quest, but then in going through the Barbados Museum I came upon a glass showcase containing a handsome model labeled "Speightstown Schooner. Gift of the Hon. Errol Barrow, Prime Minister of Barbados."

Inquiry yielded two photographs of these extraordinary vessels, two of which operated until the mid-1950s. They ran an all-sail packet service between Speightstown in the north and Bridgetown in the south of Barbados, carrying sugar, molasses, and passengers down and returning with passengers and general cargo. Since these vessels operated only locally, they were never registered, explaining why I had found no official trace of them.

I took lines off the museum model, a very careful rendition by one R. Gibbon. The run between Speightstown and Bridgetown is a beam reach sailed in the lee of a low-lying island, ideal conditions which help explain the radical rig and very high speeds attained by the Speightstown schooners. They commonly made the trip of ten nautical miles in forty-five minutes, including the two-mile beat from Pelican Shoals into the Carenage—a calculated speed of twelve or thirteen knots!

On one occasion, one of these schooners was blown off her moorings in a hurricane. She was intercepted off St. Vincent but had to be towed home because the length and low angle of her bowsprit made it impossible to sail her in the open sea. This anecdote and the high speeds mentioned are not difficult to believe if the proportions of the model are accurate. Here we find very fine lines indeed, an almost classic example of the sharp-bottomed schooner.

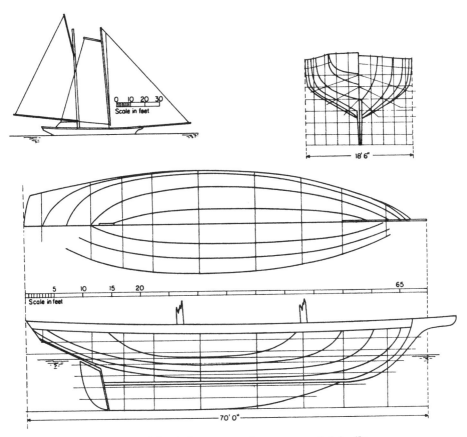

Lines of Speightstown schooner model, built
by R. Gibbon. Taken off January 1975.

Note particularly the sharp floors of the mid-section, the extreme deadrise of the stern, the nearly symmetrical waterlines and diagonals, the fine entry, and the smooth run aft that begins well forward. The false keel and deadwood are so unusual for the West Indies and the huge sail plan so radical that at first I wondered if the model builder was guilty of exaggeration. The photographs and a conversation I had with the builder of *Challenor,* last of the Speightstown schooners, confirmed that the model was, in reality, quite accurate.

Osbert Mascoll, born in 1902, learned ship carpentry from John Leacock, who had been taught in his turn by Mascoll's maternal grandfather, John Pickett. As I talked with Mascoll, he illustrated points about ship design with sketches and commented on my own sketches of the model in the museum. The Speightstown schooners carried an iron ballast false keel bolted to the keel, enabling them to stand up better to the large spread of sail. A deadwood was used in the stern on top of the keel instead of a deep tuck in the after frames, making it simpler to give the vessel "an easy bottom."

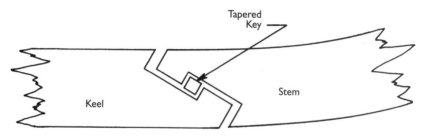

Detail of key splice described by Osbert Mascoll.

The method of setting up a vessel outlined by Mascoll was the same as those I had encountered elsewhere in the islands. The difference here was that he had a clearer and more analytical understanding of the elements of design and how they shaped the finished vessel. For example, he volunteered the information that positioning main frames farther forward on the keel gave a vessel more weather helm; that an easy bottom could be guaranteed by starting the run at two-thirds of the keel and carrying it over transom frames modeled on the main frames; that a broad stern was necessary to carry a long boom; that a "tail boat," a vessel with a counter stern, has a better turn of speed because the wake is smoother.

In designing a vessel, Mascoll told me that he used a scale half model which he took apart to get "the lofts." This was the same type of half model I had seen in Carriacou and Bequia. When asked if he learned this technique from the boatbuilder Leacock, he replied that he had worked it out himself. He also described and sketched for me a "key splice," which he used to join the forefoot of the stem to the keel. The two ends are cut as a mortise interlocked in place with a tapered key driven into a square keyway between them. The key forces the joint tight, yet leaves it both strong and flexible.

Mascoll talked easily and with an air of suppressed mirth. He was proudest of having built "the Columbus boats," replicas of *Pinta, Niña,* and *Santa Maria* used in a motion picture. For this project he had eighty men working under him, and the plans were drafted in England. In speaking of his working life, the retired builder expressed himself well and without regrets. He had built large vessels in his day; now other men built smaller vessels.

From our conversation and the other information I turned up, it was evident that the skills of boat carpentry had existed in Barbados for a good while and that vessels and boats of great merit were built there. Yet there was never a true maritime industry such as developed in Bequia, Carriacou, and Anguilla. Timber resources were scarce, and importation of vessels from elsewhere was easy and economical.

Twenty-Five

Dropping Anchor

~ ~ ~

"He trudged along, unknowing what he sought,
And whistled as he went, for want of thought."
—Dryden, *Cymon and Iphigenia*

Where you have both water and people, there you will find boats; and these boats do not occur by accident. They are built deliberately, of specific materials and to a design that is very uniform for the area and the culture of the builders. Where does this idea of what constitutes a "correct" boat arise?

At the beginning of my quest, I had certain presuppositions about the historical forces that might have influenced the evolution of watercraft design in the Lesser Antilles. My first reality check came when I found that the builders themselves rarely had any views on origins. As my journeys unfolded, I became confused about the very nature of the question. Did it even have an answer, and why was I asking it in the first place?

From the beginning, my interest in West Indian sailing craft had a historical bias—I wanted to know not only what boatbuilding was going on at the time, but what had gone on before and where it had come from. Behind this bias, I later came to realize, there lay both an inspiration and a motive.

The inspiration crystallized out of a manuscript, translated from Danish, of a 1792 report by Johan Lorentz Carstens to the King of Denmark concerning the state of the Danish colony at St. Thomas. Embedded in a magma of self-serving drivel and detail about flags flown and salutes fired, there were nuggets of information on social practice and usage among the Creoles and slaves, including the remark that, "In the harbor there are often seen sailing craft of a speed and grace which are unknown in Europe."

Now, the implications of such a remark are everything or nothing, depending on one's frame of mind. I chose to take it as evidence that fast sailing vessels were a West Indian innovation. From my arrival in St. Croix I had heard West Indian character and capacities maligned more or less non-stop by outsiders such as myself. Everyone has shortcomings, naturally, including

West Indians. But the complaints were often senseless, generally unsympathetic, and always boring. I was heartily sick of them and in a revisionist mood, actively looking for something that could be pointed out as a unique production of the native creativity of the islanders. I seized eagerly upon Carstens's remark, and made it a priority of my study of present-day boatbuilding to corroborate the suggestion I saw there.

Thus, as you've seen, my inquiries had a strong bias toward the historical aspects of boatbuilding. Never mind that the fast sailing vessels seen by Carstens were probably "Bermudan"—sharp-bottomed, sloop-rigged vessels built in Bermuda, Jamaica, and the Chesapeake as early as 1707. And never mind that this design was probably carried to the Lesser Antilles by the buccaneers when the Spanish drove them out of Hispaniola. Never mind, in short, that the proportions and characteristics of fast sailing sloops and later schooners were already taking shape when the ancestors of the builders I knew were still slaves, given no opportunity to learn anything as pernicious as boatbuilding. My mind was already made up, and all I needed were a few pliable facts to support my conclusion.

These few facts proved more elusive than I had imagined. Take for example the story of Captain Bligh and the Tortola sloop, an early favorite in the historical sweepstakes. William Bligh, best known as the rigid disciplinarian who provoked/suffered (circle your choice) the mutiny on the *Bounty*, was also the ablest navigator of his day. After his disastrous first attempt to transport breadfruit seedlings to the West Indies, Bligh returned to Tahiti in 1792 in the *Providence* and this time succeeded.

On this voyage, so the story goes, the *Providence* called in Tortola, where local shipwrights came aboard and measured one of the ship's yawls (a yawl was an open boat carried on deck by the naval vessels of that day and used when filling water casks or bringing aboard stores). The form of the yawl was accordingly copied by laying a stick across the gunwales and carving a notch to mark the beam at each one-foot interval on the keel. This, continues the story, is why in Tortola the boats are designated by the length of the keel instead of by the length overall.

This bit of cultural history seemed to me to tie the distinctive design of the Tortola sloop to one of the well-known personalities of the day, as well as to the epoch-making arrival of the breadfruit in the West Indies. It was very plausible, very circumstantial, and not difficult to verify, since I was able to find a detailed biography of Bligh, by Mackaness. According to this account, Bligh and the *Providence* arrived January 23, 1793, in St. Vincent, their first port of call in the West Indies, where several breadfruit seedlings were delivered to the Royal Botanical Gardens in Kingstown. A scrawny and generally unimposing specimen said to be the original transplant still grows there, while its descendants abound throughout the islands—a daily boon to thousands and clearly well worth the two attempts and a mutiny that its arrival required.

After a week's stay in St. Vincent, the *Providence* proceeded to Port Royal, Jamaica, arriving there on February 5—a voyage of 940 nautical miles made in six days. There is no mention in the biography of an intermediate stop in Tortola or any other island—perhaps because there simply was not time. An average daily run of 157 miles is already unusually good for a downwind passage in a ship that could not have been careened since Tahiti. To detour to Tortola and stop even for a few hours would have added 160 miles to the trip and subtracted at least one day from the sailing time, requiring an average of 220 miles or more per day—an occurrence so unlikely that it would surely have been noted in the log.

Alas, another good theory aground on the hard rock of fact! By this time, however, I had found that all the sloops and schooners in the islands were built according to a few simple rules of proportion. These rules accounted for the broad similarity of vessels built throughout the island chain: depth in the hold equal to one-half the beam; beam equal to one-fourth the length between perpendiculars; keel equal to one-half the length between perpendiculars.

Since ultimately these proportions constituted the design of a vessel, I decided to concentrate my inquiries on this simple and concrete matter of proportions instead of the abstract concept of "origins." Feeling suitably devious and infinitely subtle, I began to ask builders where they had gotten their rules of proportion. Response was only slightly improved by my new approach; now there was a pregnant pause before the shake of the head or the shrug. Very occasionally, an especially patient individual would take the time to explain that the rules were developed so that vessels would be "right."

Then one hot afternoon while working on *Skywave*, Uncle Nappy seemed in a talkative mood, and I posed my question. His response was immediate and triumphant.

"The Bible," he said. "It the Bible, Douggie. The Lord told Noah how to build the Ark and is the same way we building our own vessel."

By a masterful effort I refrained from dancing on the deck, but at quitting time I hastened aboard *Eider* to thumb the ship's Bible and find the operative passage in Genesis 6:13–15 where, in the measured cadences of the King James translation, the rules of proportion were set forth:

> And God said unto Noah, The end of all flesh is come before me; for the earth is filled with violence through them; and, behold, I will destroy them with the earth.

Make thee an ark of gopher wood; rooms shalt thou make in the ark, and shalt pitch it within and without with pitch. And this is how thou shalt make it: the length of the ark three hundred cubits, the breadth of it fifty cubits, and the height of it thirty cubits.

The units were unfamiliar, but since it was the proportions that mattered it was easy to determine that the Ark was built on a one-to-six ratio, rather than the one-to-four that was pretty constant for the islands. My disappointment was keen. Another good story had fallen apart, and it meant discarding a certain amount of good copy that was already swirling in my mind—something endearing about how a reverence for and knowledge of Holy Scripture among these people had found beneficial expression in their daily lives and accomplishments.

My frustration in the matter of origins continued until I gradually learned to distinguish between trading vessels and small craft. By now you are aware that the sloops and schooners of the Lesser Antilles are broadly similar in their general proportions and other characteristics no matter where built. By contrast, small craft are highly variable in type and are often very specific to their locale. As I turned my attention to the origins of small craft, the problem resolved itself into smaller components, and in several instance the origins were either self evident or easy to infer.

The *gommiers, yoles, canots, pirogues,* and sailing canoes make an obvious starting place, since they are the truly original small craft of the islands. For the reasons given earlier, there seemed little doubt that all these types were derived from the Carib dugout canoe, modifications having occurred mostly in response to local scarcity of logs large enough for hollowing. Dugouts, or some trace or derivative, occur on all the larger, higher islands from Guadeloupe southward to Trinidad, the islands where the Caribs were established and held out longest against European encroachment. The present users of these dugouts are Europeanized West Indians of African descent, who speak or have recently spoken a French-Creole dialect.

The two-bow boats of Bequia are another example of a local type whose origins are essentially self evident, particularly since two of these double-enders were still engaged in whaling during my time in the islands. Without wanting to belabor the obvious similarity to the Nantucket whale boats, I wondered how closely I could pinpoint this connection by a combination of local lore and historical sources.

One afternoon during the construction of *Skywave,* the talk was of whaling (a whale had been landed that morning), and Haakon commented, "It was Captain Dunham what learned them boys whaling."

Two years later, I made a trip through New England and Nova Scotia trying to establish a relationship between North American fishing schooners and West Indian trading vessels. At the Whaling Museum in New Bedford, Massachusetts, while looking through the photo archive for whaling vessels that might have been seen in the West Indies, I somewhat sheepishly mentioned the name Dunham to C.F. Purrington, the museum's archivist, adding immediately that I supposed the clue was too small to be of any use. With an expressive sniff, Purrington turned to a card file he had compiled of personal names and other information about persons known to have gone whaling out of New Bedford. The name Dunham, John A., appeared as if by magic—master of the schooner *William A. Grozier,* which whaled out of New Bedford under Dunham's command from 1888 until 1903. In that year George Dunham became master of the *Grozier,* continuing until 1911, when he became the owner and master of the schooner *Ellen A. Swift* until she went missing in 1919.

Purrington then produced, from another file, crew lists for several of the voyages of the *Grozier* and the *Swift,* which included many familiar Bequia names—Olliverre, Sargent, Kydd, and Hazell—entered as residents of St. Vincent, Bequia's administrative center. The clear inference was that the Dunhams, father and son, had been sailing from New Bedford with a skeleton crew and picking up Bequians for the heavy work of whaling.

These names and dates were still fresh in my mind one morning a few months later, as I waited on the deck while the *Rosarene* made final preparations to sail to Trinidad. A light-eyed, brown-skinned woman who introduced herself as Lozina Kydd struck up a conversation by asking if I had seen the whale that was landed two days earlier.

"My father was Timothy Kydd, and he was Captain Dunham's harpooner," she confided proudly. "He was the onliest man ever to strike a right whale."

When I expressed my interest, she smiled and told the child at her side to "go 'long there." She told me that after each voyage, when the whale ship came back to Bequia to discharge the crew, Captain Dunham always stayed for a week or two with the Kydd family.

"And my mother, you know, she make a little mistake with Captain Dunham. Timothy Kydd is only my adopted father. And Captain Dunham did love me more than all he other children, though we never see each other. He was coming for me the next time, but the ship get lost in the Gulf Stream. That must be 1921 on the way to Bequia. He was taking me to live with Frankie Brown, that is on Cape Cod."

I listened quietly, without prompting or mentioning any of the names. The pattern, possibly including the "little mistake," was not, I imagine, uncommon in the closing days of whaling. As petroleum replaced whale oil for lighting, whaling became less profitable and New Bedford whalers began to sail with skeleton crew to some island near a whaling ground and there engage a local crew for whaling. As berths in whale ships dwindled and then disappeared, the step from serving in a whale ship to whaling from a shore station was a natural one.

There remains, however, the question of why the Dunhams chose Bequia for crew, and here another influence appears in the form of Old Bill Wallace.

In 1911 a young American named Frederic Fenger made a voyage in a sailing canoe from Trinidad to Puerto Rico, described in a fascinating book entitled *Alone in the Caribbean*. On his trip northward, Fenger stopped off for nearly a month with some Bequia whalers operating from a small islet south of Carriacou (the head harpooner of this crew, incidentally, was named Jose Olliverre). Fenger arrived in Bequia to deliver to Old Bill Wallace a letter informing Wallace of his son's death on a whaling voyage several years earlier. Wallace was a Scot who went whaling as a youth, then invested his savings in a sea island cotton plantation on Bequia. When cotton failed, Wallace returned to what he knew best: He built whale boats, enlisted a crew, and established a shore-based whale fishery in Bequia.

It was Old Bill Wallace, then, who formed the essential link between the skills of whaling and those of boatbuilding—the two skills necessary for the establishment of a whale fishery, and growing out of that, a boatbuilding culture. This in turn would become the rootstock upon which a schooner-building industry would be grafted around the turn of the century.

Continuing for the moment with the subject of small craft, we turn next to the beach boats of the Leeward Islands and Barbados. When I asked Emile Gumbs, owner of the *Warspite* and later Premier of Anguilla, about the origins of the beach boat type, he simply shrugged and replied, in a very commonsense vein, that he had always supposed the early settlers knew how to build boats just as they knew how to build houses or perform any other everyday operation.

A very reasonable suggestion, though somewhat difficult to verify. The islands where the beach boats are found—Anguilla, St. Martin, St. Kitts, Nevis, Montserrat, Barbados, and, with a modified sailing rig, St. Lucia—all share the English language and, with the exception of St. Lucia, have always been predominantly English in outlook. Thus, the archetype of the beach boat should be found somewhere on the shores of England, Scotland, or Wales. It would have been interesting to pursue this matter, but I was not able to find any catalog of boat types for these shores with which to compare my lines.

Another research topic left open for the eager anthropologist.

The case for *le canot saintois*—used in the Iles des Saintes, St. Barts, and in St. Thomas by French-speaking immigrants from St. Barts—is similar to that of the beach boats. The type seems to have come to the islands along with the French settlers. I wrote to M. Bernard Cadoret, editor of the French maritime journal *Le Petit Perroquet*, sending photographs of *le saintois* and requesting information about possible antecedents. He replied that French local boat types are not well cataloged but suggested that my photos most closely resemble the small craft found along the French Atlantic coast between Nantes and La Rochelle. This accords pretty well with the local tradition that the inhabitants of the Saintes came from the region around the mouth of the Loire. *Le saintois* was the most highly finished of any boat type I found in the islands, and among American colonial shipbuilders "finished after the French manner" indicated a high standard of building.

We have now accounted for all the local small craft except the Tortola sloop. I had hoped that leaving it until last would somehow make the riddle easier to solve. Forlorn hope, I should say, because the Tortola sloop is a bit of an anomaly. To begin with, it is not really a "sloop" in island terms, since it is not gaff-rigged. On the other hand, it is a little large to fit the island definition of a "boat," which requires that it be pulled ashore when not in use. And there is nothing about the Tortola sloop indicating any relationship with types found on nearby islands—except, of course, the Antigua fishing sloop, avowedly patterned after the Tortola model. There is great irony in this setback, because it was the difficulty of assessing kinship of the Tortola boat that caused Professor Doran to wish someone would make a survey of all the sailing craft of the Lesser Antilles. Well, someone has now done it, and the origins of the Tortola boat are still obscure!

Aside from this frustration, plausible origins can be established for the various small craft of the islands, providing the background for a more fruitful approach to the origins of the sloops and schooners. The first step is to consider the related but simpler question of design influence. For this essential distinction I am indebted to Nils Jannesch, then director of the Nova Scotia Provincial Museum in Halifax, who pointed out that design and construction of sailing vessels are conceptually quite different, even though in the West Indies the two aspects are merged in practice.

Construction requires a detailed knowledge of tools, materials, methods, procedures, and priorities that is difficult to acquire except by apprenticeship, formal or informal. The techniques of construction are essentially conservative and change very little over time. Furthermore, there is little difference in technique between a rowboat and a schooner, as I had occasion to observe:

Haakon Mitchell, with his experience as a builder of two-bow boats, managed to produce a very creditable sloop.

Design, on the other hand, is essentially abstract and only indirectly affected by the details of construction techniques. And far from being conservative, design is flexible, innovative, and easily influenced—within limits. The distinction between these two aspects of boatbuilding means a skilled builder may achieve a workable, even pleasing vessel without benefit of a designer (this is sometimes called "vernacular" design or unselfconscious design), but a skilled designer can produce nothing without the services of a builder.

Now, I am fully aware that all master builders are to some extent designers, and that all good design requires an intimate knowledge of material and technique. I am likewise aware that design and construction did not become separate functions in shipbuilding (or in any other field) until comparatively recently. In fact, the separation had not occurred in the traditional culture of the West Indies when I was there. Design and construction in the islands were merged into the single activity of building, and my failure to distinguish between the two had had me looking for some sort of Kon-Tiki origin for schooner building. After my conversation with Jannesch, the light of day began to break all around: Just as Emile Gumbs had suggested, the techniques of construction employed on the schooner-building islands were not new and had no "origins" in the sense I searched for. They were simply borrowed from an older tradition of boat carpentry, which was itself part of the everyday skills of an earlier period. My problem, then, reduced itself to establishing patterns of design influence that had shaped the construction of the inter-island trading vessels. And in the matter of design influence, information had been accumulating all along.

There were, after all, the *Frances W. Smith* and others of her breed, retired from the hard life of a fishing schooner in northern waters to serve their remaining years among the sunny Caribees, a ready source of inspiration to island builders. If there was any doubt of this, it should have been dispelled when Haakon Mitchell answered my question about the shape of his center frames by telling me how he had copied this feature, called "tumblehome," from the Nova Scotiamen he saw in Barbados as a boy.

Emile Gumbs could recall Canadian fishing schooners coming to Anguilla to load salt as recently as 1948. In the Barbados *Register of Shipping*, the majority of sailing vessel entries since 1929 were transfers from Nova Scotia. The Dalhousie University Archives in Halifax, Nova Scotia, holds clearance papers and other port records indicating that fishing schooners had been sailing to the West Indies in the winter months since around the turn of the century— carrying flour, lumber, and especially salt fish to the islands and returning

Schooner Hattie A. Heckman, *105 tons, built in 1895 at Essex, Massachusetts. (Photo courtesy of Peabody Museum, Salem, Massachusetts.)*

with rum, molasses, and salt for the next season's fishing. Some Gloucester schooners did appear in the Barbados register, but in the off season they more frequently cleared for the Azores and Portugal.

All in all, there was ample evidence that North American fishing schooners, especially those from Lunenburg, Nova Scotia, were frequently seen in the West Indies. But did they influence local builders?

According to Nils Jannesch, the Lunenburgers were farmers until the 1860s, when they began to fish on the banks in vessels copied after Gloucester fishing schooners. Innovations in design developed in Boston and Gloucester

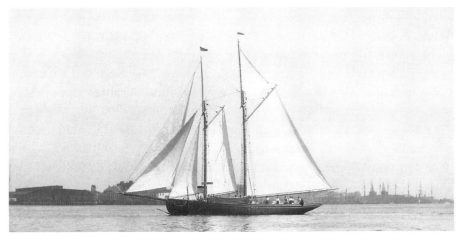

Schooner Leo, 37 tons, built in 1908 at Essex, Massachusetts. (Photo courtesy of Peabody Museum, Salem, Massachusetts.)

Schooner Emeralda, *51 tons, built in 1940*
at Friendship Bay, Bequia.

were reproduced, after a certain lag, in Nova Scotia. By means of the contacts already noted, these innovations and design characteristics finally appeared, after about twenty-five or thirty years, in West Indian vessels.

If this establishes that West Indian schooner building in this century was primarily influenced by Canadian fishing schooners, another question arises. Even in New England, fishing schooners of a recognizable modern type were not developed before the 1850s. Then what were the West Indian boatbuilders doing before they had the opportunity to be influenced?

The answer may be deduced from a bar graph I prepared from pages and pages of scrawled copies of scrawled entries in dusty volumes in hot harbor offices sprawled the length of the Lesser Antilles. It may not look like much, but it took me an entire winter, making lists, checking lists, puzzling over my own handwriting, adding, subtracting, drawing and erasing, to get all that data down on one page. And for what, you ask? Well, for this: It shows that sloops were built before schooners; that the aggregate tonnage of sloops is greater than that of schooners on all islands except Bequia; that the building of trading vessels began in the Lesser Antilles in the 1840s; that boatbuilding shows in this century two peaks corresponding to the two World Wars, separated by the valley of the Great Depression; that the building of larger vessels

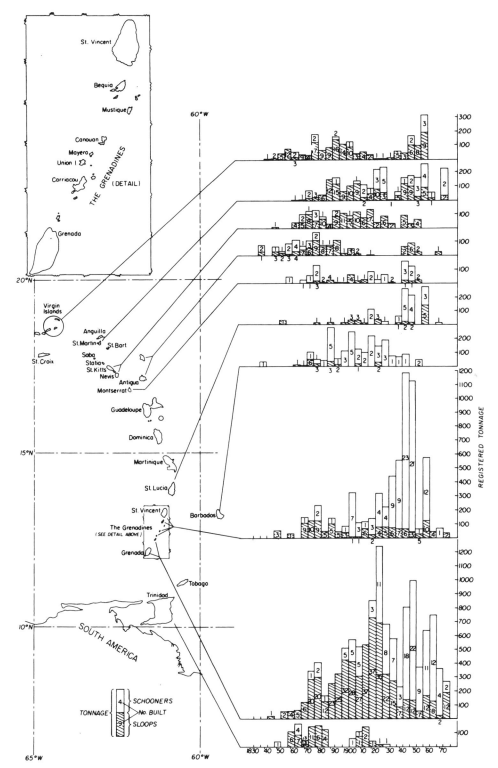

Sloop- and schooner-building activity in the Lesser Antilles, 1830–1970.
Taken from the **Registers of Shipping.**

had all but stopped by 1980; and that Carriacou and Bequia deserve additional attention to see if there is some special explanation for their markedly greater output.

In the case of Carriacou we have an excellent historical source to begin with: John Davy, a military surgeon who traveled extensively in the islands during the first half of the nineteenth century and wrote *The West Indies, Before and Since Emancipation* (1854). Davy makes several relevant references to Carriacou: Smuggling by the inhabitants was a problem as early as 1765; slaves on the island grew poultry and were selling their produce in Grenada as early as 1833 by means of small boats they built themselves; and Scottish shipwrights were brought to Carriacou to build trading vessels for landowners who wanted to sell produce in Grenada. A roll call of family names in the little boatbuilding community of Windward, Carriacou, is especially interesting in the light of the last remark: McFarlane, McLawrence, McKensie, MacLaren, McQuilken, McIntosh, Roberts, Bethel, Martineau, Mitchell, Patrice, and Fleary.

A doctoral dissertation by Don Hill of the American Museum of Natural History mentions a folk hero named John Rock who came to Carriacou from Barbados in 1888 and, according to local tradition, brought a new style in boatbuilding—the overhanging, or counter, stern. Here are all the traditional attributes of a folk hero: a stranger arriving from the east (Barbados is almost due east of Carriacou) bearing wisdom (a new method of building vessels). Even the name is poetically perfect—John Rock. All it lacks is a mysterious departure accompanied by the promise of a return at an unspecified time.

In fact, John Rock lived in Carriacou until his death in 1942, being eminently real, as I learned from the *Grenada Register of Shipping*, where the name first appeared in 1902 (builders' names were not given before 1899) as the builder of the *Island Gem*. From then until the last entry in 1941, John Rock built eleven sloops and eleven schooners—816 tons of shipping— including the first vessel described as having a counter stern. In short, the unusually large output of vessels in Carriacou may result from purely human (as opposed to economic, geographic, or historical) factors, first in the form of the unnamed Scottish shipwrights and later in the person of John Rock.

In the case of Bequia, an even more detailed and circumstantial story began to unfold when I asked Malings Compton of St. Lucia where the people of the islands had learned shipbuilding.

"I can answer that question for you," he said, while waves of silent incredulity swept over me. "In 1838 at the time of Emancipation, Sir William Snagg came out to take charge of the Island of Canouan [in the Grenadines]. With him he brought Benjamin George Compton, a shipwright and native of

Hampshire. Compton married a native woman named Albertha and had two children: a son named Benjamin in 1840 and, in 1842, a daughter named Mary Frances. Benjamin was my father [Malings Compton was born in 1898]. He learned boatbuilding from his father and taught it to me. He died in 1914, the year that I came to St. Lucia. Mary Frances married a man named William A. Mitchell, who came to Canouan from St. Vincent to learn boatbuilding from her father."

During this recitation, my skepticism melted away. Compton's account was too circumstantial to be fabricated, and it fit closely with several other pieces of information he could not have known—for example, that the *Mercantile Navy List* for 1878 contained an entry for the eighteen-ton sloop *Sir William Snagg,* built in Canouan in 1870.

Compton's account dovetailed nicely with what I knew of the Mitchell family of Bequia. The founder of the family was a shadowy figure simply called Old Mitch who had come to Bequia from elsewhere, was a boatbuilder, and had three sons. The eldest went to Panama and was never heard from again. The next, James Fitzallen, called Uncle Harry, lived in Bequia, built five schooners, and left numerous offspring. The youngest son, Romulus St. Clair, called Jack, went to Dominica and built five sloops and nine schooners. All together, the descendants of Benjamin Compton and Mary Frances Compton Mitchell had produced forty-one vessels (known to me) and two Prime Ministers. It makes an impressive contribution that, added to that of others such as Old Bill Wallace and the whalers, accounts in large measure for the high output of vessels, especially schooners, on the island of Bequia.

Where you have both water and people, there you have boats. And water flows and boats navigate and people come and go. In short there is no reason to expect that any single region should be wholly isolated in maritime matters. As a consequence, this summary can scarcely claim to be a history of boatbuilding in the Antilles, but it does represent a body of fairly detailed findings set forth as accurately as I was able. If a definitive history of the maritime culture of the Caribbean is ever constructed I hope to have furnished some planks and a frame or two.

The Last Schooner

~ ~ ~

The big tamarind tree cast a welcome shadow in the glare of the afternoon sun, strong even in February, and I was glad to stop. The road winding up from the harbor was still steep, and the view from the top still spectacular. I drank in the panorama of sea and islands, and marveled again at the sequence of events that had brought me back to Bequia after seven years away. The view of the Grenadines was unaltered, but elsewhere there was evidence of change.

Admiralty Bay was jammed as never before with yachts and yachtspeople, and the little town of Port Elizabeth had a prosperous glow that merely enhanced its original charm. I, on the contrary, was aglow from the sun and sweating freely. The intervening years had left me pudgy, and the temperate-zone winter had bleached me white.

It was 1981. I had come for a kind of personal celebration. What we knew in Oklahoma as the Oil Boom was producing in the islands a sort of related Schooner Boom, and hope ran high that working sail might yet survive.

I began my association with island boats in the early 1970s, with the assumption that the day of the island schooner was swiftly passing and that sail-powered watercraft whose form and substance were not soon recorded would disappear, unrecorded forever. As I sailed the islands measuring boats in those years, everything I saw confirmed this assumption. Outboards were replacing sails on fishing boats and small craft, and even the builders agreed that the day of the schooner was over. There were too many headaches in the schooner trade: Crew was hard to find, for the rugged life of a deck hand on a schooner appealed to few; insurance on wooden vessels and their cargo was no longer available; and finally, poor facilities and poor organization meant that there were long delays in port—schooners waiting for cargo that was simultaneously waiting for transport.

And yet, even with all the handicaps, *Skywave*, launched in 1971, had done everything that could have been hoped for her. Granted, her racing record was a little disappointing; in the 1971 Carriacou Regatta, she invari-

Sloop Skywave *arriving at Carriacou for the Regatta. August 1972.*

ably led on the downwind leg but was no match for the bigger, deeper Carriacou sloops on the wind and brought only a third place. However, Haakon was not discouraged.

"They all saying she is sail good, Douggie. Is only better sails she wanting to beat all."

The following year, with a new challenger built at Petit Martinique and *Mermaid* back from retirement, *Skywave*, even with new sails, came in fourth, and Haakon did not race her again. But as a trading vessel, *Skywave* had already begun to bring in substantial returns.

In 1974 I visited Bequia after two years' absence, making again the familiar climb up from the harbor and down toward the bay. I was some way along the beach before I noticed a new house that had joined the others in the little colony of vacation homes that had been growing in this quiet corner. It appeared Mitchell had sold some of his land, since the new house was lying up the hill from the little blue house and well inside his boundary line.

When I came into view, the younger Mitchell children, no longer small, stopped their play and came running.

"This way, Douggie, this way. Mommie been up the new house."

They led me up the hill to where Winnie waited on the verandah of a house so spacious I had mistaken it for the island retreat of some wealthy North American. Winnie proudly showed me around her house, timbered in greenheart and floored and sided with purpleheart—an extravagance of solid hardwood.

We sat on the gallery, enjoying the view and exchanging news while we waited for Haakon. Uncle Nappy had died that spring; a new daughter had been born to Haakon and Winnie; Orbin was planning to marry soon and would live in the small blue house; and Granny had a new post at the railing of the verandah. No one was around but the children, which puzzled me since there was a tan Land Rover parked just below the house. Finally curiosity overcame me and I asked whose it was.

"That Haakie's," Winnie laughed proudly, "and he done already forget how to walk." I marveled and rejoiced at the dramatic changes that *Skywave* had wrought in the fortunes of this family.

After I once again left the islands for the mainland, the Mitchells and I stayed in touch as much as time and occupation and the erratic island postal service permitted. At first we dealt mainly with the progress and problems of children and grandchildren; but then Haakon wrote that he was planning to build a schooner.

The new schooner was completed in 1981 as I was completing this book; and once again I returned to Bequia, this time for the launching of *Wave Dancer*. Granny was still at her post on the verandah, and the two older boys were married and had established households on the hillside, making four households now in the compound. Roderick, Osrick, and Carlos, who had been building gumboats when *Skywave* was built, were now putting the fin-

Schooner Wave Dancer *awaiting launching at Friendship Bay, Bequia. February 1981.*

The last schooner, Wave Dancer, *anchored just ahead of* Skywave *at Friendship Bay, Bequia. March 1981.*

ishing touches on an eighty-foot schooner, while Orbin was building a vessel of his own, and Osrick was working on the principles of celestial navigation.

One schooner does not make a fleet, and it was early yet to say that a new era was opening for working sail in the Lesser Antilles. But it pleased me at the time to think that while the skills of boatbuilding were still practiced and transmitted, "the last schooner" might mean only the one most recently launched.

~ ~ ~

Final Word

This book is translated, so to speak, from a manuscript found in a bottle. The research took place over five years of pretty good fun, from 1970 to 1975; the writing stretched into six years of intermittent agony, ending in 1981; after which the finished product languished, largely unnoticed, until the present offering took shape. Life goes on. In the intervening years I watched my two children grow to maturity and raised a whole lot of cattle; though I often lulled my children with tales of the islands, I have never been back.

When the proposal to publish this book came to me so many years after it was written, the original plan was to bring it up to date with references to the current situation. But I have found that to speak of things I know nothing about feels strange, false, and uncomfortable. We have compromised in the main with some changes of tense and the elimination of many cherished irrelevancies, doubtless to good effect. But I would like to take this moment to say to the reader that this is not a work of fiction. There is nothing said or done in it that I did not hear or see. I have rendered the lovely speech of the islands just as I heard it. If there are errors, well, then I made them; but I did my best. I listened carefully. I made good notes. To the best of my ability, I have kept faith with the West Indians whom I have known and admired.

Bibliography

~ ~ ~

Carstens, Johan Lorentz. *Account of Life among the Negro Slaves of the Danish West Indies*. Unpublished translation of unpublished manuscript, 1742.

Chapelle, Howard I. *The Search for Speed under Sail*. New York: W.W. Norton & Co., 1967.

Davy, John. *The West Indies, Before and Since Emancipation*. London: W. and F. G. Cash, 1854.

Doran, Edwin B., Jr. "The Tortola Boat: Characteristics, Origin, Demise." Supplement to *The Mariner's Mirror,* Vol. 56, No. 1, 1970.

Edwards, Clinton R. "Aboriginal Sail in the New World." *Southwest Journal of Anthropology* 21: 351-358, 1965.

Fenger, Frederic A. *Alone in the Caribbean*. Belmont, Mass.: Wellington Books, 1958.

Hall, J. Clark. *The Mercantile Navy List and Maritime Directory*. London: Spootiswoode & Co., 1853, 1857, 1863, 1898.

Hernandez de Oviedo y Valdés, Gonzalo. *Dela natural hystoria delas indias*. Toledo: Remo de Petras, 1526.

Highfield, Arnold R. *The French Dialect of St. Thomas, U.S. Virgin Islands*. Ann Arbor: Karoma Publishers, 1979.

Labat, Pére Jean-Baptiste. *Nouveau Voyage aux Isles de l'Amérique*. La Haye, 1724.

Little, Elbert L., and Frank H. Wadsworth. *Common Trees of Puerto Rico and the Virgin Islands*. Washington, D.C.: U.S. Department of Agriculture Handbook No. 249, 1964.

Mattioni, Mario. *Qui Etait le Caraïbe?* Fort-de-France: Bulletin de la Société d'Histoire de la Martinique, 1972.

Mackaness, George. *The Life of Vice-Admiral William Bligh*. Sydney: Angus and Robertson, 1951.

McKusick, Marshall. *Aboriginal Canoes in the West Indies*. Yale University Publications in Anthropology 63, 1960.

Oviedo, see Hernandez de Oviedo.

Raspail, Jean. *Secouons le cocotier*. Paris: R. Laffont, 1966.

Rigg, J. Linton. *The Alluring Antilles*. Princeton, N.J.: Van Nostrand, 1963.

Stoddard, Charles Augustus. *Cruising among the Caribees*. New York: Charles Scribner's Sons, 1895.

Stoneman, John. "The Voyage of M. Henry Challons . . . ," in *Hakluytus Posthumus or Purchas His Pilgrimes* 19. Glasgow: J. MacLehose and sons, 1906.

Treves, Sir Frederick. *The Cradle of the Deep*. New York: E.P. Dutton, 1908.

Westlake, Donald E. *Under an English Heaven*. New York: Simon and Schuster, 1972.

Index